Internationale Politische Ökonomie | 17

'Internationale Politische Ökonomie'
is edited by

Andreas Busch (University of Göttingen)
Doris Fuchs (University of Münster)
Stefan A. Schirm (University of Bochum)
Hubert Zimmermann (University of Marburg)

Tobias Leeg

When do Paper Tigers get Teeth?

Social Standards in U.S. and EU Preferential
Trade Agreements

 Nomos

Der Autor dankt der Ernst-Reuther-Gesellschaft für die großzügige Unterstützung bei der Veröffentlichung dieses Buches.

The Deutsche Nationalbibliothek lists this publication in the Deutsche Nationalbibliografie; detailed bibliographic data are available on the Internet at http://dnb.d-nb.de

ISBN   978-3-8487-4723-8 (Print)
         978-3-8452-8989-2 (ePDF)

British Library Cataloguing-in-Publication Data
A catalogue record for this book is available from the British Library.

ISBN   978-3-8487-4723-8 (Print)
         978-3-8452-8989-2 (ePDF)

Library of Congress Cataloging-in-Publication Data
Leeg, Tobias
When do Paper Tigers get Teeth?
Social Standards in U.S. and EU Preferential Trade Agreements
Tobias Leeg
245 p.
Includes bibliographic references.

ISBN   978-3-8487-4723-8 (Print)
         978-3-8452-8989-2 (ePDF)

1. Edition 2019
© Nomos Verlagsgesellschaft, Baden-Baden, Germany 2019. Printed and bound in Germany.

To Elisabeth

Acknowledgments

This dissertation would not have been possible without the support of a lot of people. Firstly, I would like to express my sincere gratitude to my advisor Prof. Dr. Susanne Lütz for the continuous support of my Ph.D. study and related research, for her patience, motivation, and immense knowledge. Her guidance helped me in all the time of research and writing of this thesis. Besides my advisor, I would also like to thank my second assessor Prof. Dr. Christian Lammert and the rest of my thesis committee, Prof. Dr. Simon Koschut, Dr. Ingo Peters and Prof. Dr. Lora Ann Viola for their interest in my work.

I would equally like to thank all my current and former colleagues from the Chair of International Political Economy at the Free University Berlin for listening, offering advice, and supporting me through the entire process of researching and writing this dissertation: Sibylle Schäfer, Christof Mauersberger, Verena Schüren, Justus Dreyling, Sebastian Schneider, Sven Hilgers and Vincent Dreher. They made the rocky road to the completion of this work a lot more fun.

Furthermore, I am grateful to the team of the Center for German and European Studies at Georgetown University for their hospitality and help during my research stay in Washington, D.C. My research has profited tremendously from this opportunity. I also want to thank all interviewees in the United States and Europe who made themselves available to discuss trade policy issues with me. Their insights contributed significantly to my understanding of the research topic.

Last but not least, I would like to thank my family for their support over the years. I am especially grateful to my mother, Christiane Leeg, for her continuous encouragement during all phases of this project. Most importantly, I want to thank Elisabeth Lastras Roldán for her love, patience and unyielding support in all aspects of my life.

Inhaltsverzeichnis

List of Abbreviations

ACTPN	Advisory Committee for Trade Policy and Negotiations
AFL-CIO	American Federation of Labor and Congress of Industrial Organizations
ALDE/ADLE	Alliance of Liberals and Democrats for Europe Group
CAN	Andean Community
CARIFORUM	Caribbean Forum of African, Caribbean and Pacific States
CCP	Common Commercial Policy
CETA	Comprehensive Economic and Trade Agreement between the EU and Canada
CFSP	Common Foreign and Security Policy
CITES	Convention on International Trade in Endangered Species of Wild Fauna and Flora
COREPER	Committee of Permanent Representatives
CSD	Civil Society Dialogue
CTE	Committee on Trade and Environment
CTPA	Colombia Trade Promotion Agreement
DAG	Domestic Advisory Group
DG	Directorate-General
DOL	Department of Labor
DR-CAFTA	Dominican Republic-Central America Free Trade Agreement
ECAT	Emergency Committee for American Trade
ECR	European Conservatives and Reformists Group
EFTA	European Free Trade Association
EMIT	Environmental Measures and International Trade group
EP	European Parliament
EPP	European People's Party Group
ESF	European Service Forum
ETUC	European Trade Union Confederation
EU	European Union
FDI	Foreign Direct Investment

FoE	Friends of the Earth
FoEE	Friends of the Earth Europe
FTAA	Free Trade Agreement of the Americas
GAERC	General Affairs and External Relations Council
GATS	General Agreement on Trade in Services
GATT	General Agreement on Tariffs and Trade
GDP	Gross Domestic Product
GOP	Grand Old Party (Republican Party)
Greens/EFA	Greens/European Free Alliance
GSP	Generalized System of Preferences
GUE/NGL	European United Left/Nordic Green Left
ICC	International Criminal Court
ILO	International Labor Organization
INTA	Committee on International Trade
IPE	International Political Economy
IR	International Relations
ITO	International Trade Organization
ITUC	International Trade Union Confederation
KIC	Kaesong Industrial Complex
KORUS PTA	Korea-United States Preferential Trade Agreement
LAC	Labor Advisory Committee
LDCs	Least Developed Countries
MEA	Multilateral Environmental Agreement
MEP	Member of the European Parliament
MFN	Most-Favored Nation Principle
NAAEC	North American Agreement on Environmental Cooperation
NAALC	North American Agreement on Labor Cooperation
NAFTA	North American Free Trade Agreement
NAM	National Association of Manufacturers
NFTC	National Foreign Trade Council
NGO	Non-Governmental Organization
NPE	Normative Power Europe
NTB	Non-Tariff Barrier
OECD	Organization for Economic Co-operation and Development
OEP	Open Economy Politics Approach
OPZ	Outward Processing Zone
PAC	Political Action Committee

PTA	Preferential Trade Agreement
PTPA	Peru Trade Promotion Agreement
RTAA	Reciprocal Trade Agreements Act
S&D	Progressive Alliance of Socialists and Democrats
SICA	Central American Integration System
SPS	Sanitary and Phytosanitary measures
STR	Special Trade Representative
TAA	Trade Adjustment Assistance
TPA	Trade Promotion Authority
TPC	Trade Policy Committee
TPP	Trans-Pacific Partnership
TREMS	Trade-related Environmental Measures
TRIMS	Agreement on Trade Related Investment Measures
TRIPS	Agreement on Trade Related Intellectual Property Rights
TTIP	Transatlantic Trade and Investment Partnership
TUCA	Trade Union Confederation of the Americas
UNCED	United Nations Conference on Environment and Development
UAW	United Automobile Workers
UNICE	Union of Industrial and Employers' Confederations of Europe
US	United States
USCIB	U.S. Council for International Business
USITC	U.S. International Trade Commission
USMCA	United States-Mexico-Canada Agreement
USTR	United States Trade Representative
WTO	World Trade Organization
WWF	World Wildlife Fund

1. Introduction

'No country is doing more than the United States to push for strong labor and environmental provisions in international trade agreements. While some other countries talk about labor and the environment in the context of trade, only the United States is actually doing something to integrate these topics as an active part of its trade agenda.'
Robert Zoellick, U. S. Trade Representative[1]

'The EU has always rejected a sanctions-based approach to labour standards – and that will continue. But equally, we can do more to encourage countries to enforce basic labour rights, such as the ILO core conventions, along with environmental standards - not simply in principle, but in practice. Co-operation and social dialogue are certainly important. Transparency, through an independent mechanism, will also help us highlight areas where governments should take action against violations of basic rights.'
Peter Mandelson, EU Trade Commissioner[2]

Preferential trade agreements (PTAs) have become the 'centrepiece of trade diplomacy' in the 21th Century (Heydon and Woolcock 2009: 3).[3] PTAs are international commercial agreements that remove trade barriers between PTA signatories in order to promote economic integration between them. In contrast to the multilateral trade regime which is based on the most-favored nation (MFN) principle, PTAs are inherently discriminatory. They reduce trade barriers for PTA members but not for non-members. Trade economists therefore disagree whether, and if so to what extent, PTAs improve welfare and whether they serve as building or stumbling blocks for multilateralism (Bhagwati 2008; Baldwin 2006). In any case, PTAs are con-

---

1 Statement of U.S. Trade Representative Robert B. Zoellick before the Committee on Finance of the United States Senate, Washington, D.C., March 9, 2004.
2 Intervention by Trade Commissioner Peter Mandelson at the EU Decent Work Conference, Brussels, December 5, 2006.
3 I use the term of preferential trade agreements (PTAs) instead of regional trade agreements (RTAs) or free trade agreements (FTAs) throughout this study because PTAs are not always regional and usually do not stipulate the removal of all trade barriers between PTA members.

sidered second-best solutions to multilateral trade liberalization (Manger 2009: 2). Due to the lasting stalemate of the multilateral 'Doha Development Round', however, their number has steadily grown over the last two decades. Until the creation of the World Trade Organization (WTO) in 1995 only about 50 PTAs were in force worldwide. By 2015, by contrast, no less than 446 PTAs were notified to the WTO (Kim, Mansfield, and Milner 2016: 323).

The United States (US) and the European Union (EU) are the biggest economic blocks of the world and among the main drivers of this development (Horn, Mavroidis, and Sapir 2010: 1565-1566). Until the mid-1990s, the US had only signed two bilateral PTAs, namely with Israel (1985) and Canada (1988), and one regional PTA, the North American Free Trade Agreement (NAFTA) with Mexico and Canada (1994).[4] Since then, though, the US has concluded PTAs with Jordan (2001), Chile (2004), Singapore (2004), Australia (2005), Morocco (2006), Bahrain (2006), the Dominican Republic and Central America (DR-CAFTA) (2006), Oman (2009), Peru (2009), Colombia (2012), Panama (2012) and South Korea (2012).[5] Furthermore, in 2015 the US concluded negotiations for the Trans-Pacific Partnership (TPP), a mega-regional PTA that included 12 Pacific Rim countries (the United States, Australia, New Zealand, Canada, Mexico, Peru, Chile, Singapore, Brunei, Vietnam, Malaysia, and Japan) (Donnan and Sevastopulo 2015). However, Donald Trump formally withdrew the US from the TPP in January 2017 as one of his first official acts as U.S. President (Schott 2017). Instead, the US renegotiated NAFTA with Canada and Mexico and announced the conclusion of a follow-up treaty named United States-Mexico-Canada Agreement (USMCA) in October 2018 (Politi, Sevastopulo, and Webber 2018).

Different forms of politically motivated bilateral and regional trade accords have long been an integral part of EU trade policy as well (Eckhardt and Elsig 2015: 970). Since the mid-1990s, however, the EU has increasingly negotiated also commercially-driven PTAs with countries like Mexico (2000), Chile (2003) and South Africa (2004). After a short moratorium on PTAs in the early 2000s, the EU has launched a series of bilateral and region-to-region negotiations since 2007 (Woolcock 2007). To date, the EU's new activism has resulted in PTAs with the Caribbean Forum (CARIFO-

---

4 The US-Canada PTA was superseded by NAFTA in 1994.
5 The dates refer to the year of the PTA's entry into force.

RUM)[6] (2008), South Korea (2011), Central America (2013), Peru and Colombia (2013), Georgia (2016), Moldova (2016), Canada (CETA) (2017), Ukraine (2017), Ecuador (2017) as well as in the signing of PTAs with Singapore, Vietnam and Japan which are still awaiting ratification. With the Transatlantic Trade and Investment Partnership (TTIP), the EU and the US also strived for a mega-regional trade pact since 2013 that would have covered 40 percent of world trade in services and one third of global trade in goods (Hamilton 2014: 82). However, negotiations have been freezed and the conclusion of a full-fledged EU-US trade accord under the current U.S. President Donald Trump seems unlikely.

But not only the quantity of U.S. and EU PTAs has changed over the last years. Modern PTAs of the US and the EU are qualitatively different from older trade pacts. Due to their enhanced bargaining power in bilateral and regional settings, the US and the EU have managed to include rules and disciplines in their PTAs with third states that are not covered by the WTO (WTO-extra provisions) or expand the depth and breadth of existing WTO rules ('WTO+' provisions). Therefore, regulatory issues such as trade in services and trade-related aspects of intellectual property rights as well as investment protection and competition policy form the core of the new U.S. and EU PTAs (Horn, Mavroidis, and Sapir 2010: 1566-1567). Most remarkable is, however, that U.S. and EU PTAs nowadays consistently contain provisions that aim to protect workers and the environment. These issues were long considered 'non-trade issues' by many countries and therefore could not be integrated into the multilateral trading system (Suranovic 2002).

Yet, these so-called social standards of U.S. and EU PTAs differ considerably regarding their scope and enforcement mechanism.[7] The scope of labor and environmental provisions in U.S. PTAs is generally more limited than in EU PTAs. The US eschews making reference to a number of key international labor and environmental conventions in its PTAs due to the simple fact that itself - in contrast to the EU or EU member states - has not ratified them (Kelemen and Knievel 2015; Weissbrodt and Mason 2014). More surprisingly is, however, that the US and the EU have opted for fundamentally different enforcement mechanisms for the social standards in their respective PTAs.

---

6 CARIFORUM is a subgroup of the ACP states and serves as a base for economic dialogue with the European Union.

7 In absence of a more suitable term, I use social standards to refer to labor as well as environmental provisions in PTAs throughout this study.

1.1 The Enforcement Mechanisms of U.S. and EU PTA Social Standards: A Policy Puzzle

Social standards in U.S. PTAs can be enforced by imposing economic sanctions just like all purely economic provisions of U.S. trade agreements. The EU, by contrast, forgoes any coercive elements in relation to the enforcement of PTA social standards and relies exclusively on soft mechanisms that follow the logic of dialogue and persuasion. In the words of international labor law expert Jeffrey Vogt (2014: 144): 'Unlike in the U.S. (…) model, there is no fine or sanction of any kind. If the parties cannot resolve their disagreement about the application of the chapter, there is nothing else to be done'. The same holds true for the environmental provisions in U.S. and EU PTAs (Jinnah and Morgera 2013: 333). This is remarkable, since the EU's general approach for dispute settlement in PTAs has shifted since the early 2000s from traditional 'diplomatic' consultations towards a US-style quasi-judicial model of adjudication that involves trade sanctions as a last resort for enforcement (Garcia Bercero 2006: 383). Even though the US and the EU hardly ever resort to sanctions in PTA disputes in practice, both consider it necessary to have them as a stick in case amicable settlements of disputes are not possible (Interview record #3, 2015). Why would the EU, in contrast to the US, abstain from sanction mechanisms when it comes to social standards? This book therefore poses the following, puzzling research question:

Why did the US enshrine sanction-based social standards in its PTAs while the EU opted for a cooperative approach?

The most obvious explanation for the difference in the enforcement mechanism of U.S. and EU PTAs' social standards is that there exist different ideas about the effectiveness and appropriateness of the respective enforcement model on both sides of the Atlantic. The preference of the US for punitive social standards could be interpreted as a reflection of the broader American legal tradition, known as 'adversarial legalism'. U.S. methods of policy implementation and dispute settlement are in general more adversarial and legalistic, relying more on threats and legal lawsuits than legal systems in Europe and other developed countries where dispute resolution is more informal, cooperative, and opaque (Kagan 2003). As a consequence, Americans could view social standards without punitive sanction mechanisms as inconsequential. Europeans, by contrast, might consider cooperative activities more expedient than coercive measures. Advocates of the 'Normative Power Europe'-theory have long depicted the EU as being fundamentally different from other powers such as the US. As a different kind of international actor the EU would generally prefer dialogue, consultation and non-coercive matters to diffuse norms to the international system (Manners 2002). According to Manners, the projection of norms is likely to be more 'normatively sustainable' if it involves 'persuasion, argumentation, and the conferral of prestige or shame' (Manners 2011: 235) 'rather than coercion or solely material motivations' (Manners 2009: 792).

This would be also in line with the arguments of advocates of a 'managerial enforcement model' for international agreements. Chayes and Handler Chayes (1995: 3), for instance, argued that for the promotion of compliance with international regulatory agreements, such as conventions of the International Labor Organization (ILO) and multilateral environmental agreements (MEAs), sanctions are 'likely to be ineffective when used'. Since they assumed that breaches of international labor or environmental standards rarely flow from deliberate disregard, a 'cooperative, problem-solving approach' would be better suited to tackle the root causes of non-compliance. Therefore, compliance strategies should focus on the actual causes of non-compliance and 'manage' these through positive means, consisting in a blend of transparency, dispute settlement through non-binding recommendations, and capacity-building (ibid.: 22-25). Following this logic, the cooperative approach for social standards of the EU could be interpreted as a manifestation of the EU's unique international identity or as a result of the different ideas EU actors held about appropriate and effective measures.

There are, however, a number of problems with such explanations. First, as pointed out by George Downs et al. (1996), sanctions might not always be required to ensure cooperation but they are crucial when strong incentives exist for non-compliance. This would be the case where treaties require states to depart significantly from what they would have done in the absence of the treaty. In labor and environmental policy, non-compliance can in fact be caused by a lack of know-how or resources especially in the case of low-income countries. In these instances, dialogue and cooperation can indeed contribute to the elimination of such grievances. Inadequate labor and environmental protection can, however, also be the result of purposeful governmental policy. Especially governments of developing countries are assumed to have strong incentives to keep production costs low by avoiding costly labor and environmental regulations (Chan 2003). However, improving social and ecological conditions in a third country through persuasion alone requires the cooperation and goodwill of its governments. But as Barrett (2003) pointed out in the context of MEAs, changing a country's behavior through an international treaty requires to restructure its incentives: either non-compliance must lead to penalties or compliance must offer rewards. In the EU approach for social standards, however, non-compliance neither entails the danger of sanctions nor does compliance hold out the prospect of additional material gains.

The sanction-based approach of the US, by contrast, dramatically increases the costs of violating standards and thereby could promote compliance in third states regardless of the preference of their governments. Coercive measures immediately simply allow for a better control of other governments' behaviors (Hafner-Burton 2005). Renouncing coercive elements for social standards, by contrasts, entails the risk that they dwindle to little more than 'paper tigers' if third country governments lack political goodwill and cooperativeness. In its unilateral trade policies, the EU seems to acknowledge this fact. As discussed in more detail in chapter two, access to the EU's internal market through its GSP system is conditional on the adherence of beneficiary countries to certain labor (and environmental) requirements (Orbie and Tortell 2009). In addition, since 1995 the EU includes a so-called 'essential element clause' in all trade agreements that enables the EU to suspend market access in the case of grave human rights violations (Bartels 2013). It short, it cannot be maintained that the EU generally considers coercive measures ineffective or inappropriate for value-based objectives in trade policy.

Second, scholars have noted an increasing 'globalization of American law', meaning the spread of American legal style to other jurisdictions including the EU affecting especially the most internationalized areas of regulation and legal practice (Kelemen and Sibbitt 2004; Kelemen 2011). As pointed out above, the EU has as well proceeded in trade policy from diplomatic means for dispute resolution to a quasi-judicial model of trade adjudication (Garcia Bercero 2006: 383; Elsig and Eckhardt 2015: 26-29). This follows the general international trend towards more legalistic forms for the enforcement of international trade rules, relying more on formalized dispute resolution procedures that can result in the authorization of retaliatory actions, such as the imposition of sanctions (Porges 2011; Davis 2012). Nowadays, the reliance on formal dispute resolution procedures and economic sanctions to enforce trade rules is not an American peculiarity but the international norm (De Biévre and Poletti 2015; Dür, Baccini, and Elsig 2014; Allee and Elsig 2014). The renunciation of sanction-based social standards by the EU is therefore astonishing, since dispute settlement procedures for commercial provisions do not differ fundamentally between recent U.S. and EU PTAs (Woolcock 2014: 731). As a consequence, social standards in U.S. PTAs appear to be more mandatory than the ones in EU PTAs (Vogt 2015: 850; Jinnah and Morgera 2013: 335). Hence, the US, and not the EU, seems to be the forerunner of the promotion of labor and environmental standards through trade policy.

The predominant theoretical approaches in International Political Economy (IPE) seem to be unable to explain this puzzling and even counterintuitive observation. Constructivists could expect the EU to be the more vigorous advocate of international labor and environmental standards. In the US, ideas that view interventions of the state in the workings of the free market with skepticism are far more widespread than in Europe. Therefore, the US is often portrayed as an agent of laissez-faire (or neoliberal) capitalism in the international system (Kotz 2015). The 'European social model', by contrast, grants the state a greater role especially with regard to economic, employment and social policies (Orbie et al. 2009).

In a 2005 communication on 'European Values in a Globalised World', the European Commission itself acknowledged that the 'European model' diverges sharply from the rest of the world inter alia because 'Europeans have greater expectations of the state than their equivalents in Asia and America' (European Commission 2005: 4). In face of the mounting international economic integration, EU policy-makers have repeatedly stressed the need to 'manage' globalization by setting global standards that cushion possible negative effects of a globalized world economy (Jacoby and Meunier 2010).[8] In a 2004 communication on 'The Social Dimension of Globalisation', the Commission noted that the 'EU has long pursued policies, both at home and internationally, which seek to ensure that economic and social progress go hand in hand' and that the EU 'can and should make an active contribution to harnessing globalisation' (European Commission 2004).

In fact, the EU has proven to be a strong promoter of international labor standards both inside and outside of Europe (Johnson 2009; Kissack 2011; Kahn-Nisser 2016). In 2009, the member states of the EU had ratified on average 68 ILO conventions, ranging between 109 ratified by Spain and 32 by Estonia (Orbie et al. 2009: 105). More importantly, the EU member states have a perfect record of ratifying the ILO core conventions (Kissack 2009: 103). This stands in stark contrast to the US that seems to prefer a more unfettered version of globalization since it is reluctant to sign up to

---

8 Policy-makers are defined as those involved in drafting, amending and adopting policies, either from the executive or from the legislative arm of government.

international conventions that aim to flank economic globalization with social and environmental safeguards. Of the total 189 ILO conventions, for instance, the US has only ratified 14, including only two of the eight core conventions (No. 105 on forced labor and No. 182 on the worst forms of child labor) (Weissbrodt and Mason 2014: 1842-1843). This exemplifies the widespread notion that the US has the less protective labor regulations in the developed world, while European countries have among the strictest labor laws worldwide.

In the field of environmental policy, the difference in the level of regulatory protection between the US and Europe is less pronounced than in the area of labor. However, again the EU seems to prioritizes environmental and health concerns more systematically over economic interests inter alia through the application of the 'precautionary principle' (Vogel 2012: 266-270). Moreover, the EU has long taken over the leadership role in international environmental policy from the US (Kelemen and Vogel 2010; Vogler and Stephan 2007; Oberthür and Roche Kelly 2008). From the late 1960s until the late 1980s, the US had been one of the strongest and most consistent supporters of international environmental treaties but has managed to ratify only two important MEAs since 1989. In June 2017, President Trump even announced the withdrawal of the US from the Paris climate accord despite heavy international criticism (Shear 2017).

The EU and/or its member states, by contrast, signed and ratified 13 MEAs in the same time period, including the Paris climate accord. Since the 1992 UNCED 'Earth Summit' in Rio, the EU has successfully established a reputation as the leader in multilateral environmental governance, while the US has increasingly been perceived as a laggard in multilateral environmental negotiations (Kelemen and Vogel 2010; Brunnée 2004). Therefore, it seems inexplicable at first sight why in trade policy the EU does not use all available means to promote the labor and environmental objectives which it obviously fully supports in other fora.

Realist approaches that stress the importance of power in international economic relations are equally unable to explain why the enforcement mechanism of U.S. and EU PTAs' social standards diverge so sharply. Due to their large markets both the US and the EU are major powers in the global economy that are equally able to determine the content of a PTA with third states. In 2015, the Gross Domestic Product (GDP) was worth $16229 billion in the EU and $17947 billion in the US. Consequently, the GDP value of the EU and the US represented 26.18% and 28.95% of the world economy respectively. As major economic powers they are equally capable of influencing regulations of third countries. According to Drezner (2007: 32) this might happen unintentionally since 'a sufficiently large internal market drastically reduces a government's incentives to switch its standards, creating a set of expectations that encourages other actors to switch their regulatory standards'. Major economic powers, however, can also resort to economic coercion since they 'can use the threat of complete or partial market closure to force recalcitrant states into switching their regulatory standards' (ibid.). Sanction-based social standards in U.S. PTAs are a clear example of the use of American market power to set at least a minimum standard for trading partners' labor and environmental regulations.[9]

Academics have long stressed that the EU is also a regulatory power in international economic relations. David Vogel (1997) was among the first who argued that the EU is able to influence rules beyond its borders thanks to its large internal market and its high levels of product regulations especially with regard to environmental protections. Chad Damro (2012: 682) equally noted that the EU can be 'best understood as a market power Europe that exercises its power through the externalization of economic and social market-related policies and regulatory measures'. The Commission itself stated in a 2007 document on the external dimension of the Single Market that 'in many areas (…) the EU is looked upon as a regulatory leader and standard-setter' with the Single Market being 'a tool to foster high quality rules and standards' (European Commission 2007). It is therefore puzzling why the EU, in contrast to the US, does not use the weight of its huge market to improve labor and environmental standards in third states through its PTAs' social standards.

Liberal theories of international politics that stress the importance of the preferences and influence of societal actors (e.g. Moravcsik 1997) as well have difficulties to explain the different approaches of the US and the EU. Both the US and Europe have vibrant civil societies that long have been vocal about the necessity of strict labor standards and environmental regulations in view of increasing international economic exchange (Dryzek et al. 2003; Hafner-Burton 2009). However, the influence of labor groups on politics can be assumed to have significantly decreased over the last decades, especially in the US. Even though trade union membership is in decline

---

9 'Product standards' automatically prevent that products that don't comply with certain requirements are being sold. 'Process standards', such as labor and environmental standards, by contrast, do not concern the characteristics of the final product but its production process. Therefore, process standards have to be actively enforced.

both in Europe and the US (Visser 2006: 44), the average union density for the EU27 still stood at 25.1% in the mid-2000s (European Commission 2008: 20). The proportion of unionized workers in the US, by contrast, halved from about 25% in the mid-1970s (Baldwin 2003: 7) to only 12.5% in 2004 (Visser 2006: 46).[10] Hence, the labor movement should actually be more influential in Europe than in the US. Environmental organizations, on the other hand, have become serious political actors both in the US and Europe (Bomberg and Schlosberg 2013; Dryzek et al. 2003).

However, only in Europe has the environmental movement succeeded in bringing 'green' political parties into governmental responsibility (Müller-Rommel and Poguntke 2002). Through the participation of 'ecological' parties in government coalitions of several key EU member states, environmental advocates gained more direct influence over public policies in Europe (Burchell 2014; van Haute 2016; Bomberg 2005). In fact, within the EU the European environmental movement has managed to establish the most stringent regulations for environmental protection of the world (Vogel 2012). The American environmental as well as labor movement, by contrast, compete for influence with the U.S. business community, which has significantly increased its political power since the 1990s (Drutman 2015) and generally opposes costly labor and environmental regulations (Kraft and Kamieniecki 2007). Hence, the societal demand in Europe for the protection of workers and the environment in trade policy should be equally, if not more, pronounced than in the US. Therefore, at first glance it remains inscrutable why the EU seems to lag behind the increasingly proactive stance of the US in the promotion of international labor and environmental standards through trade.

Since the existing academic literature lacks a profound, systematic and nuanced explanation for this disparity, the present study attempts to develop a framework that can account for their respective chosen approaches. This book explains these different approaches by the way societal interest groups, institutional actors and the rules that regulate their interactions influence trade policy choices. It develops a theoretical framework that places domestic political variables and the trade-policy-making process in the US and the EU at the center of the analysis. Thereby, it challenges constructivist explanations that are based on the respective identity of the US and the EU as international actors as well as realist notions that emphasize the importance of power disparities. Instead of modeling the US and the

---

10 The ratio of unionized workers in the private sector which is subject to stronger international competition is even lower.

EU as unitary actors in international economic relations, this study empha-
sizes the importance of the societal preferences and the institutional setting within which trade policy is made for explaining political outcomes.
The remainder of this introductory chapter sets out the characteristics of
trade policy and politics in the 21th century and presents the major argument of the book.

1.2 Trade Policy and Politics in the 21th Century

Over the last decades, the world trading system has experienced a profound
transformation. Successive rounds of negotiations within the framework of
the General Agreement on Tariffs and Trade (GATT) reduced tariffs for industrial goods among GATT members to minimum levels. Therefore, the
Tokyo Round (1973-79) expanded the scope of GATT negotiations to so-
called non-tariff barriers (NTBs) (Dymond and Hart 2000: 24). With the
Uruguay Round (1986-1994) the focus of the international trade agenda
shifted entirely from tariffs and quotas ('at-the-border-issues') towards national laws and regulations that obstruct the free exchange of goods and
services ('behind-the-border-issues').

Ever since, regulatory issues such as services, investment measures and
intellectual property rights, have dominated international trade talks at
least between industrialized countries. Scholars have termed this new form
of trade policy the 'post-modern trade agenda' (Dymond and Hart 2000;
Falke 2005), 'regulatory trade agenda' (De Biévre 2006; Hocking 2004) or
'deep trade agenda' (Young and Peterson 2006; Melo Araujo 2013). But not
only the substance of international trade policy has changed significantly.
The creation of the WTO as successor to the GATT in 1995 was accompanied with the establishment of quasi-judicial dispute-settlement proceedings in trade which made the rules that govern international commerce
much more binding. Due to the 'legalization' of trade rules, domestic legislation which is believed to be incompatible with international trade rules
can now be effectively challenged (Abbott and Snidal 2000).

The increased intrusiveness and bindingness of international trade rules
has induced traditional interest groups active in trade politics to elaborate
new concerns and demands. Business groups pressured governments to set
international rules in a wide range of policy areas within the world trading
regime. This development resulted inter alia in the agreements on Trade
Related Intellectual Property Rights (TRIPs), Trade Related Investment
Measures (TRIMs), Sanitary and Phytosanitary (SPS) measures and the

General Agreement on Trade in Services (GATS) (Young and Peterson 2006: 799). Labor unions and NGOs, on the other hand, have sought to address not only internal economic regulations of WTO members but also social regulations relating to human rights, labor standards, health and safety measures, and environmental protection. Concerns are not only raised about painful economic adjustments associated with trade liberalization but equally about the compatibility of international trade rules with broader public policy objectives, such as decent work conditions and environmental protection.

Hence, the enhanced scope of trade policy also brought a number of new actors into trade policy-making that previously were active in other public policy fields (Young and Peterson 2006). Environmental NGOs, for instance, started to engage in trade politics since they shared labor unions' fear that the extended breadth and enforceability of trade rules would come at the expense of environmental (and workers') protection. This is because existing international labor and environmental treaties, such as ILO conventions and MEAs, often lack the strict enforcement mechanisms that make international trade rules so assertive (Elliott and Freeman 2003: 102-104; Eckersley 2004: 24). Therefore, labor and environmental groups have long demanded enforceable social standards in trade agreements to counteract the perceived uneven treatment of commercial and labor as well as environmental matters in global governance.

However, reaching trade agreements at the multilateral level has become increasingly difficult even without discussions on social standards. The membership of the WTO has expanded significantly and now includes increasingly assertive emerging economic powers like Brazil, China and India. This has broken the decades-long supremacy of the US and the EU in global trade governance (Hopewell 2015; Narlikar 2010). Furthermore, the extensive negotiation agenda of the current WTO 'Doha Development Round' often requires difficult domestic reforms from WTO members (Jones 2010). Numerous developing countries, however, are increasingly wary of the expansion and legalization of international trade rules since they fear this will restrict their space to deploy effective development policies (Wade 2003; Gallagher 2008).

As a consequence, the US, the EU and other states eager to advance international trade liberalization have increasingly concluded PTAs outside of the WTO. The spread of ever more comprehensive PTAs, however, has raised fears that such a development could result in a 'spaghetti bowl' of PTAs containing increasingly incompatible regulatory requirements (Bhagwati 2008). Yet, separate from trade negotiations the US and the EU have undertaken several efforts of regulatory coordination since the 1990s in order to create a more integrated international market place (Lütz 2011). This is of particular importance since they jointly account for about a third of world trade and according to Sapir (2007: 12) produce together around 80% of the rules that regulate the functioning of world markets. Therefore, they are often viewed as the 'regulators of the world.'

U.S. and EU authorities began to cooperate more closely both formally and informally within the framework of the 1995 'New Transatlantic Agenda' and the 1998 'Transatlantic Economic Partnership.' In 2007, the US and the EU established the 'Transatlantic Economic Council' as a further step in transatlantic political coordination. These initiatives were all aimed at dismantling existing differences in regulatory approaches and preventing the emergence of new ones (Pollack and Shaffer 2001; Egan 2005; Steffenson 2005). The efforts to increase regulatory convergence across the Atlantic culminated in the launch of the TTIP negotiations in July 2013. TTIP should explicitly serve as a 'global regulatory blueprint' (Bollyky and Bradford 2013) or 'gold standard' (Dadush 2013) for future trade deals. In the light of the decline of their own relative power position vis-à-vis rising economic powers like China, the US and the EU see TTIP as a strategic chance to shape the future rules of global trade together (Hamilton 2014) 'by using the combined leverage of their consumer markets' to 'ensure that producers worldwide continue to gravitate toward their joint standards' (Bollyky and Bradford 2013).

The EU and the US agree that labor and environmental standards must be part of this 'gold standard' for trade agreements (Akhtar and Jones 2014: 37). Both consider such provisions necessary to protect the relatively high levels of European and American labor and environmental standards and 'level the playing field' for competition with low-wage countries that usually do not have equally stringent regulations. As a consequence, such standards are already regular features of recent U.S. and EU PTAs even though most third countries oppose social standards in PTAs for fear of losing their sovereignty over labor and environmental legislation and experiencing a reduction of their comparative advantage (Burgoon 2004; Suranovic 2002). As pointed out above, the approach the US and the EU have chosen in previous PTAs to ensure the compliance of their trading partners with labor and environmental standards, however, differs fundamentally. The disagreement over the design of social standards persisted also in the ill-fated TTIP negotiations (Inside US Trade 2016). In face of the increasing transatlantic efforts to converge global trade governance this can appear puzzling. One might expect that their respective models already correspond especially because the US and the EU so far have concluded PTAs with many of the same countries. This study sets out to explain why this is not the case.

1.3 *The Argument of the Book*

In this study I argue that the diverging models of social standards in U.S. and EU PTAs are not the result of different views over the effectiveness or appropriateness of certain enforcement measures held on the two sides of the Atlantic. Rather they are the result of the political process of trade policy-making in their respective political systems. The US and the EU both face an international environment which is predominantly hostile towards social standards in trade since most countries fear that stricter labor and environmental legislation will reduce their comparative advantage (Burgoon 2004). Therefore, including social standards in PTAs will be the more difficult the more enforceable these provisions are. Yet, the US and the EU should be equally capable of carrying through their demands in international negotiations due to their comparable relative market power vis-à-vis negotiation partners (Clark, Duchesne, and Meunier 2000). Hence, domestic political factors appear to be decisive for their chosen approach.

To put it in a nutshell, the study argues that the greater responsiveness of policy-makers to interest groups and the greater powers of parliamentary bodies in trade policy in the US, facilitates the influence of labor and environmental groups, while the EU trade policy-making system diminishes their impact. As a consequence, the shape of social standards in U.S. PTAs correspond more closely to the preferences of labor and environmental groups than the corresponding provisions in EU PTAs. Both in the US and Europe, the issue of social standards pits business and labor groups against each other in trade politics, since social standards potentially affect the long-term relation between capital and labor. The increasing comprehensiveness of U.S. and EU PTAs, however, has also attracted a number of new actors to trade politics that have primarily non-economic goals and mainly worry about the implications of strict trade rules on their general public policy objectives (Young and Peterson 2006). Environmental NGOs are the most relevant of these new actors for this study.

More important for the explanation of the divergence in the design of U.S. and EU social standards' enforcement mechanism is, however, how societal preferences are channeled through the institutions of a political system. Institutions can be defined as the rules that regulate the interactions of actors in a political system. They shape policy choices by influencing the responsiveness of policy-makers to societal interest groups and by determining how decision-making power is divided among different institutional actors. Thus, the institutional determinants of trade policy choices can be classified along two dimensions: (1) a vertical dimension that concerns the link between societal actors and policy-makers and (2) a horizontal dimension that identifies how the relations among institutional actors are organized.

In democracies, societal actors and policy-makers are mainly linked through elections. Since policy-makers can be assumed to be rational actors that seek to remain in office, electoral incentives crucially influence their preferences (Kerremans and Martins Gistelinck 2009). As a general rule, the size of a policy-maker's constituency strongly determines his preferences. National constituencies induce office-holders to promote the economic and strategic interests of country as a whole. Therefore, executives usually support free trade and oppose provisions which jeopardize the conclusion of PTAs. Policy-makers in legislatures, by contrast, are elected in small electoral districts and, hence, are accountable to few interest groups with narrow interests. Therefore, the concerns of trade skeptical groups, including labor and environmental advocates, have greater chances to be heard in legislatures like the U.S. Congress and the European Parliament (EP) than in executive bodies like the U.S. administration and EU member state governments. The influence of trade skeptical groups should be even weaker on the European Commission, which acts as the EU trade policy executive, since it is not elected in general elections.

The strength of the link between interest groups and representatives in legislative bodies, however, additionally depends on the type of electoral system and the nature of the electoral competition. Electoral systems with proportional representation and party-centered electoral competition allow for less control of individual legislators through interest groups than majority voting systems and candidate-centered electoral competition (Rickard 2015). As a consequence, labor and environmental groups should have more influence on law-makers in the U.S. Congress than on Members of the EP (MEPs).

The final shape of social standards in PTAs depends on the institutional structure of the political system within which trade-policy is made (Postnikov 2014). In both the US and the EU, the authority to negotiate trade agreements has been delegated from institutions that represent diverse interests to the most centralized level of government (Clark, Duchesne, and Meunier 2000). In the US, however, Congress can set detailed negotiation objectives before granting negotiation authority to the executive. Moreover, the U.S. legislature votes by simple majority which gives individual lawmakers disproportionate influence on policies in close votes since they can make their consent subject to certain conditions (Destler 2005). Trade politics in the EU, by contrast, is executive-dominated (Zimmermann 2007). The Commission itself is in charge of elaborating negotiation mandates. These proposals have to be acceptable to all member states since the Council votes on granting negotiating mandates and the approval of negotiated agreements de facto by consensus. This tends to produce results that represent the lowest common denominator of member states' positions. The EP as the only directly elected EU institutions, by contrast, is excluded from the formulation of negotiation objectives and can merely intervene in the ratification stage through a simple up-or-down-vote (Woolcock 2011). As a consequence, social standards in EU PTAs correspond more closely to executives' preferences for 'soft' standards that make negotiations at the international level easier.

1.4 Chapter Overview

The book is organized as follows. Chapter 2 explores the linkage of trade agreements with labor and environmental standards and aims to define the dependent variable of the study. It starts by summarizing the academic and political debate over the need and purpose of social standards in trade policy. The section identifies the 'race-to-the-bottom' hypothesis as a disputed but influential theoretical foundation behind the call for labor and environmental provisions in PTAs. In the subsequent section, I delineate the treatment of labor and environmental issues within the multilateral trading system. It shows that despite repeated efforts of the US and the EU, social standards did not find their way into WTO rules. The subsequent section demonstrates, however, that both the US and the EU use social standards in their unilateral trade preference schemes. The subsection aims to illustrate that in their respective unilateral General Systems of Preferences (GSP) both make use of coercive methods of enforcement. Ultimately, chapter 2 outlines the respective approaches of the US and the EU for social standards in PTAs that have a fundamental different logic of enforcement.

In chapter 3, I define the theoretical framework of my research and specify the independent variables. In order to do this, I first review the existing literature on trade politics and social standards. Then I propose a domestic politics theory of compliance mechanisms' design of social standards in PTAs. The analytical framework follows basic assumptions of the Open Economy Politics approach (OEP) that has been widely used to analyze traditional 'at-the-border' trade policies. However, I propose some modifications to OEP's basic assumptions concerning interest groups, since the content and process of the 'new trade politics' is different to traditional trade politics. I then define societal preferences, the responsiveness of policymakers and the form of institutional delegation as the central explanatory variables and formulate a number of theoretically grounded hypotheses. At the end of the chapter, I deal with crucial questions of methodology and case selection. In the study I apply the process tracing method to three different negotiation processes of the US and the EU respectively. Negotiations with three countries or country blocks (Central America, Peru/ Colombia and South Korea) with which both the US and the EU concluded PTAs within a relatively short time period were chosen as cases in order to control for the possible influence of negotiation partners.

In chapter 4 and 5, I subject the propositions developed in chapter 3 to empirical scrutiny. In chapter 4 on U.S. PTAs and in chapter 5 on EU PTAs, I follow the same way of proceeding to investigate the influence of societal preferences and institutional factors on the design of social standards. I start by delineating the institutional framework within which U.S. and EU trade policy is made. Next, I identify the trade policy preferences of societal actors and of policy-makers in the legislative and executive branch. In a third step, I analyze three cases of PTA negotiations of the US and the EU in order to recognize patterns regarding how the interaction of the different institutional actors during trade negotiations influenced the design of social standards in PTAs. In the conclusion, I summarize the main findings of the empirical analysis with a view to highlight the extent to which these fit with the expectations set out in chapter 3. Moreover, I consider the explanatory power of alternative explications and present first research results regarding the functioning of social standards in U.S. and EU PTAs.

2. The Linkage of Trade and Social Standards

Social standards constitute integral elements of recent U.S. and EU PTAs. This fact alone is astonishing. Many other states fiercely reject the integration of meaningful labor and environmental provisions into the international trade regime. The US and the EU, therefore, had to push through the inclusion of social standards in PTAs in many cases against considerable resistance at the international level. The present chapter aims to shed light on the controversy over social standards in international trade and to define the dependent variable of the study. It starts by outlining the different views proponents and opponents hold in the debate over whether labor and environmental standards should be linked to trade agreements.

The subsequent section delineates the largely unsuccessful attempts to integrate labor and environmental issues into the multilateral trading system. The chapter then describes how the US and the EU use social standards in their unilateral and bilateral trade policies. The section shows that the enforcement of social standards in U.S. and EU unilateral trade instruments follows the same fundamental logic. They make market access conditional on the adherence to certain requirements. The enforcement mechanisms of U.S. and EU social standards in bilateral and regional settings, however, diverge sharply. The US has persistently opted for a coercive approach, where the violations of obligations can result in monetary fines or trade sanctions. The EU, by contrast, applies a cooperative approach which forgoes punitive measures but attempts to secure compliance by dialogue and cooperation. The final section summarizes the central ideas of this chapter.

2.1 The Controversy over Social Standards

The advancement of globalization over the last decades has raised fears in the developed world over the possible downsides of increased economic competition with developing countries. Critics argue that the lower labor and environmental standards in poor countries generate an unjust competitive edge at the expense of workers and the environment that goes beyond the legitimate exploitation of comparative advantages in production costs. In this view, trade liberalization has led to significant job losses in developed nations due to a sharp rise of imports from countries with unacceptable production methods. In addition, the growing mobility of capital has increased the bargaining power of firms vis-à-vis workers and resulted in falling wages in the manufacturing sector of rich countries. Workers in industrial nations would be compelled to accept wage cuts or risk job losses due to the relocation of entire production sites to countries with lower manufacturing costs. Therefore, the trade policy debates in the economically advanced world since the 1990s were characterized by recurrent calls for provisions aiming at the improvement of labor and environmental standards in developing countries. According to advocates, ensuring adherence to labor and environmental regulations in the global south would create a 'regulatory level-playing field' between the industrial and developing world that would permit fairer competition (Lee 1997: 175).

Furthermore, exponents of the 'race-to-the bottom' theory claim that the persistence of serious differences in the level of labor and environmental standards would create strong downward pressures on national regulations. Developing countries would have strong incentives to weaken domestic labor and environmental legislation further in order to attract foreign direct investment with low production costs. Industrial countries, on the other hand, would become reluctant to strengthen their labor and environmental regulations – the 'regulatory chill' thesis – or would be even compelled to join the 'race-to-the-bottom' for fear that their relatively high standards currently in place could trigger capital flight (Chan 2003; Rodrik 1997). Since the liberalization of trade and investment has significantly facilitated the movement of corporate activities across national borders, advocates of this view argue that labor and environmental protection requires strict regulations not only at the national but at the international level (Langille 1997: 37-38). International conventions for the protection of workers' rights and the environment already exist, mainly in the form of ILO conventions and MEAs. Critics argue, however, that these instruments often lack 'teeth', that is effective enforcement mechanisms to ensure compliance with the obligations of the respective treaties (Hepple 2008: 238; Eckersley 2004).

ILO conventions indeed generally forgo punitive economic sanctions as enforcement mechanism. Instead, the ILO traditionally relies on 'soft' measures to achieve compliance (Langille 2005: 413). The ILO supervises the application of its conventions through its elaborate supervisory mechanisms and publicizes violations of standards to shame countries into improving matters. Furthermore, the ILO provides incentives for compliance in the form of technical assistance. Even though Article 33 of the ILO constitution also foresees the possible use of coercive measures, that provisions has hardly ever been used (Elliott and Freeman 2003: 95-104). According to Standing (2008: 367), over the last two decades the effectiveness of the international labor regime has been further undermined by the ILO's shift towards a 'promotional' approach to standards. This would have replaced binding law with less effective 'soft law'.

MEAs equally have the reputation of being toothless paper tigers. In fact, most MEAs avoid trade restrictions as enforcement tools. A few MEAs, however, include trade-related provisions in different forms (Barrett 2003: 163). They, for instance, ban the trade of endangered species or restrict trade to avoid the spread of pests and diseases. Others use trade measures to promote participation. MEAs that make use of trade instruments such as the Montreal Protocol have been found to be notably effective in reaching their objectives (Benedick 2009: 243-244). In general, however, MEAs also 'work in accordance with the voluntarist tradition of international law and proceed on an *ad hoc*, issue-by-issue basis by inducing cooperation and generally avoiding punitive sanctions and courts' (Eckersley 2004: 24). This is also because the use of trade sanctions might run in conflict with rules of the WTO.

Therefore, MEAs provide only a very fragmented form of governance. The international trade regime, by contrast, has evolved into one of the world's most powerful regimes in terms of its ability to attract members and discipline them. The legal prescriptions of the WTO and PTAs are backed up by a sophisticated dispute resolution mechanism and effective sanctioning tools. Consequently, Robyn Eckersley (ibid.), an expert on trade-environment issues, observed: 'Judged in terms of size and teeth, we might regard the WTO as a large tiger and MEAs as a ragged collection of small cats'. In turn, labor law scholar Bob Hepple (2008: 238) noted with regard to international labor conventions: 'Social rights are like paper tigers, fierce in appearance but missing in tooth and claw'.

Most labor and environmental advocates therefore insist that international labor and environmental rules have to be linked to the enforcement mechanism of trade agreements in order to make them equally binding as commercial obligations. Liberal economists, by contrast, usually oppose the idea to link social standards to trade measures. They argue that free trade itself will eventually lead to economic growth, higher income levels and consequently to the improvement of labor laws and higher investment in environmentally friendly production processes (Bhagwati 2000, 1995). Linkage proposals would be counterproductive as they threatened to reduce most developing nations' only comparative advantage of low production costs. Moreover, the empirical evidence for the 'race-to-the-bottom' hypothesis is mixed at best. Several studies found that economic openness does not lead to the degradation of labor or environmental standards (Wheeler 2001; Karp 2011; OECD 1996; Madani 1999; Jaffe et al. 1995).

David Vogel (1997) even argued that market integration with powerful and wealthy 'green' political jurisdictions leads to a 'race-to-the-top' among trading partners in environmental, health and safety regulations. A comprehensive 1996 study by the Organization for Economic Cooperation and Development (OECD) found that trade liberalization equally leads to the improvement of core labor standards (OECD 1996). Most liberal economists therefore suspect no altruistic motives behind the push for social standards in trade policy. Instead, they view them as a new form of 'disguised protectionism' by industrialized countries. Social standards would aim at diminishing the advantage of developing nations by imposing costly regulations on them which are inappropriate for their level of economic development. Developing countries would therefore rightly oppose attempts to link labor and environmental issues to trade arrangements in order to protect their advantage in manufacturing costs (Tsogas 1999: 357).

The 'race-to-the-bottom' hypothesis, however, has retained great influence in trade policy debates (Drezner 2001). This is probably because outright protectionist stances have become more and more delegitimized in industrial countries (Siles-Brügge 2014). Depicting trade liberalization as a threat to worker rights and environmental standards instead can help to transform the economic case against free trade into a moral case. Hence, the last decades have increasingly witnessed the creation of 'Baptist-bootlegger coalitions' in trade policy debates. The term describes coalitions between groups that profit economically from certain policies and other groups that favor the same policies on moral grounds (Yandle 1983).[11]

Environmentalists (and labor rights' advocates) can be considered Baptists who pursue their cause not for economic gains but due to their ethical convictions. Unions that fear the economic consequences of trade liberalization for their members, by contrast, resemble bootleggers that benefit from the status-quo. Besides directly demanding protectionism for their industry branch, they increasingly make their arguments against stronger economic exchange with developing countries also on moral grounds. By embarking on this strategy, their opposition to trade agreements appears to

---

11 The metaphor goes back to the prohibition in the US of the 1920s, when Baptists and bootleggers both supported the alcohol ban, but for different reasons.

stem not from their own economic interests but from their ethical concern for workers (and the environment) at home and abroad. Hence, using the Baptists' moral case against free trade lowers the costs of favor-seeking for the bootleggers. Since this discursive strategy has become an important political tool, it is often difficult to distinguish which groups promote social standards out of moral convictions or for their own benefit.

The central moral argument of supporters is that the ILO's four core labor standards have long been internationally recognized as fundamental human rights which aim to protect the life and well-being of workers. Accordingly, all states of the international community are obliged to respect these rights regardless of their level of development. The linkage of labor standards with trade agreements would therefore be a legitimate and effective way to ensure compliance. While environmental issues do not possess the status of human rights, environmentalists point out that an international consensus has long emerged about the need for transnational solutions of environmental problems and the central role trade can play in this context. At the 1992 UN Conference on Environment and Development (UNCED), the 'Earth Summit' in Rio, the delegates signed the 'Agenda 21' which states that 'an open, multilateral trading system, supported by the adoption of sound environmental policies, would have a positive impact on the environment and contribute to sustainable development' (UNCED 1992). Environmentalists claim therefore that the link between trade and the environment has been long established within the concept of 'sustainable development.'

Critics of social standards generally concede that a broad international consensus about the principles and objectives in labor and environmental legislation exists. They dispute, however, that the universality of specific labor practices and environmental rules is accepted worldwide. A legitimate diversity of cultural values, economic conditions or theoretical assumptions would entail diverging labor and environmental laws in different regions. In this view, labor and environmental laws are national public policy choices that are not directly trade-related and therefore must not be subject to international trade rules. The prescription of international standards in labor and environmental legislation would violate the sovereignty of nation states or even constitute a form of neo-imperialism (Bhagwati 2007: 47).

Furthermore, skeptics are concerned that labor and environmental issues would overburden the multilateral trade agenda. In the light of most developing countries' refusal to discuss these issues in trade fora, insisting on their incorporation in the WTO could jeopardize the conclusion of multilateral trade agreements altogether. In addition, accepting labor and the environmental issues in trade discussions would open up the door for ever more trade-unrelated issues entering WTO negotiations. Since multilateral negotiations are already highly complex, the world trade system should rather focus on the original goal of dismantling trade barriers and leave other issues for more specialized organizations (Scherrer 1998: 66). Owing to these irreconcilable positions and the consensus requirement of the GATT/WTO, labor and environmental matters found only to a very limited extent entrance into the multilateral trade regime. Below, I will briefly elaborate on the fate of labor as well as environmental issues in the GATT/WTO system.

2.2 Labor and the Environment in the Multilateral Trading System

Labor and environmental standards are usually grouped together as 'fair trade concerns' although they seem to constitute fundamentally distinctive issue areas at first glance. This follows from the fact that they are supposedly both at risk of being subjected to a 'race to the bottom' in a globalized world economy. In addition, disregard of fundamental labor and of environmental norms is both regarded as morally reprehensible. Hence, 'fair trade' demands involve economic as well as ethical considerations (Howse and Trebilcock 1996).

During the 1990s, social standards emerged as a key issue on the agenda of the newly established WTO. At the time, growing trade and investment flows between the global north and south fueled fears over the consequences of increasingly fierce competition among countries with different regulatory levels. In addition, the growing interconnectedness of the world through new communication and media channels led to an increased public awareness in industrial nations of intolerable labor conditions, such as the exploitation of child labor or sweat shop labor, and environmentally harmful production practices in developing countries (Lee 1997: 176). As a consequence, the WTO came under increasing pressure to address labor and environmental matters. The following sections delineates the fate of labor and environmental issues in the multilateral trading system in more detail.

2.2.1 Labor in the GATT/WTO-System

The controversy over the linkage of labor standards with international trade agreements has intesified over the last two decades. However, it is far from new. The debate dates back more than 150 years to the times of the Industrial Revolution in Europe (Addo 2002: 286; Charnovitz 1987: 565). The creation of the ILO in 1919 can also at least partly be traced back to concerns about the effects of international trade on labor standards (Lee 1997: 174). The 1944 'Declaration of Philadelphia' which restated the aims and purposes of the ILO reaffirmed the need to ensure that the development of international trade does not come at the expense of workers' rights (Haworth, Hughes, and Wilkinson 2005: 1942-1943). Equally, the 1948 draft 'Havana Charter' of the ill-fated International Trade Organization (ITO) compromised an article on labor standards. The ITO, however, never came to existence. Instead, the GATT formed the basis of multilateral trade liberalization in the following decades although it was only intended to be a provisional agreement. Except for the issue of prison labor in Article XX, the GATT made no reference to labor regulations (Wilkinson 1999: 169).

The multilateral trade system therefore remained silent on the fundamental relation of trade and labor standards for many decades. However, as early as 1953 U.S. President Dwight D. Eisenhower had unsuccessfully proposed to include a provision to the GATT rulebook that outlawed unfair labor standards (Charnovitz 1987: 574). The issue re-emerged during the Tokyo Round (1973-1979), where tentative discussions on labor standards as a future matter of the GATT where held, again mainly on the initiative of the US (Hughes and Wilkinson 1998: 375). During the Uruguay Round (1986-94), the US requested the establishment of a working party that should look into labor issues in the GATT Council meetings in 1987 and 1990. The US, however, failed both times to gather sufficient support among other governments (Waer 1996: 25). In a last effort to include labor in the Uruguay Round, the US and some other developed nations sought an explicit recognition of the importance of labor issues in the final declaration of the Marrakesh Ministerial in 1994. Yet, even this modest approach foundered on the fierce resistance of most developing countries (Dymond 2001: 102).

In 1996, the issue labor standards was raised once again at the WTO's first Ministerial in Singapore and became subject of heated debates. Due to a concerted effort, developing countries succeeded in blocking any effort to link labor issues to the WTO rulebook. With the 'Singapore Ministerial Declaration' developing countries sought to finally put an end to the social clause debate. The Singapore Declaration committed the WTO membership to a broad acceptence of core labor standards, but simultanously emphasized that the ILO, and not the WTO, would be the right forum to adress labor standards (Haworth, Hughes, and Wilkinson 2005: 1945). Paragrapgh 4 of the 'Singapore Ministerial Declaration' reads:

> 'We renew our commitment to the observance of internationally recognised core labour standards. The International Labour Organisation (ILO) is the competent body to set and deal with these standards, and we affirm our support for its work in promoting them. We believe that economic growth and development fostered by increased trade and further trade liberalisation contribute to the promotion of these standards. We reject the use of labour standards for protectionist purposes, and agree that the comparative advantage of countries, particularly low-wage developing countries, must in no way be put into question. In this regard, we note that the WTO and ILO Secretariats will continue their existing collaboration.'[12]

Outside the WTO, however, efforts for the definiton of an internationally recognized set of core labor standards accelerated. Already in 1995, the 'Copenhagen World Summit for Social Development' had defined a set of 'fundamental workers' rights', based on seven international labor conventions. Subsequently, the ILO launched a campaign for their universal ratification (Addo 2015: 109). In 1998, the ILO adopted the 'Declaration on Fundamental Principles and Rights at Work', which identified four core labor standards. The principles were based upon a set of fundamental workers' rights which were already enshrined in eight international labor conventions. Table 1 provides an overview of the four ILO core principles and the corresponding ILO conventions as well as their ratification status in the US and EU member states.

---

12 WTO Singapore Ministerial Declaration, December 13, 1996.

Table 1: ILO Core Labor Principles and Corresponding ILO Conventions.

ILO Core Labor Principles	Corresponding ILO Conventions	Conventions ratified by the US	Conventions ratified by the EU member states
1. freedom of association and effective recognition of the right to collective bargaining	Convention No. 87 on freedom of association and protection of the right to organize (1948); Convention No. 98 on the application of the principles of the right to organize and to bargain collectively (1949).	-	x
2. the elimination of all forms of forced or compulsory labour	Convention No. 29 on forced or compulsory labour (1930); Convention No. 105 on the abolition of forced labour (1957).	-	x
3. the effective abolition of child labour	Convention No. 138 on the minimum age for admission to employment (1973); Convention No. 182 on the prohibition and immediate action for the elimination of the worst forms of child labour (1999).	x	x
4. the elimination of discrimination in respect of employment and occupation	Convention No 100 on equal remuneration of men and women workers for work of equal value (1951); Convention No. 111 on discrimination in respect of employment and occupation (1951).	-	x

Source: Author's own compilation.

This set of standards has increasingly served as a point of reference for advocates of linking trade agreements with labor obligations.[13] Observance of the 1998 ILO Declaration's core labor standards is obligatory to all ILO member states wether or not they have ratified the corresponidng conventions (Alston 2004: 458). While the 1996 WTO Singapore Declaration had raised hopes among linkage opponents that labor standards were off the table, the 1998 ILO Declaration consolidated the view among proponents that, irrespective of the development stage of economies, the adherence to a certain floor of labor standards was an internationally agreed objective.

---

13 The EU itself cannot ratify any ILO Convention, because only states can be parties to it.

Therefore, advocates continued to push for a greater role of labor concerns in the multilateral trade system. In the run up to the Seattle WTO Ministerial in 1999, the US, the EU, and Canada submitted proposals for the consideration of labor issues. While the US proposed that the WTO should adopt a work programme including the establishment of a 'Working Group' to adress trade and labor issues, the EU aimed at establishing a 'joint ILO/WTO Standing Forum on trade, labor and globalization questions' (Dymond 2001: 102).

Developing countries like India, Brazil and Morroco, however, rejected both proposals from the very beginning. The trade-labor controversy reached its height when U.S. President Bill Clinton mentioned in an newspaper interview the possible use of trade sanctions to enforce labor standards shortly before the Seattle ministerial conference (González Garibay 2011: 175). The resulting outrage among developing countries, along with the inability of the EU and the US to reach agreement on agriculture, ultimately led to the failure of the Seattle Ministerial. Consequently, no solution for the trade-labor dispute was found. At the launch of the 'Doha Development Round' in Doha, Quatar in 2001, however, a second ministerial declaration was issued in which labor standards were adressed. It confirmed the basic statement of the Singapore declaration. The Doha Declaration absolved the WTO of any responsibility for labor standards and emphasized that the appropriate location for such discussions was the ILO. This signalled a general acceptance of the closure of the social clause debate inside the WTO. Hence, the current round of multilateral trade negotiations commenced with labor issues being explicitly excluded (Haworth, Hughes, and Wilkinson 2005).

2.2.2 Environment in the GATT/WTO System

Both the 'Havana Charter' and the 1947 GATT treaties remained largely silent on environmental issues. Only Article XX of the GATT permits unilateral trade restrictions for various reasons, including environmental protection, under certain circumstances. Paragragh (b) of Article XX establishes an exception for measures 'necessary to protect human, animal or plant life or health', and paragraph (g) for measures 'relating to the conservation of exhausible nautral resources is such measures are made effective in conjunction with restriction on domestic production or consumption'. A first tentative attempt to include environmental considerations more fully in the world trade regime was the creation of the so-called Environmental

Measures and International Trade (EMIT) group in 1972. EMIT aimed at examining potential conflicts between trade liberalization and measures for pollution control. Yet, like in the case of labor standards, developing countries were wary of expanding GATT rules to environmental issues which they perceived as potential new barriers to trade. Hence, the EMIT group never convened until 1991. However, a number of contoversial rulings of the GATT/WTO dispute settlement panel triggered a serious public debate about the compatibility of international trade rules and national measures to protect the environement (Charnovitz 1992: 336).

Most notably was the complaint against the US brought by the Mexican authorities to the GATT dispute settlement procedure in February 1991. In the 'tuna-dolphin dispute', Mexico challenged restrictions on the import of Mexican tuna that were imposed by the US on the grounds that the methods applied by Mexican fishers to catch tuna failed to meet the dolphin protection standards under the U.S. Marine Mammal Protection Act which aimed at avoiding dolphins being trapped into fishings nets (González Garibay 2011: 175). The dispute panel found the measure to be in violation with GATT rules, since Article XX allowed governments to restrict imports on the grounds of their physical characteristics or performance but not to discriminate on the basis of how a product is produced. The panel ruling created a stir among environmentalists and fuelled fears that the imperatives of accelerating trade liberalization are being allowed to take precedence over environmental regulations (Haworth, Hughes, and Wilkinson 2005: 117).

The increased public awarness of the potential conflict between environemtal and trade rules was reflected in the preamble of the agreement establishing the WTO. It states that trade should be conducted 'while allowing for the optimal use of the world's resources in accordance with the objective of sustainable development, seeking both to protect and preserve the environment and to enhance the means for doing so' (WTO 1994). Initially considered only a symbolic acknowledgment of the issue, the WTO's Dispute Settlement Body in fact relied on the preamble to justify later rulings in environmental disputes. Most notably, the 2001 ruling in the 'shrimp-turtle case' overturned in a sense the tuna-dolphin decision and established that under certain conditions states could take unilateral actions to protect a resource in the global commons (Newell 2005: 117).

While these developments seemed to have expanded the room for the pursuit of environmental goals trough unilateral actions inside the WTO framework, the compatibility of MEAs with international trade rules has become the major subject of disputes in the trade-environment debate. Several MEAs incorporate trade measures as means of controlling trade in environmentally harmful products, securing compliance with treaty requirements or enforcing the respective agreement. The crucial question, however, of what prevails when obligations of international trade law and international environmental law run into conflict remained unclarified. According to Abdel Motaal (2001: 1216) concerns have particularly been raised with respect to the following MEAs:

Table 2: Central MEAs in Trade-Environment Debates.

Major Multilateral Environmental Agreements (MEAs)	Ratified by the US	Ratified by the EU
The Convention on International Trade in Endangered Species (CITES) (1973);	x	x
The Montreal Protocol on Substances that Deplete the Ozon Layer (1987)	x	x
The Basel Convention on the Control of Transboundary Movement of Hazardous Wastes and their Disposal (1989)	x	x
The Framework Convention on Climate Change (1992)	x	x
The Convention on Biological Diversity (1992)	-	x
The International Tropical Timber Agreement (1994)	x	x
The Rotterdam Convention on the Priot Informed Consent Procedure for Certain Hazardoues Chemicals and Pesticides in International Trade (1998)	-	x
The Kyoto Protocol (1997)	-	x
The Cartagena Protocol on Biosafety (2000)	-	x
The Stockholm Convention on Persistent Organic Pollutants (2004)	-	x
The Paris Climate Agreement (2016)	-	x

Source: Author's own compilation.

Environmentalists predominantly presume that the expanding comprehensiveness of trade rules restrict the scope of MEAs and ultimatly undermine their effectivness. They therefore demand that environmental obligations must explicitly take precedence over economic rules in case of conflict. In view of such criticism, the GATT members reconvened the dormant EMIT group in 1991 on initiative of the European Free Trade Association (EFTA) member states. The EMIT group was mandated to examine the relationship between a number of MEAs (the Montreal Protocol, the CITES agreement and the Basel Convention) and GATTs principles concerning TREMs, the transparancy of national environmenal regulations affecting trade, and packaging and labelling issues (González Garibay 2011: 177).

Efforts to include environmental safeguards in trade rules became more concrete at the end of the Uruguay round, when the EU pushed for last minute negotiations in order to integrate environmental provisions into the emerging WTO. However, developing countries, such as Malaysia, Mexico, Colombia, and Brazil, rejected any institutional structure dealing with the environment inside the WTO. Hence, merely a reference to the concept of sustainable development was included in the preamble of the 'Marrakech Agreement' establishing the WTO. In addition, the EMIT group was replaced by the Committee on Trade and Environment (CTE). The CTE was mandated 'to identify the relationsship between trade measures and environmental measures, in order to promote sustainable development and to make appropriate recommendations on wheter any modifications of the provisions of the multilateral trading system are required.'[14] However, the CTE did not manage to reach any conclusions on such modifications due to the persistant hostile stance of developing countries regarding new trade-related environmental measures (Brack 2004: 231-232).

At the launch of the 'Doha Round' in 2001 delegates agreed that the relationship between trade and MEAs should be part of the negotiation agenda. Furthermore, the CTE should continue its work on the effects of environmental measures on market access. Yet, discussions on trade and environment were entirley sidelined again at the Cancún Ministerial of 2003, when attention shifted on higher profile issues such as agriculture and services (ibid.: 234). Nevertheless, many environmentalists continue to advocate for the use of WTO's sanctioning mechanism to enforce international environmental obligations. Thereby, the WTO could overcome the chronical weakness of many international regulations on the environment that rely mostly on 'soft law' and avoid punitive sanctions. Yet, developing countries have resisted such an approach on the ground that the WTO would have neither the mandate nor the competence to engage in the area of environmental policy (Motaal 2001: 1219-1220). Hence, efforts to include a full-fledged 'environmental clause' into the multilateral trade system have failed, just like in the case of labor. In addition, the relationship between multilateral trade rules and MEAs remains largely unsettled.

---

14 WTO: Trade and Environment Decision of 14 April 1994.

2.3 Social Standards in U.S. and EU Trade Policy

At the sight of the failure to include labor and environmental standards in the multilateral trading regime, a number of mostly industrial countries began to attach such obligations to their unilateral and bilateral trade arrangements. In such settings they enjoyed greater bargaining leverage than on the multilateral level. As a consequence, about one-third of PTAs entered into force between 2005 and 2013 contained labor provisions according to research of the ILO (2013: 23). Figure 1 shows how labor provisions in PTAs have increased since the early 1990s.

Figure 1: *Number of Labor Provisions (LPs) in Trade Agreements (TAs) (1995-2016).*

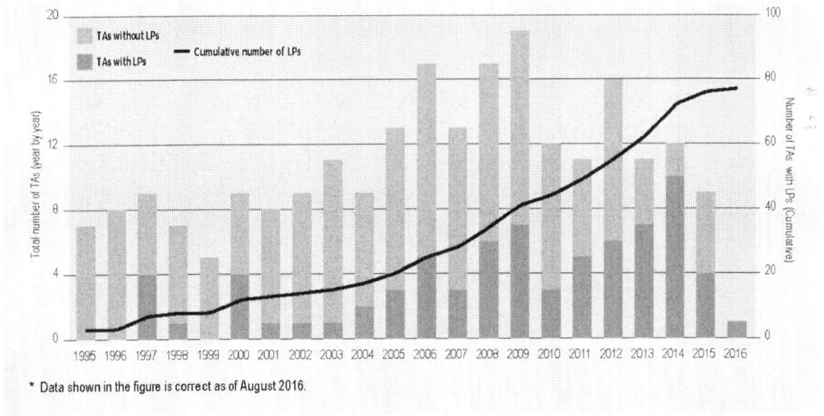

* Data shown in the figure is correct as of August 2016.

Source: (ILO 2017)

Equally, George (2014) found that 40 percent of regional trade agreements that became effective between 2007 and 2012 comprised substantive environmental provisions. Berger et al. (2017) even found that today around 85 percent of all PTAs already contain environmental provisions in some form or shape. As Figure 2 shows, each PTA included around 60 different environmental provisions by 2015 on average.

Figure 2: Average Number of Environmental Provisions in PTAs (1947-2015)

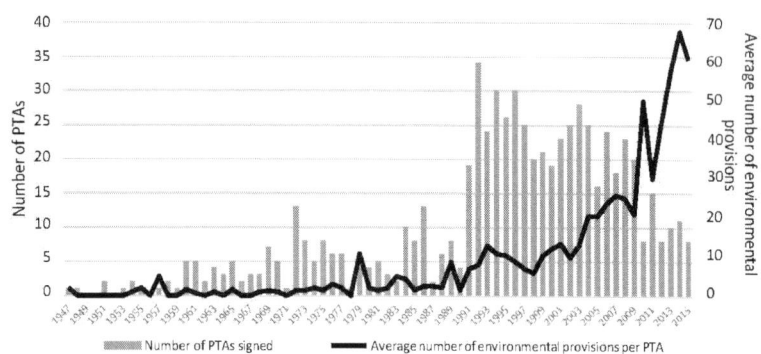

Source: (Berger, Brandi, and Bruhn 2017)

The US and the EU have been among the major drivers of this trend. Initially, they only attached labor-related conditionalities to their unilateral preference schemes (GSP) where they could basically dictate the terms of contract. Nowadays, however, ambitous chapters dealing with labor and environmental obligations constitute also part of reciprocal U.S. and EU trade agreements.

Despite these similarities, however, U.S. and EU social standards differ broadly speaking in two important ways: 1. in their scope and 2. in their enforcement tools. While the content of labor and environmental clauses in U.S. and EU PTAs changed considerably throughout the 2000s, their different underlying enforcement principle remained by and large unchanged. The EU prefers a soft approach with non-coercive means of enforcement, such as dialogue and consultations with governments and non-governmental organizations. As opposed to this, the US continuously opted for a punitive approach for its social standards, which allows for financial penalties or trade sanctions in order to compel compliance. In what follows, I outline (1) the largely similar U.S. and EU approaches to enforcement of social standards in their unilateral trade policies and (2) their distinct approaches for enforcement in bilateral and regional settings.

2.3.1 Social Standards in U.S. and EU Unilateral Trade Preference Schemes

Both the US and the EU have implemented General System of Preferences (GSP) programs since the 1970s that give unilateral, nonreciprocal, and preferential tariff treatment to products imported from designated countries in order to promote economic growth in the developing world. Over time, however, the US and the EU have made the unilateral access to their markets increasingly conditional on the adherence of beneficiary states to certain requirements regarding labor or the environment. In 1984, the US started to incorporate labor provisions in its GSP scheme that established a country's compliance with internationally recognized labor standards as one of GSP's eligibility criteria.

Similar labor provisions have been inserted by the US into other unilateral trade instruments, such as the Caribbean Basin Initiative (1983), the Caribbean Basin Recovery Act (1990), the Andean Trade Preference Act (1991), the Andean Trade Promotion and Drug Eradication Act (2002) as well as the African Growth and Opportunity Act (2000). Hence, in all unilateral U.S. trade preference instruments the failure of beneficiary states to adhere to certain labor standards is sanctionable by the withdrawal of access to the U.S. market (Jones 2015). Interestingly, however, the US to date has not introduced any environmental conditionality in its unilateral preference schemes.

The EU equally promotes social objectives in its GSP scheme through a 'carrots and sticks' approach that offers considerable incentives for compliance but also entails the threat of meaningful sanctions in case of violations. The introduction of social conditionality in the EU GSP scheme began in 1995 with the incorporation of punitive labor provisions. The provisions allowed for the withdrawal of trade preferences in case of infringements of the ILO conventions No. 29 and 105 concerning forced labor. In 1998, the EU also incorporated incentive-based provisions that provided additional preferences for countries that effectively implemented the ILO conventions No. 87 and 89 concerning freedom of trade unions and No. 138 concerning child labor. With the GSP revision of 2001 the EU extended the legal basis of both the withdrawal and the incentive clause to correspond with all the eight ILO core conventions.

In 2005, the incentive regime was reformed into the GSP+ system that granted more favorable market access than the conventional GSP to 15 countries that had ratified and effectively implemented 16 human rights conventions, including the eight ILO core conventions, and at least 7 (out of 11) conventions on environment and good governance by the end of

2008.[15] The withdrawal of GSP preferences, however, was possible in the case of 'serious and systematic violations' of the principles laid down in the labor and human rights conventions. In 2012, the EU's GSP system was once more revised this time inter alia enhancing the monitoring mechanisms and adding the implementation of the climate change convention as a prerequisite (Portela and Orbie 2014: 65-66).

In sum, in their unilateral trade preferences schemes both the US and the EU reserve the right to deny developing countries access to their markets if these do not comply with certain labor standards. In case of the US, the compliance of a beneficiary country with the GSP eligibility criteria is scrutinized in annual reviews carried out by the U.S. administration. Labor has been the single most frequently raised issue in these annual reviews. Over the years, the threat of losing GSP preferences has compelled many beneficiary countries to improve their observance of worker rights. The failure to do so in other cases led to the temporary suspension of GSP benefits for countries such as Burma, the Central African Republic, Chile, Maldives, Mauritania, Paraguay, Sudan and the Syrian Arab Republic or even the permanent termination of GSP access as it was the case with Liberia and Nicaragua. The compliance of a country with the EU's GSP eligibility criteria is not reviewed on an annual basis and therefore access to the EU market is somewhat more stable than in the case of the US. Nevertheless, the EU has also suspended GSP benefits on the grounds of labor rights abuses in two cases, namely for Myanmar in 1997 and for Belarus in 2007 (Vogt 2015).

Most recently, the US suspended trade privileges under GSP for Bangladeshi products in June 2013 in reaction to the collapse of a garment factory building in Dhaka that killed more than 1,100 people and made the headlines internationally (Sokou and Schneider 2013).[16] The EU equally threatened the Bangladeshi authorities to withdraw trade preferences the country received under the EU's 'Everything but arms' scheme for least-developed countries (LDCs) (Bilby 2013). In the end, the EU abstained from suspending the preferential access after the Bangladeshi government

---

15 The relevant environmental conventions are: Montreal Protocol on Substances that Deplete the Ozone Layer; Basel Convention on the Control of Transboundary Movements of Hazardous Wastes and Their Disposal; Stockholm Convention on Persistent Organic Pollutants; Convention on International Trade in Endangered Species; Convention on Biological Diversity; Cartagena Protocol on Biosafety; Kyoto Protocol to the UN Framework Convention on Climate Change.

16 The step was criticized as largely symbolic since textiles, the main Bangladeshi export product, were already excluded from the U.S. GSP scheme.

strengthened the protection of workers under the Bangladeshi labor code in reaction to the combined pressure from the EU and the US (Greenhouse 2013). The incident exemplifies that even though the EU seems to be more cautious in actually applying trade sanctions than the US (Orbie and Tortell 2009; Greven 2005; Vogt 2015), it does acknowledge in its unilateral trade policies the value of having the stick of economic sanctions in order to influence the behavior of foreign governments. Therefore, it can seem all the more surprising that the EU forgoes any coercive elements in relation to social standards in its bilateral and bi-regional trade policy. The US, in contrast, applies the same logic of conditionality in its bilateral and regional as in its unilateral trade policies.

2.3.2 Social Standards in U.S. Preferential Trade Agreements: The Coercive Approach

In 1994, the US set the precedent of linking labor and environmental issues to a trade accord with side agreements to NAFTA. The US-Jordan PTA of 2001, however, was the first U.S. PTA that fully incorporated labor and environmental clauses in the main body of the treaty. To date, the US has ratified overall 13 PTAs, compromising 19 countries, which contain labor as well as environmental provisions. Following Bolle (2013: 3), the labor and environmental provisions in U.S. trade agreements can be categorised into four models on the basis of the vatiation of their enforcement mechanisms:

1. Labor obligations under NAFTA are not part of the main body of the agreement. They are adressed instead in a subsequently added side agreement, namely the North American Agreement on Labor Cooperation (NAALC). Under NAALC parties agree to enforce their own labor laws. However, only a Party's 'persistent pattern of failure' to effectively enforce 'its occupational safety and health, child labor or minimum wage technical standards' is enforceable with sanctions. Furthermore, that failure must be trade-related and covered by mutually recognized labor laws (Bolle 2013: 3). By contrast, NAFTA did contain broad textual statements of support for environmental protection and reproduced the GATT's environmental exemptions. Most strikingly, however, was that NAFTA included a list of MEAs whose provisions would supersede NAFTA's in the event of conflict. The only enforceable obligations with regard to the environment, however, also can be found only in a side agreement, the North American Agreement on Environmental Cooperation (NAAEC). Mirroring the labor pro-

visions, under NAAEC only the 'persistent pattern of failure by a Party to effectively enforce its environmental law' can result in monetary penalties and ultimatly trade sanctions (Condon 2015: 107). Both labor and environmental provisions of the side agreements have different dispute settlement procedures than the main agreement. In addition, there are limits placed on monetary enforcement assesesments, with the suspension of benefits for non-compliance (Bolle 2013: 3; Condon 2015: 109).

2. The PTA with Jordan was the first U.S. trade agreement to directly incorporate labor and environmental standards in the body of a trade accord. With regard to labor, the parties 'reaffirm their obligations as members of the ILO and their commitments under the 1998 'ILO Declaration on Fundamental Principles and Rights at Work' and its follow-up'. The Parties 'shall strive to ensure that such labor principles and the internationally recognized labor rights set forth in paragraph 6 are recognized and protected by domestic law'. These internationally recognized labor rights are largely identical with the ILO core principles but exclude the fourth ILO core norm and list 'acceptable conditions of work with respect to minimum wages' instead. Hence, in contrast to NAALC, the focus lies on international labor standards rather than on national labor laws (Gantz 2011: 23). In the article on the environment, parties commit themself not to 'fail to effectively enforce' their environmental laws 'in a manner affecting trade'. No references are made, however, to MEAs. Most strikingly is that all labor and environmental provisions are subject to the same dispute settlement mechanism as commercial obligations, and hence, are equally enforceable by sanctions (Bolle 2013: 3; Gantz 2011: 21-22).

3. The seven U.S. PTAs ratified between 2002 and 2006 also refer to the list of internationally recognized worker rights defined by the US in the labor chapter. However, only the failure 'to effectively enforce' existing national labor laws 'through a sustained or recurring course of action or inaction, in a manner affecting trade between the parties' can lead to retaliatory actions. The formulation of the environmental obligations parallels the labor chapter. Violations initially would lead to capped financial penalties of up to $15 million annually. If the violating party fails to pay this fine, trade sanctions can be applied (Bolle 2013: 3).

4. All U.S. PTAs entered into force after 2007 require signatories to 'adopt, maintain, and enforce' the ILO core labor standards as stated in the ILO 1998 Declaration in their laws and practices. In the environment chapter, parties commit to 'adopt, maintain, and implement laws, regulations, and all other measures to fulfill its obligations' under a specified list of MEAs. Furthermore, parties to the agreements refrain from lowering their

labor and environmental standards. With regard to enforcement, the same dispute settlement procedures and possible sanctions apply for labor, environmental and commercial disputes (Gantz 2011: 38). Tableb 3 provides an overview over all U.S. PTAs since the early 1990s and the different models of U.S. social standards.

Table 3: Labor and Environmental Provisions in U.S. PTAs (1994-2018).

Model of Social Standards	Preferential Trade Agreement (in force)	Reference points of social standards	Enforcement mechanism
1	NAFTA (side agreements NAALC/ NAEEC) (1994)	National labor and environmental laws	Fines up to US$ 20million /0.07 of total trade volume (goods)
2	Jordan (2001)	ILO 1998 Declaration; national environmental laws	Regular trade sanctions under the regular dispute settlement mechanism of the agreement
3	Chile (2004) Singapore (2004) Australia (2005) DR-CAFTA (2006) Bahrain (2006) Morocco (2006) Oman (2009)	National labor and environmental laws	Fines up to US$ 15 million in the case of non-application of national labor and environmental law; trade sanctions in the event of non-payment
4	Peru (2009) Panama (2012) Colombia (2012) South Korea (2012) USMCA (not yet in force)	ILO 1998 Declaration; specified list of MEAs	Regular trade sanctions under the regular dispute settlement mechanism of the agreement

Source: Author's own compilation.

To sum up, social standards in U.S. PTAs have consistently relied on the threat of sanctions for enforcement with a tendency towards an ever more equivalence between commercial and social obligations. Furthermore, the US routinely sets preconditions for PTAs that require negotiation partners to undertake extensive reforms of their domestic labor and environmental legislation. Hence, even before entering into a trade agreement, the US uses conditionality in order to influence domestic regulations of trading partners. However, the US engages as well in cooperative measures in the context of PTAs to improve labor and environmental conditions in partner countries. In fact, the U.S. government provided a combined total of $275 million between 2001 and 2013 for labor-related capacity-building projects (GAO 2014: 15) and another $151 million between 2004 and 2013 for environmental cooperation activities (GAO 2014: 28) in PTA partner countries.

In general, the cooperative activities related to U.S. PTAs have not changed much over the years. U.S. PTAs usually list a set of priority areas for cooperation. In addition, further initiatives for the improvement of labor rights have been developed outside the legal PTA framework, for instance, in the case of CAFTA-DR and the US-Colombia PTA. Central American governments prepared a 'White Paper' to adress labor concerns in the region before the U.S. Congress enacted implementing legislation for CAFTA-DR. In the case of the US-Colombia PTA, the American and Colombian government agreed in 2011 to the 'Colombian Action Plan Related to Labor Rights' in order to promote the protection of international labor standards, prevent violene against labor leaders, and prosecute the perpetrators of such violence. The 'Labor Action Plan' listed nine issue areas with regard to labor rights, that Colombia had to adress before the PTA could be put to the vote in the U.S. Congress (GAO 2014: 12). With regard to the environment, the US has been working together with partner countries facing environmental challenges under the framework of the PTA as well as under environmental cooperation agreements and related programs (GAO 2014: 29).

These measures, however, require the voluntary cooperation of partner governments in order to achieve the desired results. The advantage of sanction-based clauses is that signatories can be compelled to fulfill their obligations regardless of their own preferences. In contrast to cooperative activities, the coercive character of U.S. labor and environmental provisions ensures that partner countries cannot simply walk away from labor and environmental commitments they have made by signing the trade agreement.

2.3.3 Social Standards in EU Preferential Trade Agreements: The Cooperative Approach

Labor and environmental provisions in EU PTAs did not follow a standardized approach for a long time. Instead, they were tailored to specific types of trade agreements. Following Van den Putte et al. (Van den Putte et al. 2014: 41-42) two phases can be distinguished broadly with regard to how the EU integrated social objectives in its trade agreements: PTAs for which the negotiations begann between 1995 and 2001 and PTAs negotiated since 2006, the so-called 'new generation' of trade agreements. The EU-

South Africa and EU-Chile FTAs can be considered as transition cases between the old and new generation of EU PTAs with regard to their social standards.

1. EU PTAs of the first phase incorporate only very vague references to cooperation on social matters. The Euro-Mediterranean Association Agreements of the EU negotiated under the umbrella of the 'Barcelona Process' since the mid-1990s do not contain references to ILO labor standards or MEAs. They merely forsee dialogue and cooperation on selected narrow, technical labor and environmental issues (Addo 2015: 235). Equally, the more commercially driven PTA with Mexico (2000) contains no labor and and only narrow environmental provisions (Grynberg and Qalo 2006: 641). Hence, social standards in these early PTAs, if exisiting, had more the character of declerations of intent than of binding obligations.

2. The EU-South Africa PTA (2004) can be considered a milestone for the inclusion of labor standards into EU trade agreements since it contained for the first time references to ILO core labor standards, eventhough only in a declaratory manner. The provisions regarding the environment remained largely unchanged and made no mention of MEAs. The Cotonou Agreement (2000), which is no PTA itself but provides the legal framework for cooperation between the EU and the ACP countries (African, Caribbean and Pacific states) for the period between 2000-2020, again lists the four ILO core labor standards but makes no reference to MEAs.

With the EU-Chile PTA (2003), though, the EU began to systematically include entire chapters on labor and the environment in its trade accords, although still in a comparatively limited way. With regard to labor, Article 44 of Title V requires for the first time in an EU PTA that the contracting parties recognize the ILO core labor standards articulated in the relevant ILO conventions (Addo 2015: 237). The article specifically states that signatories 'give priority to the creation of employment and respect for fundamental social rights, notably by promoting the relevant conventions of the International Labour Organisation covering such topics as the freedom of association, the right to collective bargaining and non-discrimination, the abolition of forced and child labour, and equal treatment between men and women'.[17] Furthermore, the agreement requires the parties to cooperate on environmental issues but makes no mention of MEAs. The PTA even incorporated an institutionalized civil society dialogue on social issues. Violations of labor and environmental provisions, however, could on-

---

17   EU-Chile PTA, Title V, Article 44(1.).

ly be dealt with by governmental consultations and not be enforced by sanctions.

3. Beginning with the EU-Cariforum PTA (2008), labor and environmental issues in EU PTAs were fundamentally upgraded through the inclusion of a broad 'sustainable development chapter' that covers both labor and environmental issues. EU provisions in the new generation of PTAs go beyond the content of U.S. PTAs, since they not only refer to the ILO 1998 Decleration but encourage parties to ratify the ILO core conventions. In addition, environmental provisions in the new generation of EU PTAs explicitly refer to a list of MEAs, which is much more comprehensive than the corresponding list in U.S. PTAs (Jinnah and Morgera 2013: 332).[18] However, EU agreements also recognize the right of each of the signatories to establish their own levels of labor and environmental protection and to adopt or modify their relevant laws and policies.

With regard to enforcement, the EU still solely relies on cooperative mechanisms for the enforcement of its social standards. At the outset of negotiations the EU is required to prepare a 'sustainable development impact assesment' that gives a forecast of the anticipated social and environmental consequences of the agreement. Beginning with the EU-Korea PTA (2011), EU social chapters aditionally require the creation of civil society fora such as a 'Joint Consultative Committee'[19] or 'Domestic Advisory Groups'[20], comprising environmental organizations, labor groups, business organizations and other relevant civil society stakeholders, that should provide advice on the implementation of labor and environmental provisions. The 'sustainable development chapter' is legally binding through the use of a specialized dispute settlement procedure. In the event of dispute over a subject covered by the 'sustainable development chapter' parties can request governmental consultation over the issue. If the matter cannot be settled at this stage, parties can resort to a panel of experts. The expert panel can seek information from the conflicting parties, the Domestic Advisory Group(s) and international organisations, such as the ILO, during its examination of the matter. The rulings of the expert panel, though, have a purely recommendatory character and derogations are not punishable by sanctions (Addo 2015: 246; Jinnah and Morgera 2013: 333). In the EU-CARIFORUM agreement, by contrast, the regular dispute settlement used for

---

18 The EU-Korea FTA (2011), however, does not include a list of MEAs but only obligates parties to enforce MEAs to which they are signatories.
19 EU–Central America Association Agreement (article 10).
20 EU–Republic of Korea, EU–Peru/Colombia and EU–Central America PTAs.

commercial issues applies, but the suspension of trade concessions is explicitly ruled out (Bartels 2013).

The areas of cooperation vary greatly from agreement to agreement concluded by the EU since they appear to be tailored to the specific needs of the respective partner country. In the context of recent agreements the EU funds specific labor rights capacity-building projects aimed at building the expertise of government officials to enforce labor laws. It funds, for instance, a project called the 'Joint Initiative on Corporate Accountability and Workers Rights' to attempt to improve workplace conditions in global supply chains. Furthermore, the EU works closely with the ILO on a number of similar capacity building projects. In contrast to the US, however, the EU does not require specific reforms of domestic labor or environmental legislation from negotiation partners in the context of PTA negotiations (Interview record #22, 2015).

Despite considerable variations with regard to the scope of labor and environmental provisions of EU PTAs over time, there seems to be a high level of continuity in the underlying enforcement mechanism for these provisions. In no EU PTA a clear linkage is established between market access and compliance with labor or environmental standards. In contrast to the coercive approach of the US where the threat of sanctions is used in order to compell compliance, the focus in EU PTAs is rather on information exchange and technical assistance with the aim of improving domestic legislation. Hence, the EU approach fails to address the central shortcoming of the existent international labor and environmental regime: its lack of a powerful enforcement mechanism.

Table 4: Labor and Environmental Provisions in EU PTAs (1997-2018).

Model of Social Standards	Preferential Trade Agreement (in force)	Reference points of social standards	Enforcement mechanism
1	Palestinian Authority (1997) Mexico (2000) Morocco (2000) Israel (2000) Algeria (2005) Cameroon (2009)	No Reference to ILO instruments nor to MEAs	Cooperation and/or dialogue on selected issues related to labor and the environment
2	South Africa (2004) Cotonou (2000) Chile (2003)	ILO Core Conventions; no reference to MEAs	Cooperation and/or dialogue on various labor and environmental issues

Model of Social Standards	Preferential Trade Agreement (in force)	Reference points of social standards	Enforcement mechanism
3	CARIFORUM (2008) South Korea (2011) Peru/Colombia (2013) Central America (2013) Georgia (2016) Moldova (2016) Ecuador (2016) Ukraine (2017) Vietnam (not yet in force) Singapore (not yet in force) Canada (not yet in force) Japan (not yet in force)	ILO Core Conventions; ILO 1998 Declaration; MEAs	Intergovernmental consultations, civil society dialogue and non-binding recommendations of expert panels; derogation not punishable by sanctions

Source: Author's own compilation.

2.4 Concluding Remarks: Same Ends, Different Means

The present chapter explored the role of social standards in international trade policy over the last two decades. Even though there is little empirical evidence for the relation of liberalized trade and the diminishing of labor and environmental standards, activists' calls for binding international rules in these issue areas had a profound impact on trade policy debates. All efforts by the US and the EU to include social standards in the WTO, though, foundered on the persistent resistance of developing countries. Due to their enhanced bargaining power in bilateral and regional settings, however, the US and the EU have managed to systematically integrate social standards in their PTAs since the early 2000s.

The reference points of the social provisions in U.S. and EU PTAs initially varied considerably. Nowadays, they typically refer to internationally agreed norms, such as MEAs and ILO norms instead of self-selected standards. With regard to enforcement mechanisms of these standards, however, the EU and the US show a high degree of continuity. In all U.S. PTAs, violations of labor or environmental clauses can lead to monetary penalties or even the partial suspension of market access. The EU, by contrast, consistently relies on dialogue and cooperation mechanisms for enforcement of social provisions in its PTAs and explicitly rejects a sanction-based approach. Hence, while both prefer to achieve improvements of labor rights and environmental protections in partner countries through dialogue and cooperative activities, only the US reserves the right to resort to coercive measures in case trading partners fail to comply with their labor and environmental obligations. The US therefore seems to be more resolute in promoting labor rights and environmental protection abroad than the EU.

In sum, the US uses both coercive and cooperative measures to promote labor and environmental goals through its PTAs. The EU, by contrast, forgoes coercive means to ensure compliance with social standards, and confines itself to soft enforcement tools. Both soft and hard measures bear the potential of improving labor and environmental conditions in partner countries Yet having the option of reverting to the threat of trade sanctions as a last resort provides social standards with a higher level of obligation. It remains therefore puzzling why the EU as a self-declared champion of international labor and environmental standards voluntarily opted for renouncing punitive measures, while the US turned into a pioneer in this area. Thus, the aim of this study is to identify the causes behind the divergence in the enforcement mechanisms of U.S. and EU social standards in PTAs. The central research question is therefore: Why did the US enshrine sanction-based social standards in its PTAs while the EU opted for a cooperative approach?

3. A Domestic Politics Approach to PTA Social Standards

The outcome of international trade negotiations depends on the relative bargaining power of the states (or trade blocs) involved and the effects of their domestic politics on the international bargaining process. The US and the EU have large markets of comparable size, which enables both equally to determine the content of PTAs with third states. Consequently, the diverging design of social standards in U.S. and EU PTAs must stem from the respective characteristics of their domestic trade policy-making processes. This chapter presents a theoretical framework that seeks to explain how the preferences of societal interest groups as well as the attributes of the institutional setting that channels their demands influence negotiation outcomes in trade talks of the US and the EU with third states.

The chapter begins by reviewing the relevant academic literature on the political economy of trade policy-making and social standards in PTAs. The subsequent section delineates the theoretical framework that will guide the analysis in the following empirical chapters. The section develops a domestic politics theory for the design of social standards' enforcement mechanisms that draws on key assumptions of the 'Open Economy Politics'-approach (OEP). OEP offers the advantage of integrating theories of interest formation based on the theory of international trade, theories of collective action, and theories of political institutions (Lake 2009). Thereby, it allows us to understand how societal and institutional factors combined shape governmental decisions over foreign economic policy. Applied to a comparative study of trade-policy making in the US and EU, such a framework should enable us to identify the factors that were decisive for the different design of social standards in U.S. and EU PTAs. The chapter concludes by addressing the pivotal methodological issues of case selection, operationalization, and data collection.

3.1 Trade Politics and Social Standards: A Literature Review

Numerous studies have already explored labor and/or environmental standards in U.S. and EU PTAs. They unexceptionally noted the fundamental differences that underlie the U.S. and EU models (Addo 2015; Grandi 2009; Grynberg and Qalo 2006; Horn, Mavroidis, and Sapir 2010; Jinnah and Morgera 2013; Scherrer et al. 2009; Greven 2005; ILO and IILS 2013; Elliot 2011; R. V. 2011; Berger, Brandi, and Bruhn 2017; ILO 2017). However, these studies remain largely descriptive and do not seek to explain the reasons behind these different approaches. In order to do so, a thorough review of the relevant theoretical literature on trade policy-making in the field of International Relations (IR) and International Political Economy (IPE) seems essential.

Constructivist scholarship appears to offer a straightforward explanation for the distinct approaches of the US and the EU to social standards. Ian Manner's (2002) often-cited concept of 'Normative Power Europe' (NPE) shaped the notion of the EU as a distinct kind of international actor. The EU would pursue normative goals with normative means instead of imposing its self-centered interests on others by coercion like nation states. The soft enforcement mechanism of social standards in EU PTAs could be interpreted as a manifestation of the EU's general preference for non-coercive means in international relations. However, on closer examination it becomes clear that the EU does not generally shrink back from using economic sanctions in international relations. On the contrary, 'restrictive measures' are in fact the principle foreign policy tool of the EU in the framework of the Common Foreign and Security Policy (CFSP) (Portela 2009).[21] In trade policy, the EU equally does not generally refuse to use economic coercion to reach value-based objectives. In its unilateral General System of Preferences (GSP) the EU requires beneficiary states to comply with a number of conditions regarding human and labor rights as well as governance (Portela and Orbie 2014). In the event of non-compliance, beneficiary countries can lose their access to the EU market.

Hence, constructivist explanations that are based on the different identities of the US and the EU as international actors can be ruled out. Therefore, the rationalist literature on the political economy of trade policy moves to the fore. This body of literature is vast and can be broadly divided into systemic - or international-level - and domestic political approaches. Systemic approaches hold domestic politics constant since they treat all states as unitary, rational actors. International-level theories assume that the conditions of the international systems decisively determine actors' policy choices. Several studies have identified international competition as the reason behind the recent spread of regional and bilateral PTAs (Aggarwal and Fogarty 2004; Baldwin and Jaimovich 2012; Baldwin 2006; Sbragia 2010). Another line of research focuses on the impact of actors' relative

---

21 'Restrictive measures' is synonymous with economic sanctions in EU jargon.

bargaining power on the outcome of trade negotiations (Narlikar 2004; Lee and Wilkinson 2007; Singh 2008; Schirm 2010).

Relative power in international trade politics is largely determined by the size of an actor's internal market. Since small economies are often heavily dependent on market access to larger foreign markets (Manger and Shadlen 2012), the latter are better placed to shape the terms of an agreement (Drezner 2007). Both the US and the EU can be defined as 'Great Powers' in international trade politics due to their comparable, enormous economic weight vis-à-vis other trading nations (Behrens and Janusch 2012). In other words, they are both 'rule-makers' instead of 'rule-takers' in international economic relations. Therefore, they should be equally able to design social standards in PTAs according to their preferences. Hence, systemic approaches are incapable of explaining variations in these provisions between U.S. and EU PTAs. Since differences in bargaining power cannot account for their diverging social standards, we need to shift our attention towards the domestic political dynamics behind trade policy choices of the US and the EU.

Domestic politics-theories of trade policy-making again can be subdivided in two categories: Society-centered and state-centered approaches. Society-centered approaches proceed from the assumptions of the 'pressure group model' that was developed by Schattschneider (1935) in his pioneering study on the Smoot-Hawley tariff act. This line of research considers the competition for influence among societal groups to be the decisive variable to explain a country's foreign economic policy choices (Moravcsik 1997). The central assumption of this model is that trade policy decisions invariably produce winners and losers in the domestic economy. According to standard economic theory, consumers invariably gain from trade liberalization since they profit from cheaper imports (Suranovic 2010). However, consumers generally fail to overcome collective action problems and to get organized since their gains are diffuse. The costs of trade liberalization, by contrast, are concentrated. Therefore, losers are better placed to mobilize and influence public policy formulation (Olson 1965).

As a result, many society-centered approaches assume that interest group pressures are inevitable biased towards protectionist forces (Bailey, Goldstein, and Weingast 1997; Evans, Jacobson, and Putnam 1993; Moravcsik 1993). However, as Milner (1991) has shown also actors with concentrated gains through trade liberalization organize and wield strong influence in trade politics. Thus, trade politics is characterized by the competition among different special interest groups with conflicting demands. A main point of contention in society-centered approaches is whether the central line of conflict runs between capital and labor or between the different sectors of an economy (Milner 1999). Irrespective of these disagreements, societal approaches have difficulties to explain the extensive liberalization of international trade that has occurred over the last decades (Alt et al. 1996). Hence, the influence of interest groups seems to be a necessary but not a sufficient condition to explain trade policy choices of states. Therefore, we have to consider also the institutional characteristics within which trade policy is made.

In contrast to societal approaches, state-centered theories focus on the role of political institutions in the aggregation of societal preferences. According to these theories, institutional structures grant different trade policy actors diverging degrees of influence during the policy formulation process. Consequently, different institutional settings can produce distinct policies. A major difference of political systems lies in the degree of autonomy from special interest groups they grant to policy-makers in different positions of government (Katzenstein 1977; Rogowski 1987). Some institutional rules give interest groups great influence on the political stances of policy-makers. Others leave decision-makers much more leeway in setting policy (da Conceição-Heldt 2013).

Many trade policy scholars agree that the size of policy-makers' constituencies heavily influence their relationship with interest groups and, hence, their preferences. Large constituencies induce policy-makers to focus on the supraregional welfare and on strategic objectives in trade policy. Smaller electoral districts, by contrast, are more concerned about the impact of a policy on their own electoral district. Therefore, concentrating trade policy competences in the executive branch is believed to reduce the influence of concentrated interests and to result in a more liberal trade policy. Greater involvement of parliamentary bodies on the formulation of trade policy, by contrast, should lead to more protectionism. This is because legislators are assumed to be more susceptible to protectionist pressures from their local districts (Haggard and Kaufman 1995; Haggard and Webb 1994; Baldwin 1986; Lake 1988; Milner 1988; Frieden and Martin 2003; Mansfield and Busch 1995; Destler 2005; Bailey, Goldstein, and Weingast 1997; Haggard 1988; Goldstein 1993).

Nevertheless, not only constituency size seems to influence policy-makers' preferences. The nature of the electoral system and party politics matter as well (Mansfield, Milner, and Rosendorff 2002; Epstein and O'Halloran 1996; Schnietz 2000; Keech and Pak 1995). Furthermore, institutional rules equally determine which branch of government is best placed to achieve its preferred outcome (Rogowski 1999; Haggard 1988; Milner and

Kubota 2005; Milner and Rosendorff 1997). Tsebelis' (1995) veto players approach is frequently used by researchers in quantitative studies to explain countries' varying degrees of openness to trade (Mansfield, Milner, and Pevehouse 2007; O'Reilly 2005; Milner and Mansfield 2012; Henisz and Mansfield 2006). It is assumed that the more domestic veto-players exist, the more difficult it is for governments to pursue trade liberalization. These studies, however, solely examine the conditions under which states are more likely to enter into trade agreements. They treat PTAs as if they were all identical in scope and depth. Some recent quantitative studies, by contrast, have explored variations in institutional features of PTAs (Kucik 2012; Eckhardt and Elsig 2015; Kohl, Brakman, and Garretsen 2016; Dür, Baccini, and Elsig 2014; Baccini, Dür, and Elsig 2015). Few scholars, however, have used so far qualitative methods to explore selected differences of PTAs provisions. A notable exception is Hafner-Burton (2005) who compared labor and human rights standards in EU and U.S. trade agreements.

Few studies, however, have attempted to provide explanations for the variations in the design of social standards in PTAs to date. Behrens and Janusch (2012) examined the PTA negotiations of the US and the EU with Mexico and Chile and concluded that their chosen approach for human rights, labor and environmental standards cannot be explained by normative convictions but rather domestic politics. Kerremans and Gistelinck (2009) based their explanation for the difference in U.S. and EU PTA's labor standards on the different role political parties play in the US and Europe. Postnikov (2014), by contrast, identified the different patterns of delegating negotiating power from the legislative to the executive branch in the EU and the US as the central variable for explaining the differences in the design of social standards in U.S. and EU PTAs. These studies deliver valuable starting points for our understanding of the domestic political dynamics behind social standards in PTAs. However, in my view, they tend to focus too narrowly on one variable - political parties or the delegation from the legislature to the executive - to fully grasp the underlying causes in the variation in the design of social standards. Following Hafner-Burton (2009), who compared the emergence of labor standards in U.S. PTAs with human rights standards in EU PTAs, the present study will therefore apply a more elaborated domestic politics approach as the theoretical framework. Building on the OEP literature, the study will consider both societal preferences and institutional characteristics as explanatory factors.

Besides answering the central research question, this study attempts to contribute to our understanding of how domestic political processes shape the design of trade agreements more generally. Several researchers (Poletti and De Biévre 2013; da Conceição-Heldt 2013) have pointed out that there is a lack of comparative focus in the literature on domestic trade policy-making. Most studies are limited to one actor, usually the US or the EU. Research on U.S. trade policy routinely deals with the impact of divided government (Lohmann and O'Halloran 1994; O'Halloran 1994), the electoral system (Mansfield and Busch 1995; Rogowski 1987) or interest groups (Bailey, Goldstein, and Weingast 1997; Destler and Odell 1987). Most research on EU trade policy instead attempts to get to grips with the unique multi-level nature of EU trade politics (Collinson 1999; Dür 2006; Dür and Zimmermann 2007; Frennhoff Larsén 2007, 2007; Young and Peterson 2014; Meunier 2005; Woolcock 2011; Zimmermann 2008). EU trade policy research would benefit tremendously from explicit controlled comparisons with other political systems. Comparisons with the US promise to be especially fruitful since the literature on the functioning of the domestic trade policy-making process in the US is the most developed. Furthermore, the international framework conditions for both actors are quite similar.

There are already some studies that do compare trade policy-making in the US and EU, mostly focusing on the delegation of negotiation authority from the legislature to the executive (Clark, Duchesne, and Meunier 2000; da Conceição-Heldt 2013; De Biévre and Dür 2005; Zimmermann 2007; Leeg 2018). As da Conceição-Heldt (2013: 590) points out, more such qualitative cross-country studies are needed to better comprehend the complex interaction of executives, legislatures and interest groups in foreign economic policy-making. Yet, grounding EU trade policy research more firmly in the comparative politics approach entails several difficulties. It requires comparing the political systems of a traditional nation-state like the US with a sui-generis supranational entity like the EU.

However, scholars have noted that the EU's quasi-federal structures, its bicameral legislature, extensive judicial review and its separation of powers make the EU resemble more closely the US than any European nation state (Menon and Schain 2006; Fabbrini 2007). Furthermore, Meunier (2005) has argued that the delegation of negotiation authority to the executive branch in EU trade politics was intentionally modeled after the U.S. system. Hence, comparisons between the EU and the US in trade policy-making are not impracticable. They require, however, the utilization of abstract conceptual tools in order to take into account the different institutional contexts of the US and the EU. The following section intends to develop such a theoretical framework that is applicable for both the US and the EU despite the wide discrepancies of their respective political system.

3.2 Theoretical Framework

As the literature review above shows, trade politics is a well-researched field in IPE. We therefore have now a relatively good understanding of many aspects of current trade politics. From the multitude of insights from these perspectives, the OEP approach emerged by the late 1990s as an influential paradigm that now guides research among many IPE scholars. It originally emerged in the context of traditional trade policy that focuses on the distributional consequences of customs policy. Meanwhile it has been fruitfully extended to other areas of foreign economic policy, such as monetary and financial relations (Frieden 1988; Bernhard, Broz, and Clark 2003), foreign direct investment (Jensen 2006; Pinto and Pinto 2008), foreign aid (Milner 2006; Lundsgaarde 2013; Milner and Tingley 2010), regulation (Richards 1999), corporate governance (Gourevitch and Shinn 2005), and global governance (Kahler and Lake 2003). This study attempts to refine the basic assumptions of the OEP approach in order to make it usable for the analysis of the shaping of social standards' enforcement mechanisms in PTAs.

Research within the OEP framework proceeds in three analytical steps: Initially, it derives the interests of societal actors over economic policy from their position within the international economy. Hence, the distributional consequences of trade liberalization are seen as the decisive factor for the position interest groups take in trade politics. However, modern-day trade policy no longer exclusively deals with the erection or dismantling of tariff barriers. Instead, it focuses on domestic regulations that might obstruct the free flow of goods across borders (Woll and Artigas 2007). Therefore, any theoretical approach for modern trade policy requires considering not only the distributional effects of trade liberalization but also the implication of strict international trade rules for interest groups' general public policy objectives. In a second step, researchers analyze how domestic political institutions aggregate these societal interests into 'national' policy preferences. Finally, researchers examine, when necessary, how states with diverging preferences bargain to reach an agreement. Thereby, OEP allows to understand the emergence of political outcomes from 'the most micro- to the most macro-level in a linear and orderly fashion' (Lake 2009: 225).

Preferences of Societal Interest Groups

The basic point of departure for research within the OEP framework is to determine the interests, or policy preferences, of relevant societal interest groups. This is because costs and benefits created by dismantling trade barriers are believed to be diffuse for the general public. They are concentrated, however, for certain societal groups directly affected by trade policy decisions. Only actors anticipating such concentrated costs or benefits can be expected to overcome collective action problems and have sufficient incentive to invest resources in trying to influence policy. Therefore, well-organized groups with concentrated interests dominate trade politics (Olson 1965). Interest groups are assumed to be rational, goal-oriented and utility driven actors. In classical OEP research, the expected redistributive income effect is the major determinant of interest groups' preferences in trade politics, since trade liberalization is irrevocably associated with significant distributional consequences (Frieden 1991, 1999).

As a result, policy-makers are subject to pressures stemming from different interest groups with colliding preferences. Put simply, actors that benefit from a policy are expected to lobby political decision-makers in order to obtain that policy. Actors that lose from a policy, by contrast, should try to prevent such a policy from materializing (Frieden and Martin 2003: 128). However, the theory of international trade yields contradictory conclusions concerning how tariff reductions will redistribute income. In the Heckscher-Ohlin model with two factors and complete factor mobility, the Stolper-Samuelson-theorem predicts that trade liberalization benefits the abundant factor and harms the scarce factor (Stolper and Samuelson 1941). Hence, the main political conflict in trade policy is assumed to arise between capital and labor. In the factor-specific model, on the other hand, the Ricardo-Viner theorem indicates that trade liberalization benefits the export-oriented industries and harms import-competing sectors. Hence, capital and labor of an industrial branch should be united for or against trade liberalization depending on whether their industry expects to profit or loose (Alt and Gilligan 1994). The empirical evidence for either model, however, is mixed (Beaulieu 2002, 2002; Magee 1980; Magee, Brock, and Young 1989; Irwin 1994, 1996; Balistreri 1997).

Therefore an increasing consensus has emerged in the literature on trade policy preferences that the explanatory power of the two competing theorems depends on the time horizon (Magee, Brock, and Young 1989). The Ricardo-Viner theorem is believed to be better at forecasting the effects of trade policy decisions in the short-term. The Stolper-Samuelson-theorem, by contrast, has its strengths in predicting trade policy preferences in the long run (Rogowski 1989). Since the focus of this study are social standards in PTAs, I assume that the Stolper-Samuelson theorem serves as the appropriate heuristic tool to describe the cleavages among societal actors. This is because the issue of social standards is not tied to the distributional consequences of a particular PTA, but rather affects the long-term relation between capital and labor. The establishment of strict international rules for labor and environmental protection should benefit workers in industrialized countries in the long-run since its shields them from unfair competition of products that are made under conditions incompatible with internationally recognized minimum labor and environmental standards. In addition, social standards on the international level shield domestic labor legislation from downward pressures in an increasingly globalized world economy.

Consequently, different coalitions between industry sectors might emerge in the context of different PTA negotiations due to the specific distributional consequences of the respective agreement. The cleavages between proponents and opponents of social standards, however, should be stable over the investigation period. Business groups are expected to stand to gain from trade liberalization and therefore should favor the swift conclusion of PTAs. Enforceable social standards, however, don't offer economic gains for them. Quite the contrary, the coupling of commercial agreements with labor and environmental obligations could be obstructive to the goal of trade liberalization (Suranovic 2002). Not only developing countries' governments are extremely wary of the entanglement of trade with labor and environmental issues. Thus, aiming at agreements including such provisions can protract PTA negotiations or even lead to their failure.

In addition, such regulations could have adverse effects for the potential profits of firms operating abroad. They might also strengthen such costly regulations at home. Consequently, the central demand of export-oriented business organizations towards decision-makers can be assumed to be to strive for the extensive opening of foreign markets through PTAs devoid of serious labor and environmental regulations. Import-competing business groups, by contrast, stand to lose from freer trade and consequently seek protectionist measures. However, instead of demanding social standards such industries should seek targeted protective tools such as tariffs and quotas that are tailor-made to their specific needs (Milner 1988). Hence, only export-oriented business groups can be expected to spend resources lobbying on the issue of social standards.

Labor unions can be equally split with regard to particular PTAs. Unions whose members stand to gain from a PTA through the rise of exports should welcome the conclusion of the agreement. Unions of import-competing sectors, by contrast, who fear the opening up of the domestic market will affect their workers negatively through increasing pressures on wages or job losses, by contrast, should oppose trade liberalization. The labor movement, however, can be assumed to be united when it comes to preserving or extending regulations for the protection of workers. As a consequence, labor unions in import-competing sectors should seek strict social standards in PTAs as protections against cheap imports and the shifting of production to low-cost countries. Labor unions in export-oriented sectors should be equally supportive when trade agreements protect national labor regulations against international competitive pressure and contribute to the establishment of an international binding labor rights regime. After all, labor unions formed in the first place to protect workers from unbridled market forces. Therefore, labor in advanced industrialized should be uniformly in favor of enforceable social standards in trade agreements.

However, a purely economic theory of preference origins has difficulties to explain why environmental groups spend resources attempting to influence trade policy (Oatley 2010: 92). Tariff reductions neither wield economic gains nor cause concentrated costs for environmental groups. Positive or negative externalities of trade liberalization affect society as a whole. According to Olson's (1965) theory of collective action problems, environmentalists should therefore not even be able to get organized in order to engage in trade policy. Environmental NGOs, however, emerged independently of trade politics. Environmentalists became organized in the industrialized world during the late 1960s and 1970s to promote environmental protection mainly through more state intervention in the economy. Private enterprises were believed to disregard the negative externalities of their economic activities for the environment. Therefore, environmental NGOs advocated comprehensive state regulations for environmental protection (McCormick 1995; Doherty 2005).

Simultaneously, the world trade regime increasingly focused on dismantling non-tariff barriers. Domestic regulations that obstruct the free flow of goods and services across borders, including environmental regulations, were subjected to strict scrutiny by international trade courts. These opposing tendencies made environmental groups inevitably critical of trade liberalization since strict environmental regulations might run in conflict with the goal of unhindered economic exchange. Hence, environmentalists became active in trade politics as they saw their policy objectives threatened by increasingly strict international economic rules (Young and Peterson 2006). Nowadays environmental groups constitute influential stakeholders in trade politics although they did not form based on the distributional effects of trade policy. Therefore, they must be necessarily incorporated in domestic political approaches. Environmental groups should oppose trade liberalization, at least unless trade agreements provide for sufficient safeguards to protect the environment. Hence, even though labor unions and environmental NGOs are frequently pitted against each other on other economic issues (Obach 2004: 47-81), they can be assumed to be on the same side in trade politics. Based on these theoretical assumptions, the following general hypothesis regarding societal preferences on social standards in trade agreements can be formulated:

Hypothesis 1: Labor unions and environmental NGOs should favor enforceable social standards in PTAs, while business organizations should oppose strict labor and environmental provisions.

Responsiveness of Policy-Makers

Deducing the preferences of societal actors, however, is only the starting point for the analysis. The domestic political institutions through which these conflicting societal preferences are mediated fundamentally shape political outcomes. Different institutional arrangements aggregate interests in different ways, and consequently, can substantially influence the weight different interest groups have in the political process. In particular, they crucially determine the responsiveness of policy-makers towards the demands of different interest groups (Krasner 1977; Lake 1988; Katzenstein 1977; Krasner 1978; Gourevitch 1986). This allows to draw conclusions about the trade policy preferences of relevant decision-makers in the legislative and executive branch.

In democracies, the transmission of societal interests to politicians happens mainly through elections. Since politicians can be assumed to be utility-maximizers whose ultimate goal is to remain in office (Mayhew 1974), office-holders tend to take political stances that increase their chances for re-election (Grossman and Helpman 1994). Hence, interest groups can exert considerable influence over policy-makers which heavily depend on them for their re-election. Therefore, policy-makers that are reliant on trade skeptical groups are most likely to take protectionist stances while office-holders with business ties should favor trade liberalization. Policy-makers that are more autonomous from interest group pressure, by contrast, have greater leeway to advance the 'national interest' and maximize the general economic welfare. Since mainstream economic theory teaches that protectionism only benefits narrow groups but inevitably creates costs for society as a whole (Krugman 1993), policy-makers that are largely insulated from interest group pressures should invariably support free trade.

The relationship between policy-makers and interest groups is primarily determined by the constituency size, the characteristics of electoral institutions and the nature of electoral competition. Constituency size matters because small and large constituencies create different incentives for policy-makers. Large constituencies are believed to reduce the impact of special interests and incline policy towards the general welfare. Since large constituencies are more likely to include losers and winners of trade liberalization, policy-makers can balance the pressures of proponents and opponents. Instead, they can keep in view the strengthening of the overall economy (Rogowski 1987). National governments, like the U.S. administration and EU member state governments, are - at least de facto - elected in one single, national constituency.[22] Therefore, they are more likely to override protectionist forces and promote liberal trade policies (Lohmann and O'Halloran 1994; Milner and Rosendorff 1997; Baldwin 1986; Lake 1988; Katzenstein 1977).[23] They are only inclined to take protectionist measures, if an import-competing industry possesses such nationwide importance that neglecting its demands could affect their re-election chances (Nielson 2003).

However, governments seek PTAs not only for economic but also for strategic reasons (Bailey, Goldstein, and Weingast 1997; Karol 2000; Aggarwal and Fogarty 2004; Briceno Ruiz 2007; Feinberg 2003; Antkiewicz and Momani 2009; Phillips 2007; Ravenhill 2010). This is particularly true in case of the US and the EU since many of their PTAs are signed with much smaller trading partners. Therefore, they have negligible economic impact on the large markets of the US and EU. Instead executives regularly pursue foreign policy objectives in trade policy and disregard narrow economic

---

22 Governments in Europe are of course not directly elected by voters, but emerge from parliamentary majorities. However, the parliamentary system prevalent in Europe creates de facto national constituencies for governments.

23 This classic assumption of the literature on U.S. trade policy, however, has been heavily challenged by the election of the openly protectionist President Donald Trump.

concerns (Karol 2000; Bailey, Goldstein, and Weingast 1997). As a consequence, U.S. and EU executives should have a clear preference for the swift conclusion of PTAs. The inclusion of social standards, by contrast, offers no immediate commercial or strategic gains but often proves to be a stumbling block in trade negotiations. Therefore, executives can be assumed to be reluctant to press for enforceable social standards that might complicate or even jeopardize the conclusion of trade agreements.

The preferences of policy-makers that are accountable to small constituencies, by contrast, are quite different. Members of legislatures are primarily concerned to promote the interests of groups that support them in their electoral districts. Hence, they are more susceptible to the narrower economic concerns of their constituencies (Rogowski 1987). Representatives who vote against their constituency's direct interests run the risk of losing their seat in parliament in the next election. Consequently, law-makers that rely on business groups tend to favor trade liberalization. Legislators that heavily depend on trade skeptical groups, by contrast, should oppose such policies. Constituency preferences on trade, however, have become increasingly heterogeneous in industrialized countries over the last decades (Hall 1998). Legislators are nowadays confronted with lobbying from a wide range of groups, including organizations representing exporting or import-competing interests, labor unions, environmental groups as well as public health and human rights advocates. Consequently, law-makers from inhomogeneous districts often face the dilemma of having to represent conflicting interests simultaneously. They are therefore compelled to engineer trade policies that deliver benefits for exporters by securing foreign market access at same time as addressing the concerns of groups critical of trade liberalization (De Biévre and Dür 2005: 1274). As a result, legislators exposed to such contradicting pressures advocate for the inclusion of strong labor and environmental standards in PTAs. These are intended to cushion possible adverse effects of trade accords and thereby allow law-makers to give their consent to trade liberalization.

This logic, however, is more pronounced in political systems with majoritarian electoral rules than in systems with proportional electoral rules. Hence, the type of electoral system and the nature of the electoral competition have to be taken into account (Rogowski 1987; Rickard 2015). In political systems with proportional electoral rules, parties receive seats in proportion to the number of votes they obtain. Candidates are rank-ordered on lists that are compiled by the party leadership. Such systems produce electoral competition that is largely party centered. The best electoral strategy for politicians is therefore to promote the national popularity of their party and ensure to be as high as possible on the party's list. As a result, in case of conflict legislators tend to emphasize the party line over preferences of their constituencies. This tends to produce relatively high party discipline, and in effect creates larger constituencies for single representatives (Rickard 2015). MEPs are elected on the basis of electoral procedures determined by national legislation of the country where they run for office. However, EU rules require that these different procedures must in any case be some form of a proportional electoral system (Strauch and Pogorelis 2011). The relatively long legislative periods of five years in the EP further mitigate the influence of interest groups on MEPs.

Political systems with majoritarian electoral rules like in the US, by contrast, tend to have candidate-centered electoral competition. Here representatives have a high incentive to promote policies that best serve their home districts (Rogowski 1987: 208). Hence, party discipline is less pronounced. Legislators are more likely to vote against policies that are beneficial for the overall economy, if they see the interests of their constituencies threatened. Members of the House are even more susceptible to their constituencies than Senators since they have smaller electoral districts. U.S. Senators represent whole federal states which is why trade liberalization receives generally more support among Senators than House members (Baldwin 1986). This difference is reinforced by the relatively long term of five years for U.S. Senators, compared to the short two-year terms of Members of the House. The latter should therefore be the most susceptible for interest groups, including labor and environmental organizations.

The dependency of individual candidates on interest groups is additionally aggravated in the US by the absence of strong formal party structures and meaningful public funding for political parties. Politicians on all levels of government have to rely heavily on interest groups for the provision of political resources, including campaign contributions and campaign aides. To finance the increasingly expensive U.S. election campaigns, candidates must collect private contributions (Nassmacher 2014: 272). Donors in the US can contribute money to the campaign funding committees of political parties or directly to individual candidates. This latter money makes candidates more independent from their party. However, the threat of reducing or withholding contributions to candidates is a powerful tool at hand of interest groups to control the actions of office-holders. But campaign contributions are not the sole mechanism through which interest groups can exert influence. Since formal party structures are weak, candidates also have to resort to the manpower and infrastructure of non-party organizations for voter mobilization in their electoral districts.

In Europe, by contrast, election campaigns are almost exclusively organized and financed by political parties. Elections for the EP are still held as separate national elections for a fixed contingent of parliamentary seats for every member state. Hence, the conduct of an EP candidate's election campaign is also in the hands of his or her national political party (Hix, Abdul, and Roland 2007: 134-136). The most important source of income for political parties in Europe are not private contributions but public funding. State funding accounts on average for 67% of the total income of political parties in Europe. Private contributions to individual candidates are, by contrast, insignificant. As a consequence, the direct influence of campaign money provision by interest groups is appreciably lower in the EU.[24]

Furthermore, candidates in Europe can rely on a strong party infrastructure and registered party members for their election campaigns and don't have to count on non-party volunteers and organizations (Piccio 2014). As a result, politicians in Europe are much more depended on their party than on private interest groups during election campaigns (Frieden and Martin 2003: 132). The electoral rules and the nature of the electoral competition in US, by contrast, give U.S. lawmakers a double incentive to represent the interests of their local constituencies. Therefore, the influence of interest groups should be weaker on MEPs than on members of the U.S. House of Representatives.

Policy-makers that are not determined through public elections are not subject to the constraint of electoral politics. Their continuance in office does not depend on the support of voters or specific interest groups. Therefore, they can develop their preferences more autonomous from societal pressures than elected public officials (Ikenberry, Lake, and Mastanduno 1988: 10). Since free trade policies are considered most beneficial for the overall economy, unelected bureaucrats tend to support trade liberalization (Zimmermann 2007). Accordingly, the European Commission's Directorate-General for Trade (DG Trade), which acts as the EU executive in trade policy, tends to ignore trade skeptical voices inside Europe and cooperates closely with groups that help to promote free trade. It can afford to do so since Commission officials don't face public elections and there is no need to collect private contributions to finance election campaigns. Quite the contrary, civil society organizations often receive money from the Commission to guarantee a more balanced interest representation at the European level (Woll 2012: 199-200).

---

24 The share of state funding as a source of the total revenue of political parties in Europe ranges from just over 20% in the UK to almost 90% in Spain.

The major currency in EU lobbying that secures lobbyists access and influence is information and expert knowledge. Since business organizations have considerable technical, specialist and politically salient information on policy issues most affecting their interests (Chalmers 2013: 39), Commission officials willingly resort to the advice of export-oriented interest groups when formulating trade policy. The importance of technical expertise has been further aggravated through the growing importance of regulatory issues in international trade policy (Woll and Artigas 2007). Other societal stakeholders cannot provide equally valuable information that help the Commission to reach its objectives and are therefore disadvantaged in EU trade politics (Dür and De Biévre 2007). Since trade skeptic groups cannot punish Commission officials in elections, Commission officials have little incentives to pay attention to their concerns (Woll 2012). Therefore, the European Commission's should have a rather technocratic approach towards trade and be critical of enforceable social standards.

In the US, trade policy is equally executed by unelected officials. The Office of the United States Trade Representative (USTR) represents the U.S. administration in international trade negotiations. The USTR, however, is short-staffed and 'operates on a shoestring budget' (Schott 2004). Therefore, USTR officials equally require input from the private sector to lead increasingly complex trade negotiations that require knowledge about regulatory barriers to trade in third countries. Consequently, USTR officials hold close working relationships with the U.S. business community that are characterized by mutually beneficial exchange of information and reciprocal learning (Woll and Artigas 2007: 130). Nevertheless, as an executive agency the USTR is directly responsible to the President and has to report regularly to Congress (da Conceição-Heldt 2011: 56). The USTR is bound by the instructions of the President which regularly stands for re-election. As a result, USTR officials are much more exposed to electoral politics than their colleagues in DG Trade. Hence, U.S. trade bureaucrats cannot formulate trade negotiation objectives as autonomous as EU trade officials.

In sum, it is well established in the literature on trade politics that electoral incentives heavily influence the stance of decision-makers (Rogowski 1987; Rickard 2015). If different branches of government have differing electoral bases, it is most likely that they have diverging policy preferences. Since the executive branch is elected in large constituencies, it is primarily concerned with the effect of trade liberalization on the economy as a whole or with foreign policy objectives. Therefore, the U.S. administration and EU member state governments should be in favor of PTAs but against strict social standards. The Commission and the USTR as un-elected bodies should be even more inclined to free trade policies and critical of enforceable social standards. Only the Commission, however, is truly free of electoral politics since the USTR is still responsible to the U.S. administration.

The members of legislatures, by contrast, are elected in small electoral districts. Therefore, they should be more susceptible to special interests. Labor and environmental positions should be most strongly advocated by legislators that depend heavily on labor and environmental constituencies. Hence, left of center members both in Congress and the European Parliament should be receptive to labor and environmental groups' demands. However, the strength of interest group influence on individual legislators additionally depends on the electoral system. The majoritarian, single-member districts in the US increases the dependence of U.S. lawmakers on interest groups. Therefore, they are more likely than MEPs to vote against the party line in case it runs in conflict with their constituencies' preferences. As result, the following hypothesis can be established on the link between policy-makers' responsiveness to interest groups and their preferences regarding social standards:

Hypothesis 2: Policy-makers who equally depend on business, labor and environmental organizations for reelection promote enforceable social standards as a way to balance these conflicting interests.

The Institutional Form of Delegation

The different electoral incentives of policy-makers within and across different branches of government are likely to result in diverging policy preferences. As a consequence, the institutional rules that regulate the trade policy-making process are decisive for political outcomes. Most influential are the rules that stipulate the voting procedure in the legislative branch and that govern the relations between the executive and legislative. Analytically, the conduct of international trade negotiations can be subdivided in three different phases: the pre-negotiation stage, the stage of the actual international negotiations, and the ratification stage (Woolcock 2005). In both the US and the EU, the authority to negotiate international trade agreements has been delegated from the legislative to the executive branch. Hence, the relationship between legislative and executive can be modeled as a principal-agent-situation in both cases, where principals mandate an agent to act on their behalf (De Biévre and Dür 2005; Meunier 2000; Nicolaïdis 1998).

The delegation of the negotiation competence to the executive has a number of advantages. It enables strategic behavior in international negotiations, enhances the credibility of commitments made in bargaining situations and enables states (or trading blocs) to speak with a single voice internationally (Dür and Elsig 2011: 329). Principals, however, usually reserve several tools to control the agent and prevent it from pursuing objectives that diverge from its own since the preferences of legislatures and executives are often not congruent. Prior to delegation, principals can restrict agents' room for maneuver to different degrees by the negotiation mandate (*ex ante* control mechanisms). Throughout the actual negotiation process, principals can institute monitoring and reporting requirements to better oversee the agent's actions (*ad locum* control mechanisms). At the end of the negotiation process, principals can exert the ultimate control by rejecting a negotiated agreement presented for ratification (*ex post* control mechanism) (da Conceição-Heldt 2013: 25).

The institutional rules that govern the delegation of negotiation authority in the US and the EU, however, differ in several respects. As a consequence, they grant different institutions diverging sway over the result of trade negotiations (Zimmermann 2007). In the US, the competence to conduct trade negotiations is delegated the U.S. Congress to the United States Trade Representative (USTR) who acts on behalf of the U.S. President. This delegation takes places through the so-called 'trade promotion authority', formerly known as 'fast-track procedure'. It enables the executive to negotiate trade agreements for a fixed period of time that are once signed brought before both Houses of Congress for a simple majority up-or-down vote without the possibility for amendments. However, through the TPA law Congress can exert considerable control over the USTR by setting binding requirements for the negotiations *ex ante*, keeping a close eye on the course of negotiations *ad locum* and *ex post* pass judgment over the final deal through the ratification requirement (Destler 2005).

In the EU, by contrast, negotiation authority is delegated from EU member states' governments in the Council of Ministers to the Commission's DG Trade. The Commission needs to obtain a separate mandate from the Council every time it intends to open trade negotiations. The EP as the second 'chamber' of the EU legislative branch and the only directly elected EU institution, by contrast, has no formal role in awarding negotiation mandates. Any negotiated agreement finally requires the approval of the Council and, since the Lisbon Treaty, the consent of the EP for its adoption. EU member states' governments which as executives are assumed to be less susceptible for special interests, consequently, still decisively determine the negotiation objectives DG Trade has to follow in trade talks (Woolcock 2011).[25]

The voting rules in the legislative branch that apply for awarding negotiation authority to the executive and ratifying negotiated agreements, however, differ as well and affect the content of PTAs. This is because voting rules are not just procedural matters but impinge upon the translation of preferences into political outcomes. Political bodies that take decisions by consensus, like the Council of the European Union, tend to produce the smallest common dominator, since each member can veto any undesired decision (Garrett and Tsebelis 1996; Meunier 2000). In political institutions where majority voting rules apply, like the U.S. Congress and the EP, by contrast, there is no need to reach an agreement everyone can agree to. In case of close votes, majority voting rules rather give undecided members greater leverage to influence the outcome according to their preferences, as both camps will tout for their votes.

As a result, majority-voting rules in the legislative branch should facilitate establishing enforceable labor and environmental standards as negotiation objectives. Swaying legislators representing conflicting interests are able to demand them from free trade advocates in exchange for their affirmative vote. Institutions where taking decisions requires (de facto) consensus, by contrast, are likely to opt for watered-down, unenforceable social clauses. Members with extreme positions, such as fully enforceable social clauses or no social clauses at all, can prevent any agreement that goes too far towards the other direction through their informal veto right. As a consequence, the following hypothesis can be derived regarding the influence of institutional settings on the design of social standards in PTAs:

Hypothesis 3: The more the institutional form of delegation empowers institutional advocates of enforceable social standards, the stronger these provisions will be in PTAs.

---

25 Most EU PTAs additionally require the ratification of all national parliaments in the EU. However, the parliamentary systems in Europe require national governments to have a majority in parliament to govern. In addition, the high party discipline in legislatures elected by proportional rules ensures that governments in Europe can usually rely on their parliamentary majorities. Therefore, ratification of EU PTAs at the national level is normally a mere formality. Since the ratification process at the national level is irrelevant, I waive to include the national ratification process into the analytical framework.

Figure 3 provides an overview over the shaping of PTA social standards.

Figure 3: The Shaping of PTA Social Standards

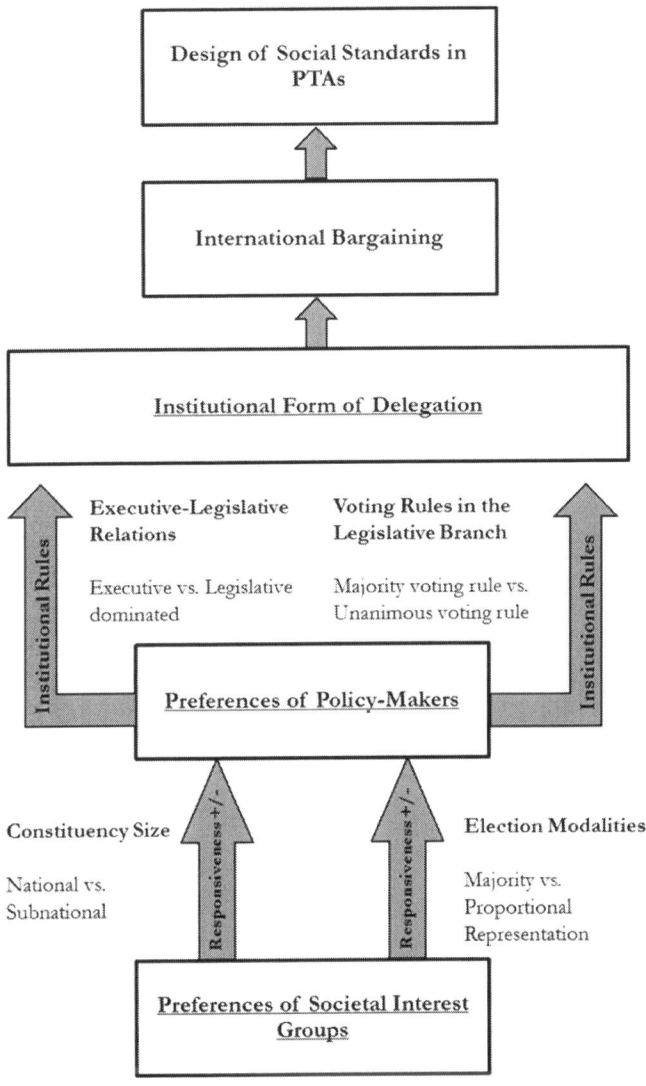

Source: Author's own compilation.

3.3 Research Design and Methodology

Qualitative research methods are generally applied to a limited number of cases in order to understand the complex interactions between explanatory variables. This proceeding allows for an in-depth analysis of the political dynamics in each case and thereby unveils the causal mechanisms that are at work and produced a given political outcome. Over the last years, qualitative methods have become increasingly sophisticated by paying more attention to the development of research designs and the selection of cases. The last section of this chapter therefore discusses pivotal methodological issues in greater detail.

3.3.1 Variables and Operationalization

The research design of this study is Y-centered since it aims at unravelling the causes behind differing political outcomes. It does not focus on the effect of one specific independent variable, but considers the interaction of several independent variables as explanatory factors for the variance on the dependent variable (Ganghof 2005: 77). As explained in chapter 2 in greater detail, social standards in U.S. and EU PTAs differ mainly along two dimensions: (1) their scope and (2) their enforcement mechanism.

Table 5: Scope and Enforceability of Social Standards in U.S. and EU PTAs.

Actor	Scope of Social Standards	Enforceability of Social Standards
United States	Narrow	Enforceable
European Union	Broad	Non-enforceable

Source: Author's own compilation.

The explanation for the divergence in the scope of U.S. and EU PTA's social standards is straight forward. The US has failed to ratify a number of central labor and environmental conventions and consequently eschews referring to them in its PTAs. EU member states, by contrast, have ratified all major ILO conventions and MEAs and therefore have no problem making them the point of reference for social standards. The variance in the enforcement mechanism – trade sanction mechanism vs. lack thereof – between U.S. and EU social standards, by contrast, is more puzzling and requires a more profound investigation. Thus, the central dependent variable of this study is the enforceability of social standards in U.S. and EU PTAs.

To explain the variance on the dependent variable, the study considers three independent variables as explanatory factors: preferences of societal interest groups; responsiveness of policy-makers; and, the institutional form of delegation. The variable 'Preferences of Societal Interest Groups' is operationalized as the policy objectives of business, labor and environmental groups in trade politics. These are observable through publications such as position papers and press releases as well as through interview responses. In the case of (enforceable) social standards, societal actors can either support or oppose such provisions in PTAs.

The second independent variable 'Responsiveness of Policy-Makers' refers to the strength of electoral links between decision-makers and interest groups. This relationship is, on the one hand, influenced by the size of the constituency in which an office-holder is elected and on the other hand by the election modalities that determine the dependence of decision-makers on interest groups' support. Policy-makers are either elected in national or in subnational constituencies. Election modalities in this study have either the form of majority representation with candidate-centered electoral competition or proportional representation with party-centered electoral competition.

The last independent variable 'Institutional Form of Delegation' is operationalized as the institutional rules that govern the interaction of executive and legislature during the three stages of international negotiations and the voting rules in the legislative branch. Possible values for this variable are executive vs. legislative-dominated process and majority vs. unanimous voting rules. Tables 6 provides an overview over the independent variables and their operationalization.

Table 6: Independent Variables and Operationalization.

Independent Variable	Operationalization	Possible Values
Preferences of Societal Interest Groups	Position of • business groups • labor unions • environmental NGOs	Support of vs. Opposition to (enforceable) social standards
Responsiveness of Policy-Makers	• Constituency Size • Election Modalities	National vs. Subnational Constituency Majority representation with candidate-centered electoral competition vs. Propotional representation with party-centered electoral competition
Institutional Form of Delegation	• Executive-Legislative Relations • Voting Rules in the Legislative Branch	Executive-dominated vs. Legislative-dominated Majority vs. Unanomous voting rule

Source: Author's own compilation.

3.3.2 Qualitative Comparative Method

This study engages in a structured, focused comparison of trade policy-making processes in the US and the EU. The method used in this study is 'structured' in the sense that it will ask a previously defined set of standardized, general questions to each case under study which is necessary to guide and standardize data collection in comparative studies. It is 'focused' in that it will take into account only the relevant aspects of the cases under examination (George and Bennett 2005: 67). Previous research on PTA formation and variations in PTA elements is mostly dominated by quantitative studies (e.g. Baccini, Dür, and Elsig 2015; Baccini 2010; Büthe and Milner 2014; Dür, Baccini, and Elsig 2014). The statistical methods of quantitative research indeed are well-suited if the researcher is, for instance, interested in the effects of different levels of trade integration on trade and investment flows in a large number of cases. Unlike qualitative case study methods, however, statistical methods are not able to examine the operation of casual mechanisms in individual cases in detail (Mahoney and Goertz 2006).

Thus, a comparative, qualitative approach is more suitable for exploring the causal relations between the domestic political dynamics of trade policy-making in the US and the EU and the design of social standards in their PTAs. In addition, the study will conduct a within-case analysis using theory-oriented process tracing (George and Bennett 2005: 205-232). The process tracing method has become increasingly popular in political science and political economy methods debates over the last years (Collier 2008; Beach 2016; George and Bennett 2005; Beach and Pedersen 2013; Falleti 2016; Trampusch and Palier 2016; Hall 2013; Bennett and Checkel 2014).

Process-tracing aims to reconstruct the course of events and the constellation of variables that led to a given outcome. In contrast to mere descriptive studies, research using the method of process-tracing is informed by propositions that identify the phenomena that are expected to manifest themselves when theories are exposed to empirical evidence (Beach 2016: 463-464; George and Bennett 2005: 223; Collier 2008). Hence, the method of process-tracing allows for an analytical causal explanation of each case, since all intervening steps in a case must be predicted by a hypothesis. The process tracing method allows to 'make *stronger evidence-based inferences about causal relationships* when we have within-case evidence of each step of the causal process (or absence thereof) in-between a cause and outcomes, [and it] gives us a better understanding of *how* a cause produces an outcome' (Beach 2016: 463). The in-depth analysis possible in case studies also leads to a higher conceptual validity compared to statistical or large-N studies (George and Bennett 2005: 19-20).

However, as any method, case study research suffers from a number of limitations. As George and Bennet (2005: 25) acknowledge, case studies remain much stronger 'at assessing *whether* and *how* a variable mattered to the outcome than at assessing *how much* it mattered.' Further downsides of small-n studies are a limited generalizability and an increased danger of selection bias (Bennett 2004: 19). The present study attempts to sidestep many of these pitfalls by paying particular attention to case selection.

3.3.3 Case Selection

The goal of this study is to explain the different design of social standards in PTAs of the US and the EU. Since qualitative research undertakes in-depth analysis of the cases under investigation, researchers are forced to a select workable number of cases from the basic population. Given the research puzzle, the universe of cases is restricted to bilateral and regional PTAs of the US and the EU that contain social standards. From this population three cases are selected both for the US and the EU that meet a number of requirements.

First, only PTAs with countries are chosen as cases with which both the US and the EU concluded trade agreements. Thereby, I control for the potential influence of the respective negotiation partner on the design of U.S. and EU social standards. This is primarily because relative market size is the most important economic factor for bargaining power in trade negotiations. Since the U.S. and EU GDP are about the same size and they constitute the world's biggest trading powers, they normally both encounter much weaker negotiation partners in bilateral and regional trade talks. Nevertheless, it is conceivable that the US and the EU made concessions with regard to social standards to certain crucial bargaining partners during negotiations. In addition, the level of existing labor and environmental protections in the respective trading partner might have induced the US and the EU to press more or less vigorously for stricter enforcement mechanisms. By holding constant the negotiating partner, I minimize the effect of the relative bargaining power and the initial labor and environmental protection in trading partners on the design of social standards in the respective agreements with the US and the EU.

Second, since the institutional framework under which PTAs have been negotiated is a crucial variable for explanation it should be held constant for the EU and the US over time. In the US, 'Trade Promotion Authority', or 'Fast-Track', is the crucial piece of legislation that stipulates the rights and obligations of the different government branches during trade negotiations. Trade negotiations conducted by the US without TPA, like the US-Jordan PTA, can be assumed to follow a fundamental different logic. In the EU, the conduct of trade negotiations is regulated by the European Treaties currently in force. With the Lisbon Treaty of 2009, EU trade policy-making experienced a series of changes. Most notably was that the new treaty granted the EP the right to vote on the approval of any negotiated trade agreement and established it thereby as an important institutional player in EU trade politics. Therefore, I only take PTAs into consideration that the US negotiated under the 2002 Trade Promotion Authority and the EU after the signing of the Lisbon Treaty in 2007.

Third, only agreements come into question that are first and foremost trade accords. The EU has concluded numerous treaties in the past that prepare countries for EU membership. While these arrangements often also entail a trade component, they usually require candidate countries to change legislation in many policy areas and therefore generate a very different political dynamic than PTAs. Therefore, only such agreements qualify as cases that liberalize trade but do not contain further requirements necessary for EU accession. Sector-specific trade accords like the US-Vietnam Textile Agreement are just as little eligible as cases.

Under these conditions, the U.S. and EU PTAs with Central America, Peru/Colombia and South Korea qualify as cases. However, it should be noted that the U.S. and EU agreements with Central America and Peru/Colombia slightly differ with regard to membership or structure. Unlike the EU-Central America Association Agreement, the U.S. PTA with Central America (CAFTA-DR) excludes Panama but incorporates the Dominican Republic instead. In case of the Peru/Colombia agreements, both the U.S. and the EU began talks for regional deals that included further Andean countries. Negotiations resulted however in two separate bilateral U.S. PTAs with Peru and Colombia, and a single EU-Peru/Colombia PTA.

These differences, however, can be considered negligible for the comparability of the cases, since they neither alter the relative bargaining power significantly nor do they change the basic characteristics of negotiation partners. Yet, these cases should be particularly informative because labor and environmental issues often stood at the center of negotiations. Besides the Latin American cases, this study also investigates the U.S. and EU PTAs with South Korea. The case is significant since these PTAs are considered to be the most elaborate agreements of both and have served as templates for other PTAs (Schott and Cimino 2013: 4-5). In addition, the different regional context and stage of economic development of South Korea should allow for an increased generalizability of the results.

Finally, the independence of the chosen cases is a crucial issue to be considered in the case selection process, since the failure to identify a lack of independence between cases entails the danger of reaching false conclusions (George and Bennett 2005: 33). For this study, it is highly unlikely that the cases are fully independent since individual trade negotiation processes usually influence concurrent or successive negotiations of a state or its competitors. Actors may learn from earlier experiences or starting conditions for negotiations simply may have changed, for instance, when a third state has already entered a trade agreement with the actor's competitor. Such learning or diffusion processes, however, do not need to undercut the value of studying partially dependent cases, if they are anticipated and taken into account. The use of process-tracing reduces the risks of studying dependent cases by inductively uncovering the linkages between cases and, in addition, can help to 'gauge more accurately how much of the variance in outcomes is explained by learning or diffusion and how much is explained by other variables' (ibid.:33-34).

3.3.4 Data Collection and Data Analysis

For this study I collected data from several sources, most notably academic literature, government documents, policy position papers of interest groups, media reports and interviews. The research process began with a thorough review and analysis of secondary sources published on the issue of labor and/or environmental standards in preferential trade agreements. Several academic studies as well as publications of international organizations, such as the ILO and the OECD, and labor and environmental groups exist that delve into the specifics of social standards in trade accords of different states (ILO and IILS 2013; OECD 2007; Grandi 2009; Draper, Nkululeko, and Tigere 2017; ILO 2017; Berger, Brandi, and Bruhn 2017). These predominantly descriptive studies prodded to the diverging enforcement mechanisms of U.S. and EU social standards and in this way assisted in the clarification of the dependent variable of this study. However, they provided little insights into the causes behind the different U.S. and EU approaches.

Therefore, in a next step I consulted official administrative documents both from the US and the EU (proposals, reports, briefing notes and other internal governmental documents) inasmuch these documents were accessible. In addition, I analyzed position papers of labor, environmental and business groups in order to gain a deeper understanding of the views of non-governmental actors involved in trade policy-making. These sources have been complemented with information from newspapers and specialized news agencies, such as *Inside US Trade* and *Agence Europe*. Since obtaining data proved to be much more difficult for the EU cases, I also relied on governmental documents of the respective negotiation partners. Furthermore, the study makes use of reporting and information from think tanks such as the International Centre for Trade and Sustainable Development (ICTSD). These materials allowed for a sound reconstruction of the bargaining processes that led to the PTAs under investigation.

Nevertheless, since certain data can only be obtained 'by going to the original sources' (George and Bennett 2005: 97), expert interviews constituted an indispensable method of data collection. Overall I conducted 32 interviews with relevant actors both in the US and Europe. The majority of interviews for the U.S. cases took place during a 2-month research stay in Washington, D.C. in March/April 2015. Most interviews for the EU cases were conducted on a field trip to Brussels in November 2015. In addition, several interviews were conducted via telephone since face-to-face interviews were not always possible. My respondents included trade-policy scholars and journalists, representatives from labor unions, environmental NGOs and business associations as well as parliamentary aides, legislators and trade policy executives both in Brussels and Washington, D.C.

The interviewees were selected based mainly on the importance of their role in the related policy processes as well as on their function in the institutions they represented. Initially, I relied on press reports and available publications to obtain names of individuals and organizations with first-hand knowledge of the subject of my research. Before and during my field research I additionally used snowball sampling procedure to identify and gain access to relevant actors. Interviews were problem-orientated and semi-structured with a basic outline, including relatively open questions. However, questionnaires were adapted to the knowledge and position of the respective interviewee and refined with information gathered over the course of time (Pickel and Pickel 2009). Depending on the respondent's expertise, I also asked additional questions or deepened the discussion on certain points.

3.4 Structure of the Empirical Chapters

In the following two empirical chapters, the theoretical framework developed above is applied to the US and EU in negotiations for PTAs. The chapters are similarly structured in order to systematically detect the causal mechanisms that produced the different approaches towards social standards in trade agreements. Both chapters begin with a brief account of the respective institutional structure within which trade policy is made in the US and the EU. Then the relevant interest groups and their preferences with regard to social standards in trade agreements are mapped out. Subsequently, I explore the nature of interest group influence on the legislature and the resulting preferences of the legislative branch. In a similar vein, I outline the preferences of the executive in both the US and the EU. Then each chapter goes on to present in detail how the interaction between societal and institutional actors within in the respective institutional setting shaped social standards in three specific cases of PTA negotiations for both the US and the EU. If the institutional differences are decisive for the diverging design of social standards in U.S. and EU PTAs as assumed, we should be able to detect repetitive patterns of institutional dynamics for the US and the EU in the three cases under investigation.

4. Social Standards in U.S. Preferential Trade Agreements

The US is anything but a champion of international labor and environmental agreements. Among industrialized countries, the US has one of the worst records on ratifying ILO conventions. To date, the country has ratified only 14 of the total 189 ILO conventions and even failed to ratify six of the eight ILO core conventions (Weissbrodt and Mason 2014: 1842-1843). In recent years, the US has become equally reluctant to commit itself to international arrangements in the field of environmental policy. Since the early 1990s, the US refused to ratify a whole range of important MEAs (Bang 2011; Kelemen and Vogel 2010; Kelemen and Knievel 2015). At the same time, however, the US became the global pioneer in promoting labor and environmental standards through PTAs. Naturally, U.S. PTAs do not make references to international conventions which the US has not ratified. However, the US stands out internationally by making PTAs' social standards enforceable through trade sanctions. In addition, the US regularly requires negotiating partners to change their domestic labor and environmental laws as a precondition for the signing of a PTA (Kim 2012). Hence, the US seems to attach great importance to labor and environmental issues in the context of PTAs.

The present chapter aims to demonstrate that this seemingly paradoxical development can be traced back to the constellation of the preferences of interest groups in U.S. trade politics and the way their interests were channeled through the institutional structure of the US. The institutional rules of the US systematically favored advocates of enforceable social standards in PTAs and thereby made such provisions established features of U.S. trade agreements. In the following section, I will first outline the institutional structure within which U.S. trade policy is made. Next, I identify the initial preferences of interest groups involved in U.S. trade policy-making with regard to social standards. The subsequent section explores to what extent these interest groups could influence the preferences of U.S. policymakers in the legislative and executive branch. Ultimately, the chapter studies the interaction of the legislative and executive branch during three separate international trade negotiations to detect which institution was able to achieve its preferred outcome.

4.1 Institutional Structure of U.S. Trade Politics

In the US, the powers to set tariffs and regulate foreign commerce lies constitutionally with Congress. The President in turn is responsible for foreign affairs and the negotiation of international treaties. This division of competences considerably complicates the conclusion of reciprocal trade agreements. Therefore, the delegation of special negotiating powers from the legislative to the executive branch has become a central characteristic of U.S. trade politics. After the disastrous experience of the protectionist Smoot-Haley Act of 1930, Congress granted the President for the first time the formal authorization to negotiate reciprocal tariff reductions with foreign countries in 1934. The Reciprocal Trade Agreements Act (RTAA) facilitated the ratification of trade agreements since it overrode the requirement of receiving a two-thirds majority in the Senate that usually applies to international treaties. Instead, the ratification of trade agreements required only a simple majority in both Houses of Congress (Bailey, Goldstein, and Weingast 1997: 310). RTAA was limited in duration, but was extended and reenacted through 11 successive Trade Agreements Extensions Acts until 1962 (Shapiro 2006: 11).

Prior to the 1962 Trade Expansion Act, the State Department was responsible for conducting U.S. trade and investment diplomacy. With the 1962 trade bill, however, Congress authorized the President to designate an individual as Special Trade Representative (STR) in order to better balance between competing domestic and international interests in formulating and implementing U.S. trade policy. The Trade Act of 1974 then gave the STR primary responsibility for trade agreements and programs established under previous U.S. trade legislation in 1930 and 1962. Furthermore, it established the Office of the STR as an agency in the Executive office of the President. In 1979, the STR was again reorganized and renamed as Office of the United States Trade Representative (USTR). Additional legislation in 1988 and 1994 further elevated the USTR's position within the executive branch and extended its authority over virtually all of U.S. trade policy. Even though the Departments of State, Labor, Treasury, Agriculture and Commerce participate in the formulation of U.S. trade policy, the USTR today constitutes the primary coordinator of U.S. trade liberalization efforts. Even though the USTR is accountable to Congress, it is as an agency of the executive branch directly responsible to the president. Since the head of the USTR is appointed by the President, the agency represents mostly the point of view of the incumbent government (O'Halloran 1994: 147).

The 1974 Trade Act established as well a new procedure for the consider-ation of trade agreements that became known as 'fast-track'. Over the last decades, the consecutive 'fast-track' bills of 1979, 1984, 1988 and 2002 have combined increased presidential competences with tightened control mechanisms for Congress (Destler 2005; De Biévre and Dür 2005; Shapiro 2006). The TPA bill of 2002 requires the implementing bill to be intro-duced in both houses of Congress, referred to the relevant committees (at minimum the House Ways and Means and Senate Finance Committee) and to be automatically approved after 45 legislative days if the bill has not been reported out of the committees. In addition, 'fast-track' allows no amendments to the implementation bill and limits the debate on the floor of each House to 20 hours. Furthermore, it requires a timely vote on the implementing bill in both Houses, no more than 15 legislative days after leaving committee. It thereby ensures that no conference committee takes places since both chambers have to vote on the same bill (Hornbeck and Cooper 2013).

The 'fast-track' legislative procedure entails a number of advantages that are essential for the U.S. administration in the conduct of international trade negotiations. First, it ensures a streamlined legislative process by es-tablishing limits on congressional prerogatives. The mandatory deadlines guarantee that trade agreements are not being held endlessly in a commit-tee without being submitted for floor vote. Second, the 'fast track' provi-sions prevent trade agreements from being picked apart by amendments that would require the renegotiation of the entire trade accord. Congress either has to accept or reject the agreement in its entity. Third, 'fast-track' rules require simple majorities in both Houses for the ratification of trade agreements instead of two-third majorities in the Senate. This substantially enhances the credibility of presidential commitments in trade politics on the international level since the uncertainty over whether or not a negotiat-ed agreement will be ratified is reduced. In return, Congress has reserved itself several oversight mechanisms to comprehensively control the execu-tive. These mechanisms can be divided into *ex ante* control through con-gressional oversight procedures, *ad locum* control through obligatory con-sultations and *ex post* control through the possibility of reversing fast-track or rejecting the agreement itself (Brainard and Shapiro 2001).

Ex ante congressional oversight procedures establish conditions the ex-ecutive branch must meet for fast-track to apply. Congress sets overall ne-gotiating objectives and industry- or issue-specific principal trade negotia-tion objectives that it expects the USTR to pursue in international negotia-tions. This enables Congress to lay down the requirements trade agreements must meet in detail even before international negotiations start. In addition, through substantial consultation requirements of the executive branch, Congress possesses considerable *ad locum* control mechanisms. Before and during trade negotiations, the USTR is obligated to consult extensively with Congress, departments, federal agencies and the private sector. Before entering into negotiations, the executive branch provides the U.S. International Trade Commission (USITC) with the articles to be negotiated. Within 90 days, the USITC informs the President about the trade agreement's likely impact on labor, consumers and industries (Hornbeck and Cooper 2013).

In addition, U.S. trade politics involve an extensive system of private sector advisory committees that provide information and advice on U.S. negotiation objectives. The system compromises the President's Advisory Committee for Trade Policy and Negotiations (ACTPN); four policy advisory committees (including the Labor Advisory Committee and the Trade and Environment Policy Advisory Committee); and 22 technical and sectoral advisory committees. These committees are composed of relevant stakeholders in the different policy areas and provide essential expertise for trade policy-makers in the executive and legislative branch (GAO 2007). The USTR also consults regularly with relevant governmental departments and congressional committees, most notably the House Ways and Means Committee and the Senate Finance Committee. Moreover, five members of each House are appointed as 'congressional advisors' by the USTR to provide advice on trade issues. These multiple channels of information exchange allow legislators to closely scrutinize the USTR during trade talks and influence the content of negotiations (Shapiro 2006: 20-21).

Ultimately, Congress has considerable *ex post* control mechanisms at its disposal. If the executive fails to meet the procedural conditions described above, Congress can withdraw 'fast-track' procedures from a particular trade agreement. This can occur if a majority in both houses passes a disapproval resolution for a failure to consult within 60 days. The House Ways and Means and the Senate Finance Committee can deny fast-track application to a trade agreement also on the basis of the 'gatekeeper committee provision'. Fast track can also generally be withdrawn through unicameral repeal at any time, since it is considered an exercise of the House and Senate's rule-making power. Lastly, fast-track's duration is limited to a period of a few years through 'sunset provisions' which enables Congress to decide anew whether to grant the executive branch fast-track in the first place. As a consequence, fast-track is a highly fragile mechanism that requires the USTR to constantly adhere to congressional guidance in trade talks (Brainard and Shapiro 2001). Even under fast-track rules Congress can, of course, reject any agreement presented by the President. U.S. negotiators must therefore unfailingly seek an international agreement that gathers enough support among representatives to be ratified. The *ex post* veto power of the legislature is therefore a credible threat for the executive branch that guarantees a substantial congressional influence on negotiation outcomes. Figure 4 displays the most important characteristics of the trade policy process in the US in a simplified form.

Figure 4: Trade Policy Process in the US

Source: Author's own compilation.

4.2 Preferences of U.S. Actors

Within the institutional framework described above, a variety of actors vie to influence political outcomes in their interest. Societal actors formulate political demands towards policy-makers in order to promote their policy objectives. Office-holders respond to these conflicting pressures differently depending on how important interest groups are for their remaining in office. Therefore, the preferences of societal and governmental actors are the basic building block to analyze the formulation of U.S. trade policy. Subsequently, the preferences of societal interest groups and governmental actors in the US with regard to social standards are examined.

Business Groups, Labor Unions and Environmental NGOs

U.S. trade politics is characterized by a firm competition between numerous interest groups that are striving to influence government policy in their respective interest. With regard to social standards in PTAs three different types of actors possess a genuine incentive to engage in lobbying activities: business organizations, labor unions and environmental NGOs. The major organizations representing U.S. business interests include the U.S. Chamber of Commerce, the U.S. Council for International Business (USCIB), the National Foreign Trade Council (NFTC), the National Association of Manufacturers (NAM), the Emergency Committee for American Trade (ECAT) and the Business Roundtable. The leading U.S. business organizations fully support trade liberalization through multilateral and bilateral trade agreements, since they expect to gain from the move towards freer trade. As a result, these groups strongly supported the Bush administration's efforts to gain 'fast track' or Trade Promotion Authority (TPA) in 2002. The U.S. Chamber of Commerce, the largest American business group, for instance, became heavily engaged in the 2002 pro-TPA campaign through public events, direct lobbying of congressmen, issue ads and other communication efforts (U.S. Chamber of Commerce 2001).

Business organizations, however, strongly opposed the linkage of trade agreements with labor and environmental standards (Interview record #15, 2015; Interview record #19, 2015). The U.S. Chamber of Commerce held the view that 'linking trade with labor and environmental rules will slow the process of trade liberalization.' Therefore, the Chamber advocated that such issues should be rather addressed in 'separate, but parallel efforts' (U.S. Chamber of Commerce 2000). In the context of the US-Chile FTA negotiations, then Chamber President Thomas J. Donohue stated that the Chamber 'will oppose the inclusion of unnecessary non-trade provisions' like social standards in PTAs (U.S. Chamber of Commerce 2000). The Chamber particularly rejected hard enforcement mechanisms for social standards, stating that 'trade agreements should not hold out trade sanctions as a remedy in response to labor and environmental disputes' (U.S. Chamber of Commerce 2003). Donohue went so far to say that the Chamber will 'oppose any free-trade agreement that has mandated, sanctions-based social issues in it' (Yerkey 2001).

Similarly, USCIB recognized 'the importance of improving worker rights in the global economy' and shared 'concerns that countries be held accountable in cases of abusive labor practices.' However, it argued that 'the most effective way to do this is to strengthen the capacity of the International Labor Organization to effectively address violations of fundamental worker rights' (USCIB 2007). Environmental issues should be likewise addressed in 'cooperative agreements parallel to, but separate from trade agreements.' With regard to bilateral and regional agreements, USCIB especially warned against 'creating precedents on non-commercial, domestic governance issues that will make achievement of multilateral trade liberalization more difficult' (USCIB 2001). The NFTC, NAM and ECAT and other business organizations held similar views (Destler 1997). In short, business organizations in the US unanimously lobbied against sanction-based labor and environmental standards. Instead, they preferred dealing with labor and environmental issues through mechanisms that were based on voluntarism and cooperation.

U.S. business organizations not only feared that enforceable social standards in PTAs would complicate trade negotiations but also that they could be used to challenge U.S. domestic labor law. Since the US has not ratified the majority of ILO conventions, its labor laws diverge from international norms in several respects (Weissbrodt and Mason 2014). As a consequence, U.S. business organizations were particularly keen to make sure that U.S. trade agreements would not make reference to ILO conventions but, if at all, to the less binding 1998 ILO Declaration on Fundamental Principles and Rights at Work (U.S. Chamber of Commerce 2007; USCIB 2007).

In contrast to U.S. business organizations, American labor expected to lose from freer trade especially with less developed economies. As a result, the U.S. labor movement has been highly critical of the U.S. governments' intensified move towards trade liberalization over the recent years. The American Federation of Labor-Congress of Industrial Organizations (AFL-CIO) is the largest federation of trade unions in the US with fifty-six national and international member unions that represent together more than 12 million workers. According to one AFL-CIO representative, the AFL-CIO does not principally oppose free trade but considers the current model of U.S. trade agreements to be inspired by an aggressive neoliberal ideology, or market-fundamentalism, which serves solely the interests of multinational cooperation but neglects the interests of American workers (Interview record #3, 2015).

For the AFL-CIO, NAFTA had been the original sin in U.S. trade policy. It supposedly led to the loss of many American jobs and the lowering of living standards of U.S. workers that kept their job through increased wage-based competition with Mexico, where fundamental labor laws would be disregarded (AFL-CIO 2002). Therefore, NAFTA in particular has served as the point of reference in all subsequent labor campaigns against

U.S. PTAs.[26] The arguments presented by the AFL-CIO to justify its opposition to most U.S. trade agreements in the last two decades can be found in statements like the following:

> 'Free trade agreements like the North American Free Trade Agreement (NAFTA) and the agreements of the World Trade Organization (WTO) are hurting U.S. workers. These agreements allow imports made under inhumane conditions to flood our market, undercutting U.S. jobs and wages. They encourage U.S. companies to scour the world looking for the lowest wages, the weakest labor laws and the most vulnerable workers' (AFL-CIO 2002).

Hence, the AFL-CIO combines an economic argument which postulates that U.S. workers are damaged by trade agreements with a moral argument according to which vulnerable workers in third countries are being exploited. Consequently, the AFL-CIO has demanded a number of pivotal changes to U.S. trade policy. The inclusion of labor provisions into trade agreements has been one of the central objectives on the AFL-CIO's trade agenda since the controversy surrounding the ratification of NAFTA in 1993 (Burgoon 2004: 198-201). The AFL-CIO insisted that labor standards in U.S. PTAs should refer to the ILO core conventions and not merely to the 1998 ILO Declaration. Most importantly, however, labor standards should be subject to the regular dispute settlement procedure of the agreement. Consequently, failure to comply with these obligations should lead to trade sanctions. The AFL-CIO took the view that certain labor problems in trading partners could and should be addressed through dialogue and capacity building. Others, however, were caused by a lack of political will of foreign governments to protect fundamental worker rights. Therefore, the sole reliance on soft measures would be insufficient. One interviewee summarized the AFL-CIO's perception of an effective enforcement mechanism as follows: 'Monitoring, pressuring and knowing that there is a threat of a stab at some point. If there is no threat, we just don't find endless conversations to be meaningful effective' (Interview record #3, 2015).

U.S. environmental NGOs generally agreed with labor unions that extensive trade liberalization entails negative effects. Many share the unions'

---

26 Mega-Regionals like the Transpacific Partnership Agreement (TPP) are often labeled as 'NAFTA on steroids' by opponents. The U.S.-EU FTAs therefore has timely been renamed from Transatlantic Free Trade Agreement (TAFTA) to Transatlantic Trade and Investment Partnership (TTIP) in order to avoid any association with NAFTA.

view that unregulated trade leads to a 'race-to-the-bottom' in social standards. But 'green' groups were of course more preoccupied with the environmental impact of trade liberalization. Especially big NGOs with broad goals, like Friends of the Earth, Greenpeace, Sierra Club and Earthwatch, categorically opposed the conclusion of trade agreements in recent years (Center for International Environmental Law et al. 2002). These organizations got involved in trade policy especially out of fear that regulations for environmental protection are increasingly being subordinated to international trade rules. Dan Seligman, trade expert of the Sierra Club, for instance, stated:

> 'We got into globalization, or the trade issue because of a new set of institutions and rules that are propagating global free trade, specifically the WTO, NAFTA, and these other major trade agreements... [T]rade agreements are rules that enhance corporate property rights at the expense of what we have considered here for the last 50 years in the United States, to be government prerogatives: to adopt and implement laws and regulations in the public interest' (Seligman 2001).

As a consequence, major U.S. environmental groups sought a number of changes to trade agreements that they believed would reduce the dangers of trade rules to the environment. Most importantly, they demanded changes to the investment rules, references to MEAs in environmental chapters and parity between the enforcement mechanisms of environmental and commercial provisions of PTAs (Center for International Environmental Law et al. 2002). Others, mostly smaller, more specialized organizations, are less critical as long as certain MEAs that are of particular interest to them become more enforceable trough their linkage to the dispute settlement procedure and possible sanctions of PTAs (Interview record #5, 2015). Both fractions, though, advocate for sanction-based environmental provisions that require improvements in environmental legislation of partner countries and make reference to MEAs.

U.S. environmental groups across the board, however, lack the financial resources and the number of members that trade unions have at their disposal. Many environmental NGOs therefore have forged alliances with unions during anti-trade campaigns where they benefit from the manpower and the financial and organizational resources of unions (Obach 2004). U.S. labor unions on the other hand profit from the collaboration with groups like environmentalists, consumer and developmental NGOs, since they help unionists to rhetorically transform the economic interests of organized workers in the US into the morally founded public interest (Destler and Balint 1999).

The U.S. Congress

The legislative branch of the U.S. government is comprised of the U.S. Senate and the U.S. House of Representatives. In both chambers, congressmen almost exclusively belong either to the Democratic or the Republican Party. Republicans are generally characterized as the traditional pro-business party, supporting free market capitalism, deregulation and free trade policies. Democrats, by contrasts, are seen as being more open to government intervention and regulation in the economy and thus less supportive of trade liberalization (Rogowski 1989; Magee, Brock, and Young 1989). The position of the main political parties in the US, however, do not seem to be the direct result of their voters' views. Polls conducted by NBC News/Wall Street Journal in December 1999, and again in March 2007, show that the percentage of people who think free trade agreements 'have hurt the United States' grew from 30% in 1999 to 46% in 2007. The percentage of people who think trade agreements 'have helped the United States' fell from 39% 1999 to just 28% in the same period. Republican voters seem to be similar critical towards trade liberalization as Democratic voters. 54% of Democratic voters said free trade agreements have hurt the United States, while only 21% said trade agreements have helped. In a September 2007 poll, however, 59% of registered Republican voters agreed with the statement that 'trade has been bad for the U.S. economy', while only 32% of those voters opined that trade has been good (cited in Rangel 2009: 382-383). With regard to social standards, another poll found that 90% of respondents (90% Republicans, 88% Democrats) supported the inclusion of labor and 93% (92% Republicans, 94% Democrats) the inclusion of environmental standards into trade agreements (Kull 2005).

Hence, voters' preferences do not directly determine the trade policy positions of U.S. legislators. Instead, the literature on congressional politics generally lists four factors that influence voting behavior of representatives in Congress: ideology, parties, interest groups and constituencies. Lawmakers of course seek to promote policies in Congress that correspond to their personal conviction and ideological orientation. Hence, they generally vote for policies that in their view further their policy goals. However, congressmen risk their reelection if they do not take into account the preferences of their core bases of support that can help to stay in power. One of these bases of support today are political parties. The role of political parties in the US for election campaigns and the organization of the legislative work has increased significantly (Pearson 2015). Therefore, U.S. lawmakers are well advised to bear the instructions of the party leadership in mind when voting. Because of the grown leverage of political parties over lawmakers' fade in Congress, the party unity scores of congressional voting have significantly risen over time. In addition, the personal policy views of representatives and their respective party have become more congruent. In contrast to earlier decades, the ideological divide in Congress today runs largely along party lines: Republicans are usually in favor of conservative, market-oriented policies, while Democrats support liberal societal positions and more interventionist economic policies (Levendusky 2009).

However, positions on individual policy questions can of course still differ between single representatives and their party leadership. This may stem from divergent views of lawmakers or pressures from interest groups or constituencies that they are exposed to. Compared to legislators in Europe, lawmakers in the US are still more dependent on direct support from interest groups and their own electoral district. When the preferences of their constituencies and important interest groups do not overlap with those of their political party, they must make tough choices. By voting with the party on controversial or highly salient issues, such as trade, they risk alienating their political base in the next election. But, if they repeatedly vote according to the preferences of local interest groups and against the party, then they may lose favor with the party leadership and risk sanctions. This explains the higher party unity scores mentioned above. Nevertheless, party discipline is still not as pronounced as in parliaments on the other side of the Atlantic. The stronger reliance on direct contributions from interest groups to finance and organize the increasingly expensive election campaigns make them more independent from their party leadership (Mutch 2016). However, it also grants interest groups stronger and more direct influence over the political positioning of single legislators. Interest groups can use the provision of campaign funds as 'carrots' or use the reduction or withholding of funds as a 'stick' in order to influence swaying legislators (Bardwell 2000).

The insecure political majorities in Congress today (Lee 2016) and the increasing polarization of congressional politics (Pierson and Skocpol 2007) has fostered partisan stalemate even on issues that once featured cross-party bipartisan coalitions such as trade. This has provided organized interests an exceptionally opportunity to influence policies in their favor. As several scholars of American politics have shown (Hacker and Pierson

2010; Gilens 2012; Page and Gilens 2017) business interests have identified this from early on and drastically increased their influence in politics through the provision of extensive campaign contributions. Beginning in the mid-1970s, business organizations gave generously to politicians of both parties. However, the amounts and way business donated money to the two parties differed dramatically. Business money went on the one hand to Republican incumbents to finance their reelection bids, but the Republican party also received large amounts for party-building efforts. These financial resources gave Republicans a massive advantage over Democrats and tied Republicans down on a pro-business agenda (Hacker and Pierson 2010). Campaigns of Republicans today continue to rely heavily on financial support from business organizations. Financial contributions of labor and environmental groups to Republicans, by contrast, are insignificant. Consequently, Republicans tend to represent business organizations' positions. Accordingly, both House and Senate Republicans firmly supported multilateral trade liberalization over the last decades as well as the conclusion of PTAs. However, they strictly opposed any reference to labor and environmental issues in trade agreements (Destler 2005; Destler and Balint 1999; Kerremans 1999, 2003). Republicans echoed business' concerns that enforceable social standards would limit U.S. sovereignty, could be used to challenge U.S. labor and environmental laws and ultimately may impede the conclusion of trade agreements (Elliott 2000a).

For Democrats in turn labor and environmental groups are key constituencies. This is because labor unions donate almost exclusively to Democrats. In the 2002 election cycle, for instance, 90% of labor Political Action Committee (PAC) contributions went to Democrats. However, labor donations are still just a small percentage of the amount Democrats get from business organizations. However, business donations largely go to individual politicians rather than to the party as an organization. In addition, business channels money mostly to influential or swing Democrats in order to affect the political balance in Congress in business' favor (Hacker and Pierson 2010). As a result, Democrats have adopted a more accommodative stance towards business in order to profit from business donations. For many Democrats, however, union money is still essential to offset the advantage Republicans have in business money (Shoch 2000: 134-136). Moreover, labor unions have reacted to the strategies of business organizations and now also use forms of campaign contributions that are highly candidate-specific and volatile (Francia 2012: 86-89).

U.S. environmental groups' contributions, by contrast, are financially insignificant for Democrats as they are for Republicans. Campaign contributions, however, do not provide a complete measure of policy input in the US. The grassroots support and endorsement of interest groups is often crucial for voter mobilization in congressional electoral districts. Democratic candidates rely heavily on the manpower of unions and groups like environmental NGOs during election campaigns (Shoch 2001; Dark 1999; Francia 2012: 83-85). In 2006, for instance, the AFL-CIO alone mobilized more than 200,000 volunteers before the congressional elections to defeat GOP congressional candidates (Eilperin 2007). Environmental NGOs in turn have learned to compensate for their lack of money by skillful coalition-building (Duffy 2012). In trade policy, they have formed a strong alliance with labor unions against trade liberalization, even though labor groups and environmental NGOs frequently disagree on other issues (Obach 2004: 61-69). Hence, congressional Democrats have increasingly taken trade-skeptical positions over the last decades in order to secure the indispensable support of labor unions and environmental groups (Shoch 2001).

Democratic congressmen, however, vary with regard to the level of opposition towards trade liberalization. In the Senate, a considerable share of Democrats consistently votes in favor of trade agreements. Senators generally represent larger and therefore industrially more diversified political units than House members. As a consequence, their re-election chances are less likely to depend exclusively upon on the support of interest groups that expect to loose from trade liberalization (Baldwin 1986). This lets them greater leeway in voting on trade issues than their Democratic colleagues in the House. In addition, elections for the Senate take place only every six years. The longer office terms further reduce their dependence on interest groups' resources and shield them from societal pressures over long periods (Shoch 2001: 24-25). Even though Democratic Senators supported enforceable labor and environmental standards in trade agreements as well they are largely concerned with the economic and strategic implications of PTAs. As a result, trade agreements usually received comfortable majorities in the Senate regardless of the shape of social standards.

Members of the House, by contrast, represent smaller political units and face elections every two years. This forces them to constantly seek the support of their constituencies. Therefore, House Democrats are more receptive to trade skeptical interest groups and more often oppose trade agreements (Destler 2005: 286). As consequence, votes on TPA and the ratification of PTAs usually have been much closer in the House than in the Senate in the last years. However, business groups represent important donors especially for leading House Democrats. Therefore, influential Democrats usually have mixed loyalties to business and to the more traditional constituencies of Democrats. Thus, they tend to design policies that are not alienating any of these constituencies. Consequently, enforceable social standards in PTAs have become a central instrument to simultaneously serve conflicting interests.

The House Democrats' call for enforceable social standards in trade agreement over the last two decades has been led by Charles Rangel (D-NY) and Sander Levin (D-MI). Both have strong ties to labor unions in their electoral districts in the Midwest and Northeast, where fears of job-loss though increased foreign competition is particularly pronounced (Destler and Balint 1999). However, they also have been high ranking members and even chairs of the House Ways and Means Committee, which is responsible for trade. In this function, they struggled that Democrats where not painted as outright protectionist, which would have put off donors from the business community (Goodman 2007).

Levin (D-MI), for instance, noted that the 2001 TPA debate 'was not primarily between 'free traders' and 'protectionists', but instead among groups that support more open and expanded trade.' He explained that there was strong bipartisan support for free trade, but a cleavage existed between those who believe 'that expanded international trade will guarantee economic and social development and that the theoretical efficient market will resolve any problems that emerge' and those who think that 'globalization [...] needs to be shaped to maximize its benefits and minimize its downsides' (Levin 2002). Therefore, Pete Stark (D-Calif.), another Democratic member of the Ways and Means Committee, argued that Democrats 'must insist on mandatory language to protect U.S. labor and environmental interests and back it up with enforced sanctions' (Stark 2001). Hence, a small group of House Democrats firmly advocated flanking PTAs with enforceable social standards as a way to reconcile business with labor and environmental groups. Many Democrats, however, opposed PTAs altogether regardless of the design of social standards therein.

The U.S. President

The executive branch in the US is de facto directly elected by voters.[27] Consequently, U.S. administrations of different political orientations usually take different political positions. However, U.S. Presidents without exception have been in favor of trade liberalization regardless of their party affiliation since the 1930s (Destler 2005; Karol 2000).[28] The strategic and overall economic value of trade agreements outweigh all other concerns for the U.S. administration. Republican and Democratic Presidents differed, however, with regard to their treatment of social standards ever since the issue entered trade policy debates. President Ronald Reagan consistently opposed the linkage of trade accords with social standards in the 1980s. This reflected the general position of his Republican party and its big business donors. Unsurprisingly, the bilateral trade agreements with Israel and Canada negotiated under his presidency in the 1980s contained no reference to labor or environmental issues (Hafner-Burton 2009: 62). His Republican successor, President George H. W. Bush, was equally opposed to link social standards to commercial agreements. Accordingly, he ignored calls to include labor and environmental clauses in NAFTA which was negotiated under his leadership. Before NAFTA could be passed into law, however, he was replaced by his democratic challenger Bill Clinton.

Bill Clinton had come out strongly in favor of NAFTA already as presidential candidate. This was well received by business organizations but put him at odds with the Democrats' traditional constituencies. In order to appease labor and environmental groups, he pledged to add protections for workers and the environment to the agreement. Hence, Clinton's support for social standards was a clear strategic choice for his presidential campaign (ibid.: 63-64). The Mexican and Canadian government, however, fiercely opposed to reopen negotiations to add social standards to the PTA (ibid.:122). Therefore, he merely negotiated side accords on labor and the environment after he had taken office in 1993. This was acceptable to Mexico and Canada since it created enough support among Democrats to get NAFTA passed in Congress. The AFL-CIO, however, criticized the labor side accord as 'political window-dressing on a bad agreement' and vigor-

---

27 In U.S. presidential elections voters actually elect members of an electoral college which elects the President. However, this is nowadays a mere formality and does not affect the results of elections.

28 The notion that U.S. Presidents regardless of party affiliation support trade liberalization became known as the 'Presidential Liberalism' thesis.

ously opposed the ratification of NAFTA (French 2006: 1014). Environmental groups, in contrast, were split in their assessment of the environmental side agreement and consequently held different positions.[29]

After the ratification of NAFTA, Clinton made several attempts to regain 'fast-track' authority. Democratic-sponsored bills that contained social standards as negotiation objectives, however, put off too many Republicans to pass. Republican-sponsored bills, on the other hand, made no or very modest references to social standards and therefore failed to gain sufficient support among Democrats (Kerremans 1999). Republicans felt vindicated in their opposition to social standards by Clinton's ill-fated efforts to put labor issues on the WTO's agenda. His initiatives to link labor to the WTO at the 1994 Marrakesh and 1996 Singapore Ministerials foundered on the vehement resistance of most developing countries. Even the modest proposal to create a working group on labor and trade inside the WTO at the 1999 Ministerial in Seattle failed spectacularly. Shortly beforehand, he had suggested in a newspaper interview that he supported the use of trade sanctions as enforcement mechanism for labor standards in trade agreements (French 2002: 286; Aaronson and Zimmerman 2008: 52).

On the bilateral level, however, Clinton managed to set the precedent of including enforceable social standards in the main body of an U.S. PTA. The US-Jordan PTA is until today the only U.S. PTA ever signed by a President without fast track/trade promotion authority. The Jordan PTA enjoyed overwhelming bipartisan support in Congress due its foreign policy significance. But Republicans made clear that the Jordan PTA's social standards should under no circumstances constitute a template for future U.S. PTAs. The Clinton administration, however, left office before Congress considered the agreement (Hafner-Burton 2009: 91-92).

In 2001, President George W. Bush arrived in office with an ambitious agenda for trade liberalization. He intended to negotiate a new WTO round, a Free Trade Agreement of the Americas (FTAA) and a dozen of bilateral and regional PTAs all over the world. However, unlike his predecessor, he clearly opposed the idea that trade agreements should be linked in any way to labor or environmental obligations. Consequently, the Bush administration watered down the US-Jordan PTA's social standards before the agreement was presented to Congress for ratification. USTR Robert

---

29 The following six environmental groups supported the agreement: National Wildlife Federation, the Natural Resources Defense Council, the Environmental Defense Fund, the World Wildlife Federation, the National Audubon Society, and Conservation International.

Zoellick and the Jordanian Ambassador to the US exchanged identical letters that made clear that the agreements' provisions, including the social standards, should not be enforced by trade sanctions. Instead, any differences should be settled through consultations (Rosen 2004: 70; Aaronson and Zimmerman 2008: 165-166). Thanks to this move, congressional Republicans were soothed and the House approved the agreement by voice vote within days after the exchange of letters. The Senate followed suit several weeks later (Lacey 2001).

In the context of the FTAA trade talks, President Bush again made clear that for him 'a free trade agreement focuses on commerce' and that he doesn't want 'labor protections to be used to destroy the free trade agreement' (Sanger 2001). For him, things were quite clear: Proponents of social standards 'don't like free trade. They're protectionists and they're isolationists' (The White House 2001). Therefore, in 2001 he advocated a trade promotion authority bill

> '[...] that's not laden down with all kinds of excuses not to trade. I want a bill that doesn't have these codicils on it that frighten people from trading with us. I like to remind people that if you're a poor nation, it's going to be hard to treat your people well. And if you're a poor nation, it's going to be hard to have good environmental policy. And trade is the best way to eliminate poverty; therefore, our trade agreements ought to be free from codicils which prevent us from freely trading' (The White House 2001).

Ironically, however, it was under the presidency of George W. Bush that the US began to systematically include fully enforceable social standards in all U.S. trade agreements. As the remainder of this chapter will demonstrate, this was not the result of the administration's preferences but of the ability of a few congressmen to incorporate these matters into the U.S. trade agenda.

4.3 Negotiation Processes

This study proceeds from the assumption that the strict social standards in U.S. PTAs are the result of the big impact pressure groups have in U.S. trade politics. If this assumption is correct, I expect to detect a strong influence of interest group especially on the legislative branch. Furthermore, the conduct of U.S. trade policy should be fundamentally shaped by the involvement of Congress. Ultimately, I expect the majority voting rule to empower a limited number of legislators to push through enforceable social standards. In the following, these suppositions are tested during the three phases of international negotiations in the case of the US-Central America PTA (CAFTA-DR), the US-Peru and US-Colombia PTA as well as the US-South Korea PTA negotiations. Since the initial proposals for social standards of the US were developed independently of individual negotiation processes, I discuss the developments during the pre-negotiation stages for the three cases in one section.

4.3.1 Pre-negotiation Stage

From the outset of his presidency, President George W. Bush was firmly committed to advance global trade liberalization. The Bush administration aimed at achieving this goal through a strategy called 'competitive liberalization', a concept developed by Bush's USTR Robert Zoellick. The strategy foresaw to advance free trade simultaneously on a multilateral, regional and bilateral level in order to overcome obstacles and create a political dynamic for liberalizing trade internationally (Evenett and Meier 2008). In May 2001, Bush officially informed Congress that he would seek trade promotion authority in an outline of his legislative agenda for international trade (The White House 2001). Even though Republicans held a majority of seats in the House, the low party-discipline in the American legislature effectively forced him to gather at least some Democratic votes. As a consequence, he had to heed the demands of congressional Democrats. Thus, he entered into talks with leading Democrats about how to address their concerns despite his initial refusal to entangle trade with labor and environmental matters (Janusch 2015: 1058-1059).

Even some major Business organizations acknowledged that there was no way around integrating labor and environmental objectives into the TPA bill. A report prepared by the Business Roundtable for the USTR stated that 'international labor and environmental issues have emerged as the principal stumbling blocks. The Business Roundtable believes [...] that the issue is no longer whether they should be addressed in international trade and investment negotiations, but rather how to address them constructively' (Business Round Table 2001: 20). In a similar vein, Bush explained in early 2001 that addressing these issues in trade agreements was a matter of political reality (Sanger 2001). As a consequence, his legislative agenda for trade included labor rights and environmental protection as negotiation objectives, but 'in a manner consistent with U.S. sovereignty and trade expansion' (The White House 2001).

The U.S. administration still attempted to avoid making social standards full-fledged and enforceable parts of trade agreements. In mid-2001, Bush's USTR Robert Zoellick pointed out 'that there are many ways to try to support international environment and labor objectives' (Business Week 2001) in trade policy but warned that 'if other countries resist this or see this as a new form of colonialism and imperialism, we're not going to be successful' (Sanger 2001). He claimed that 'other nations are more likely to work with us to improve local standards if the U.S. approach is positive and cooperative, not intimidating' (Zoellick 2001). In addition, he worried that enforceable social standards could make U.S. labor and environmental laws subject to international challenges (Inside US Trade 2001). Therefore, the administration worked on a 'toolbox to address labor and environmental issues without resorting to sanctions' (Business Week 2001). This 'toolbox' included incentives, such as the support of efforts by multilateral development banks to help countries to improve their labor and environmental conditions as well as penalties for the violation of social standards in the form of monetary fines. The money from the penalty payment in turn should be used to improve shortcomings in social standards in the respective country (Sanger 2001). In contrast to direct sanctions, monetary fines should prevent the emergence of persisting damage on the bilateral trade flows.

The Bush administration's approach was intended to help performing the difficult balancing act in the House that was necessary to gain TPA. Enforceable social standards were a prerequisite to gather sufficient democratic votes. Too strict provisions, however, would have alienated a considerable amount of Republican representatives (Interview record #11, 2015). Congressional Republicans still strongly opposed to incorporate meaningful social standards in any fast-track bill. Consequently, Phil Crane (R-IL), chairman of the Trade Subcommittee of the House Ways and Means Committee, introduced a fast-track bill in June 2001 that made no references to labor or environmental matters at all. This draft bill, however, failed to gather any support from Democrats (Sek 2003: 5).

In order to strike a compromise, the chairman of the House Ways and Means Committee Bill Thomas (R-CA) developed with several business-friendly Democratic members of the committee, including Cal Dooley (D-CA) and John S. Tanner (D-TN), a bill to delegate trade promotion authority (Hafner-Burton 2009: 96).[30] The bill established in its principal negotiation objectives that the USTR would need to 'seek provisions in trade agreements under which parties to those agreements strive to ensure that they do not weaken or reduce the protections afforded in domestic environmental and labor laws', 'to ensure that a party to a trade agreement with the United States does not fail to effectively enforce its environmental or labor laws' and to 'seek provisions encouraging the early identification and settlement of disputes through consultations' including 'compensation if a party to a dispute under the agreement does not come into compliance with its obligations under the agreement', with the right 'to impose a penalty upon a party'.

In short, social standards in U.S. trade agreements should obligate signatories not to weaken and to enforce their own domestic laws, but not international rules like ILO conventions or MEAs. Thereby, the bill dissipated concerns among Republican congressmen that enforceable social standards could encroach on U.S. sovereignty over labor and environmental legislation (Interview record #11, 2015). The failure to enforce domestic rules, however, could result in penalties. This made social standards in U.S. PTAs indeed enforceable and not just declaratory. Nevertheless, the bill fell short of what many leading Democrats had wanted. As a consequence, several Democrats, including Representatives Rangel (D-NY) and Levin (D-MI) submitted an alternative bill a day after Thomas had introduced his bill. The Levin-Rangel bill contained far more comprehensive social standards (Sek 2003: 5-6). However, it was the carefully balanced Thomas bill that managed to get the consent from both Houses. Congressional Republicans gave their consent to this bill since they were convinced through this language the Bush administration would not to push social standards too far in PTA negotiations (Interview record #11, 2015). Hence, it was a right-leaning administration that paved the way for the systematical integration of social standards in U.S. PTAs. The more left-leaning Clinton administration, by contrast, had repeatedly failed to gain fast-track authority due to congressional Republicans' opposition to bills including these issues.

In July 2002, the House passed the final TPA bill by a vote of 215 to 212. 27 of the 217 Republicans voted against the bill. However, the bill passed nonetheless since 25 of the 210 Democratic votes were recorded in favor. The Senate, by contrast, approved the TPA bill with a substantial bipartisan

---

30 Cal Dooley was a leader of the centrist 'New Democrats' faction and John S. Tanner a member of the conservative 'Blue Dogs Coalition' within the Democratic Party. Consequently, they had close ties to the business community.

majority of 64 to 34 votes in August 2002 (Destler 2005: 331-333). Hence, a small group of House Democrats could use the fast-track procedure as an effective *ex-ante* control mechanism to make sure the reluctant Bush administration would negotiate enforceable social standards in all future U.S. PTAs. The narrow political majorities in the House left no doubt that the administration would have to follow meticulously TPA's instructions if it was not willing to risk a congressional veto. Nevertheless, TPA's language still granted President Bush some leeway regarding the way of addressing worker rights and environmental issues in PTAs.

The notion that non-compliance with labor and environmental standards could result in trade restrictions encountered fierce resistance from Chile and other Latin American states, with which the U.S. were already in negotiations for a bilateral PTA and the region-wide FTAA (Charnovitz 2005). The administration therefore developed a template for social standards that was in line with TPA negotiation objectives but acceptable for negotiation partners. This template foresaw that violations of social standards would lead first to monetary fines before direct trade sanctions could be applied. USTR officials argued that this approach would meet TPA requirements, since TPA only stipulated 'equal' but not 'identical' enforcement mechanisms for all principal negotiation objectives (Inside US Trade 2002).

The US-Chile PTA of 2002 was the first agreement that was finalized under TPA. It ultimately contained the 'enforce-your-own-laws' approach and foresaw a penalty of maximal $15 million annually for the failure to do so. Only the non-payment of the fine could trigger trade sanctions. Given what was stipulated by the TPA bill, this was the lowest possible commitment to labor and environmental protections (Interview record #17, 2015). It reflected the repulsion of the Bush administration towards the inclusion of these issues in trade policy. Nevertheless, through TPA Congress possessed an effective *ex-ante* control mechanism that forced Bush's hand to include enforceable social standards even against his will (Interview record #12, 2015). The PTA with Chile containing this model of social standards proofed to be able to gather sufficient congressional support to get passed. Hence, the Chile model of social standards served the Bush administration as a template in the subsequent PTA negotiations.

4.3.2 International Negotiations and Ratification

As shown above, the U.S. Congress possessed considerable power in the pre-negotiation stage through the formulation of detailed negotiation objectives in TPA that stipulated the U.S. administration to negotiate enforceable social standards into PTAs. However, the content of PTAs still had to be negotiated at the international level. In addition, any negotiated agreement required the consent of the U.S. legislature in order to be ratified. Therefore, the following sections seek to analyze how the institutional dynamics during three separate negotiations processes shaped the design of social standards in the final agreements.

The US – Central America Free Trade Agreement (DR-CAFTA)

In January 2002, President Bush announced at the Organization of American States (OAS) in Washington, D.C. that the US would pursue an PTA with the five Central American countries of El Salvador, Guatemala, Honduras, Nicaragua and Costa Rica (Salazar-Xirinachs and Granados 2004: 225). Even though the region constituted the third largest Latin American trading partner of the US, total trade with Central America (and the Dominican Republic) in 2003 represented only 1.6% of U.S. foreign commerce. Therefore, the macroeconomic effects of the PTA with the small Central American markets were expected to be relatively insignificant for the U.S. economy. The rationale of the agreement for the U.S. administration lay rather in its geopolitical and strategic value. The PTA should reinforce the regional stability by strengthening institutional structures that are essential for democracy and the rule of law and that support the fight against terrorism, organized crime, and drug trafficking. In addition, the conclusion of the agreement should expand support for U.S. positions and increase momentum for progress in the stalled FTAA talks (Hornbeck 2005: 4-7).

For the Central Americans, by contrast, improved and permanent access of its exports to the U.S. market (especially for textile and agricultural products) was the major motivation for the agreement. The US was the largest trading partner of Central America, accounting for some 57% of its exports and 41% of its imports in 2003. Exports from Central America already enjoyed largely unrestricted access to the U.S. market under the Caribbean Basin Initiative (CBI), a unilateral trade preference program. Yet the CBI required periodic reauthorization from Congress and excluded some products that were of particular interest for the region. Central American governments additionally expected an increase of U.S. foreign direct investment (FDI) from the expanded and stable market access which would support the region's export driven development strategy (ibid.: 7).

The idea of including enforceable labor and environmental provisions in the agreement, however, was met with reluctance by the Central Americans. If at all, they wanted to address such issues in a cooperative manner in the trade accord (Interview record #2, 2015; Interview record #9, 2015). Costa Rica's trade minister Trejos, for instance, proposed that the PTA's social standards should follow the model of the Canada-Costa Rica PTA. This model does not provide for fines or trade sanctions to enforce social standards (Pruzin 2002). Leading House Democrats, however, demanded from the very beginning that the labor and environmental requirements of CAFTA should not fall back behind the conditions Central American countries had to meet in order to be eligible for duty-free preferences under CBI.

Therefore, they urged the Bush administration to go beyond the Chile model of social standards when talks were officially launched in January 2003 (Becker 2003). In their view, the labor and environmental challenges in the region were more severe than in Chile and therefore required a more ambitious approach for the PTA's social standards. Especially the poor state of worker rights in Guatemala, El Salvador, Honduras and Nicaragua gained center stage in the controversy over the agreement (Alden 2003). Congressional Democrats criticized that the proposed labor provisions would only stipulate to enforce existing labor laws but not require CAFTA countries to improve their laws in order to reflect internationally recognized labor standards. Furthermore, most House Democrats demanded that labor and environmental commitments should be subject to the same dispute settlement mechanism as the commercial aspects of the agreement. House Democratic leader Nancy Pelosi (D-CA) and five other Democrats warned that the agreement would face difficulties in winning congressional approval unless it offered stronger protections for labor rights (Inside US Trade 2003).

Since the design of labor and environmental standards proofed to be a point of contention in the negotiations from the very beginning, U.S. negotiators waited until the fourth round in Guatemala to formally table the U.S. proposals for the corresponding chapters (Inside US Trade 2003). In light of the displeasure of the Central American governments and the volatile majority situation in the House, however, the U.S. administration retained TPA's carefully drafted approach to social standards. The Central

American governments understood that ratification in the U.S. Congress could only be secured by agreeing to include social standards in the PTA (Interview record #9, 2015). However, the Central Americans agreed with the Bush administration that the focus of the social standards should be on enforcing already existing domestic laws, but not the imposition of additional obligations (Inside US Trade 2003).

In their view, labor legislation in Central America already reflected the ILO core principles. The Central American countries would merely lack the necessary resources to properly implement and enforce these laws. The CAFTA governments therefore tried to allay concerns in Congress regarding the situation of worker's rights in Central America by directly lobbying House and Senate Democrats. The Bush administration supported these efforts and promised to provide technical assistance to Central America to ensure the region's labor laws adhere to international standards. Lead U.S. negotiator Regina Vargo admitted that 'we know that we have a lot to demonstrate with regard to providing a comfort level with the laws in Central America' (Inside US Trade 2003).

Even though labor issues attracted most attention during the CAFTA negotiations, House and Senate Democrats also demanded improved environmental standards for the PTA. In October 2003, Ranking Finance Committee Member Max Baucus (D-MI) unveiled a detailed proposal that aimed at altering the stance of the U.S. administration regarding environmental provisions. The proposal sought to improve the monitoring of the agreement's environmental obligations by introducing a petition process for NGOs and creating an appeal process for investor-state proceedings. Furthermore, the proposal foresaw a detailed capacity-building process with binding goals and stable funding (Inside US Trade 2003). In November 2003, a group of 21 Senators called the Bush administration to table such an improved negotiating text on environmental standards during the last round of CAFTA negotiations. The Senators pointed out that 'strong environmental provisions are critical to Congressional approval' of the PTA (Inside US Trade 2003).

In December 2003, U.S. negotiators officially announced the conclusion of the negotiations with four of the five CAFTA countries. Costa Rica's negotiators had refused to conclude negotiations before the Costa Rican government gave its consent to critical concessions (Becker 2003). The agreed text with the remaining states also left a number of issues unresolved. Alongside the details of service commitments in several sectors and critical textile provisions, negotiators had also left the exact language on environmental rules open. Incorporating rules on appealing investment decisions and a petition process for environmental problems in the PTA as demanded by Democrats needed additional time (Inside US Trade 2003). Since these modifications did not include further punitive elements, the U.S. administration was willing to add them to the agreement. The Bush administration, however, declined to strengthen the enforcement mechanism of the labor and environmental chapters. House Republicans with textile constituencies had already expressed their discontent with the PTA's textile provisions. This made the Republican majority in the House even shakier than before (Inside US Trade 2003). U.S. lead negotiator Regina Vargo conceded that the agreement's fate in Congress would likely be 'determined by one vote' (Inside US Trade 2003). In order not to lose further Republican votes, Bush renounced any further changes to the PTA's social standards.

In January 2004, the US and Costa Rica could conclude talks after agreeing on the outstanding agricultural and service market access issues. The same month, the U.S. administration began separate trade negotiations with the Dominican Republic aiming at docking the agreement subsequently on CAFTA. The talks with the Dominican Republic were already finalized in mid-March. The Dominican government largely accepted the terms of the CAFTA text including the labor and environmental standards (Inside US Trade 2004). In February 2005, the US and its six DR-CAFTA partners additionally agreed to establish a special secretariat for petitions by societal actors to open investigations into the enforcement of environmental laws by DR-CAFTA signatories. This secretariat would directly report to the Environmental Affairs Council composed of high-level government officials from each Party. However, no trade sanctions could result from this process (Aaronson and Zimmerman 2008: 174-175).

AFL-CIO and major environmental NGOs immediately expressed their dissatisfaction with the agreement's social standards in separate letters they sent to members of Congress (Inside US Trade 2004). Consequently, leading House Democrats stepped up their efforts to press for changes to the labor and environmental provisions of the PTA. The 2004 Democratic presidential nominee John Kerry equally pledged to renegotiate DR-CAFTA in order to include 'adequate and fully enforceable protections for labor rights and environmental protections' in an effort to reach out to labor and environmental groups (Davis 2004; King 2004). As a result, the Central American governments pressured President Bush to sign the agreement as soon as possible and advance quickly with the ratification process.

On May 28th 2004, the US and the original five CAFTA states signed the agreement at the OAS in Washington, D.C. The language of the social provisions remained unchanged since the Bush administration and the Central American governments objected to further strengthen CAFTA's social standards (Reuters 2004). Honduran Labor Minister German Leitzelar argued that labor-related problems in his country such as child labor would not result from inadequate laws but from local cultural practices. Therefore, 'we shouldn't have restrictions, but programs to help change our culture.' In addition, he doubted that any change to the labor chapter would change the position of members of Congress who have longed voiced opposition to the deal (Inside US Trade 2005). Indeed, congressional Democrats were under immense pressure from their constituencies not to vote in favor of DR-CAFTA. Labor and environmental groups initiated massive congressional campaigns against the ratification of DR-CAFTA. Their lobbying activities focused mainly on House Democrats but also on some House Republicans with mixed voting records on trade. Union leaders specifically warned Democrats that they would penalize any member voting for the PTA by withholding financial support (Inside US Trade 2005).

In an effort to curb labor-related opposition among U.S. congressmen, ministers of trade and labor from the Dominican Republic and Central America presented a white book in April 2005 that laid out a strategy to improve the enforcement of labor laws in the region, listed projects they were already undertaking and asked the ILO and the International Development Bank for additional funding (Inside US Trade 2005). The U.S. administration additionally promised House Democrats to spend $160 million in appropriations over the next four fiscal years for labor and environmental enforcement capacity-building in the DR-CAFTA countries.

Since these steps were considered insufficient by most Democrats, however, President Bush focused on winning over protectionist Republicans rather than trying to build bipartisan support for the ratification of DR-CAFTA. Consequently, the Bush administration worked with individual congressional Republicans to eliminate obstacles to the passage of DR-CAFTA (Alden 2005). In the Senate, he offered assurances to Republicans with sugar constituencies to curtail sugar imports if the U.S. markets cannot absorb them. This step paved the way for the approval of DR-CAFTA in the Senate. In June 2005, the U.S. Senate passed the agreement with the narrow margin of 54 to 45 votes (Andrews 2005). In order to organize a majority in the House, Bush made a personal appeal to wavering GOP members. He made the case for DR-CAFTA especially on foreign policy grounds, arguing that the US should reward nations that support U.S. policies aiming at combating terrorism and pursuing democratic forms of government. Therefore, he urged members to think beyond the interests of their districts (Klein 2005). In addition, however, he secured votes from some Republicans by promising targeted benefits for their districts through Highway and Energy bills. Bush equally cut side-deals with Republicans representing textile and sugar districts (Financial Times 2005; Klein 2005; Andrews 2005, 2005; Swann 2005).

In order to realize the promises made to congressional Republicans, Bush's new USTR Rob Portman renegotiated key clothing provision of the accord with the six DR-CAFTA states. As a result, Rep. Sander Levin (D-MI) complained: 'If they could do it for pockets and linings, I would hope they could do it for something as important as the core rights of workers. But there has been no flexibility on their part' (Los Angeles Times 2005). The U.S. administration indeed saw no need to change the social standards of DR-CAFTA. USTR Portman claimed that 'CAFTA has the strongest labor and environmental provisions of any trade agreement ever negotiated by the United States. CAFTA is light years ahead of NAFTA, more practical and effective than current law, and is far stronger than earlier agreements' (Portman 2005).

In July 2005, DR-CAFTA passed the House with the razor-thin majority of 217 to 215 votes (Andrews 2005).[31] Faced with great pressure from their labor and environmental constituencies to oppose the deal Democrats voted overwhelmingly against it. However, 15 Democrats voted in favor and made the passage of the agreement possible (New York Times 2005). Since Republicans held the majority in the House, labor and environmental groups ultimately failed to organize a majority in Congress to stop the agreement. Labor unions immediately announced to withhold campaign contributions for the democratic incumbents that voted in favor of DR-CAFTA and work to defeat them in upcoming elections (Vieth 2005). Even though DR-CAFTA opponents failed to stop the trade deal, their fierce opposition left the Bush administration no choice but to incorporate enforceable social standards in the body of the agreement contrary to its own and its negotiating partners' preferences. But since Bush could still rely largely on a Republican House majority, he could stick to the compromise language on social standards of the TPA bill. House Speaker Nancy Pelosi (D – CA) lamented therefore: 'He has all the power of the presidency, and all we have on the House Democratic side is the fact that we are right' (Klein 2005).

---

31 For a detailed overview for voting behavior in the House see http://clerk.house.go v/evs/2005/roll443.xml..

The US-Peru Trade Promotion Agreement (PTPA) and the US-Colombia
Trade Promotion Agreement (CTPA)

In November 2003, the Bush administration formally notified Congress of
its intention to begin negotiations on a US-Andean Free Trade Agreement
with Colombia, Peru, Ecuador, and Bolivia. Talks should initially start only
with Colombia and Peru but later on also include Ecuador and Bolivia
(Villareal 2006: 1). The US aimed at reducing barriers to trade and investment between the parties to the agreement. Imports to the US from the
four countries combined only accounted for $15.5 billion, or 1%, of total
U.S. imports in 2004. Simultaneously, only 1% of all U.S. exports, or $7.7
billion, went to the Andean region the same year. Colombia alone accounted for 48% of those U.S. imports and 54% of the U.S. exports. Peru and
Ecuador split nearly all of the other half of imports and exports while Bolivia accounted only for a small share (Villareal 2005: 6). Thus, like in the
case of DR-CAFTA, the macroeconomic effects of the agreement on the
overall U.S. economy were expected to be modest. Hence, the U.S. administration again had first and foremost important strategic reasons for the
PTA. Besides creating momentum for the stalled FTAA talks, the Andean
PTA should strengthen democracy and fundamental values in the region.
By enhancing economic stability and regional cooperation, the agreement
was also thought of as a tool to combat the problem of narco-trafficking,
especially in Colombia (Villareal 2006: 2).

For the Andean governments, however, the agreement was economically
essential. Most imports from the region already entered the US duty-free
under the Andean Trade Promotion and Drug Eradication Act (ATPDEA)
and other unilateral trade preference programs. A large share of imports
also entered the US duty-free under normal trade relations. In total, only
10% of the value of U.S. imports from the four countries was dutiable in
2004 (Villareal 2005: 6). But the access to the U.S. market through unilateral programs depended on recurrent congressional renewal and was scheduled to expire at the end of December 2006. Therefore, the Andean governments aimed at gaining a more stable access to the U.S. market and attract-
ing additional foreign direct investment. In addition, products that were
import-sensitive to the US and therefore largely excluded from U.S. preferential programs should receive better access (ibid.: 3).

In the US, however, labor issues took center stage in debates over the
agreement from the very beginning. U.S. labor unions regarded the protection of worker rights as inadequate in all four Andean nations (Interview
record #3, 2015). But Colombia was considered a particular serious case,

due to the high number of assassinations and kidnappings of trade union-ists as well as the lack of adequate punishment for the perpetrators of these crimes. The International Trade Union Conference (ITUC, then ICFTU) regarded Colombia as the most dangerous place on earth for unionists at the time. But also the labor rights situation in the other Andean nations came under criticism. Ecuador, for instance, was repeatedly criticized by U.S. unions for the persistence of child labor in the country and several in-cidences of anti-union violence (Villareal 2006: 10). As a consequence, leading congressional Democrats urged the Bush administration to take unprecedented steps in the context of the PTA negotiations to address these problems. At the very least, the PTA's social standards should be made equally enforceable as commercial obligations (Janusch 2015: 1064).

Ecuador's labor rights record had already been under increased scrutiny by the U.S. administration since the review of the country's ATPDEA bene-fits in 2002. Since there existed serious doubts that Ecuador fulfilled AT-PDEA's labor requirements, the Ecuadorian government had made exten-sive promises to take additional steps to improve the protection of worker's rights. However, in the run up to the Andean PTA negotiations House Democrats claimed that Ecuador had not lived up to these promises. Therefore, they questioned the country's eligibility for ATPDEA and its participation in the Andean PTA talks (Villareal 2006: 10-11). U.S. unions even filed a petition with the USTR to withdraw ATPDEA preferences from Ecuador on the grounds of labor rights violations. As a result of the domestic pressure, the Bush administration threatened Ecuador in March 2004 to withdraw ATPDEA benefits and exclude it from the Andean PTA negotiations if the country would not begin to earnestly tackle its labor rights problems (Inside US Trade 2004).

President Bush's priority in the Andean negotiations clearly lay on get-ting a PTA with Colombia (Palmer 2004). He already faced fierce resis-tance from U.S. unions and their Democratic allies in Congress due to the innumerable killings of trade union activists in the country. Therefore, la-bor issues in Ecuador should not jeopardize the strategically important PTA. Ecuador ultimately gave in to three central demands of the U.S. ad-ministration on labor issues. In order to address the concerns of U.S. crit-ics, Ecuador hired child labor inspectors, presented a draft executive decree preventing the use of subcontractors to circumvent the right to strike and trained police officers on how to deal with striking workers. After Ecuador and Peru had also pledged to settle outstanding investments disputes that involved U.S. companies, the Bush administration declared that both would join Colombia in the imminent PTA negotiations (Inside US Trade 2004).

Negotiations were officially launched in May 2004 with a short first round in Cartagena, Colombia. Bolivia only participated as an observer in the two-day meeting that focused on identifying the particular interests and sensitives of each side (Villareal 2006: 3).[32] TPA was set to expire in June 2005 if Congress would not extend TPA for further two years. Since this was uncertain, the Bush administration aimed at a rapid conclusion of negotiations. From the very beginning, USTR officials made clear that negotiations in the labor and environmental areas would follow the standard U.S. approach despite the criticism of U.S. unions, environmental NGOs and congressional Democrats. The labor and environmental chapters of the PTA should again adhere strictly to the guidelines of the TPA bill's carefully drafted language (Inside US Trade 2004). In addition, labor rights problems in each country should be discussed in bilateral talks between USTR officials and the representatives of the respective state on the fringes of the first three rounds.

Over the next negotiation rounds serious conflicts emerged over the access of certain agricultural products and textiles to the U.S. market, investment issues and the protection of intellectual property rights, especially in the context of pharmaceuticals and biodiversity. After the fourth round in September 2004, the USTR even threatened to drop Peru and Ecuador from the negotiations if outstanding investment disputes could not be settled. While Peru subsequently took steps to show its goodwill, the dispute with Ecuador further intensified (Inside US Trade 2004). In addition, U.S. labor, human rights and environmental groups urged the USTR in a letter from September 2004 to suspend the Andean PTA negotiations and to withdraw Ecuador's trade preferences under ATPA and ATPDEA because of the government's failure to improve respect for worker rights over the past year. However, the USTR repeatedly postponed the decision over Ecuador's trade preferences in order to not affect the negotiations (Inside US Trade 2005).

In the presidential elections of November 2004 Bush was reelected as U.S. President. Simultaneously, Republicans could defend their majorities in both Houses in the congressional elections. As a consequence, the U.S. administration could maintain its stance on labor and environmental issues in PTAs and continued negotiations with the 'enforce-your-own-laws'-

---

32 Bolivia subsequently decided not to participate in the Andean PTA negotiations at all.

approach for social standards. Congressional Democrats, however, urged the USTR in a letter from February 2005 to pile the pressure on Ecuador to improve worker rights by gradually withdrawing ATPDEA benefits for the country. The letter threatened that the failure of Ecuador's government to follow through with its commitments on labor rights as well as the persistence of the country's flawed labor laws would 'undoubtly weigh into Congress' willingness to approve an FTA with Ecuador' (Inside US Trade 2005). The Ecuadorian government reacted promptly by promising to get to work on the demanded reforms right away.

Despite progress on key issues in early 2005, negotiators were not able to conclude talks as planned during the 8th round in March (Inside US Trade 2005). During the 9th negotiation round in April 2005 negotiations came to a standstill due to an internal crisis in Ecuador which culminated in the deposition of the acting President Lucio Gutiérrez. Therefore, the PTA could not be signed before the scheduled expiration of TPA. The Republican majorities in Congress, however, secured the Bush administration the approval of a fast-track extension for two years in June 2005. But it became increasingly clear that the negotiation positions of the three Andean countries were ever more disunited and negotiations proceeded at different speeds. Therefore, Peruvian President Toledo indicated that his government was ready to move ahead bilaterally if the plurilateral negotiations would lead nowhere. Indeed, beginning with the 11th round the USTR began to hold bilateral talks with each country individually to address the most sensitive issues, such as market access for agricultural products (Villareal 2006: 4).

Also on the issue of labor standards, the Andean governments opted for different paths. Peruvian President Toledo strove to create conditions that would ease the passage of the agreement in the U.S. Congress. In order to avoid a DR-CAFTA-like fight on Capitol Hill, which was ultimately decided by only on vote, he preferred to build bipartisan support for the PTA. Therefore, he proposed during a visit to Washington, D.C. in September 2005 to incorporate the ILO's core labor standards into the PTA and to attach strong enforcement mechanisms to all provisions (Villareal 2005: 12). As a consequence, labor and environmental issues were not formally addressed during the 12th negotiation round in September 2005. Instead, USTR Robert Portman consulted with members of Congress about Toledo's proposals (Inside US Trade 2005). USTR officials were equally in search of measures that would gather more support from congressional Democrats for the PTA. However, the UTSR ultimately declined to make any changes to the agreement's social standards. The majority situation in Congress left the USTR with no other choice than to stick to the carefully drafted compromise language of the TPA (Interview record #2, 2015). Hence, the detailed language of the TPA's negotiation objectives bill constituted a strong *ex-ante* control mechanism for Congress. Sander Levin (D-MI) therefore lamented the unwillingness of the USTR to compromise on labor issues. He complained that the USTR seemed to be 'stuck in cement' to the 'enforce-your-own-laws' approach (Inside US Trade 2005)

In contrast to Peru and Colombia, Ecuador showed less commitment to remove the stumbling blocks to the conclusion of negotiations. The country already stood on the brink of exclusion from the talks due to persisting investment disputes between the Ecuadorian government and U.S. companies. In addition, the government still lagged behind its pledges to reform its labor laws. Consequently, a bipartisan House delegation issued a report in September 2005 that demanded improvements of Ecuador's labor code with respect to the right to form unions and the enhancement of the governments' enforcement measures for child labor laws. U.S. negotiators threatened again to drop Ecuador from negotiations if the government would not undertake these necessary labor rights reforms (Inside US Trade 2005). As a result of the persistent pressure of the American administration, Ecuador intensified its cooperation with the U.S. Department of Labor in order to address labor-related issues (Inside US Trade 2005).

In November 2005, negotiations with Peru were on the home stretch. The talks with Ecuador and Colombia, by contrast, were stuck over IPR issues and market access for agricultural products. In particular, the U.S. administration had serious doubts about the commitment of Ecuador to enter into a comprehensive PTA (Inside US Trade 2005). As a consequence, the 13th negotiation round was the last held in a plurilateral framework. Subsequently, the US decided to end the regional negotiations and proceed with bilateral talks in order to take account of the different states of negotiations (Villareal 2006: 4). The talks with Peru could already be closed at the first round of bilateral negotiations in December 2005. The U.S. administration consequently used Peru's early acceptance of the agreement as leverage to urge Colombia and Ecuador to sign on to similar terms (Weitzman 2005; Blustein 2005). As a result, negotiations were also concluded with Colombia after two additional, intensive rounds in late February 2006. The bilateral negotiations with Ecuador began belatedly in March 2006. The talks were hampered from the beginning by the pending investments disputes between U.S. companies and the Ecuadorian government. In the end, the US suspended the PTA talks with Ecuador indefinitely in May 2005, after the Ecuadorian government had cancelled an oil contract with a U.S. company and seized the firm's assets (Inside US Trade 2006). Consequently, the US signed bilateral PTAs with Peru and Colombia in April and November 2006 respectively.

After the signing of the PTAs with Peru and Colombia, USTR Robert Portman initiated a bipartisan outreach to garner support for the congressional passage of the agreements. Congressional Democrats still insisted that the US should accept Peru's offer to require signatories to the trade accords to comply with the standards of the ILO. However, USTR Portman again dismissed all calls to strengthen the labor provisions of the agreements and insisted that 'the TPA provisions that I live by' only require countries to enforce their own labor laws (Inside US Trade 2006). Instead, the USTR tried to convince Democrats from the progress made by Peru and Colombia on labor-related problems and the appropriateness of the existing U.S. approach to labor standards. The US, Peru and Colombia aimed at a rapid ratification of the PTAs. However, a conflict over the elimination of import restrictions on American beef held up the congressional consideration of the agreements for months (Inside US Trade 2006).

Prospects for a smooth ratification of the PTAs with Peru and Colombia darkened after the congressional elections of November 2006 when Democrats won the majority in both Houses (Palmer 2007). Most importantly, 16 trade-friendly House Republicans were replaced with trade sceptical Democrats. Since no seats moved into the free trade direction, the balance of power in Congress shifted in favour of the opponents of trade liberalization (Destler 2007: 3). Hence, the Bush administration could no longer rely on a Republican majority to pass trade agreements. Instead, he had to respond even more to Democratic concerns. The Democrats openly threatened to reject the Colombia and Peru deals if labor standards were not upgraded in these agreements (Callan 2007). As the new chairman of the Ways and Means trade subcommittee Sander Levin (D-MI) put it bluntly: 'Now, we're in the majority, and they have to step up to the plate' (Goodman 2007).

Consequently, USTR Susan Schwab immediately engaged in discussions with congressional Democrats on how to move forward the pending trade agreements after the 110th Congress had taken up its work in January 2007. House Speaker Nancy Pelosi (D-CA) wanted to bring about a significant shift in U.S. trade priorities but still avoid that Democrats were painted as protectionists (Toner 2007). She tried to balance the interests of trade skeptical Democrats from the declining industrial areas of the Northeast and Midwest and their more business-friendly party comrades from the prosperous areas of the East and West Coast. The latter had become more and more responsive to the export interests of the financial, high technology, health, pharmaceutical and entertainment industries in their districts due to these industries' substantial campaign contributions. The former, by contrast, relied on the support of unions and other trade-skeptical groups and consequently had campaigned on a scathing critique of U.S. free trade policy (Weisman 2007). Before the first meeting between USTR Schwab and the Democratic leadership, 39 of the 42 newly elected House Democrats wrote a letter to the House Ways and Means Committee Chairman Charles Rangel (D-NY) in which they underlined their criticism of the current American trade policies:

> 'Vital to our electoral successes was our ability to take a vocal stand against the Administration's misguided trade agenda, and offer our voters real, meaningful alternatives to the jobkilling agreements, such as CAFTA, that the majority of our opponents supported' (cited in Destler 2007: 1).

As a result of the dwindled support for free trade in the House, the U.S. administrations was now willing to reconsider their trade policy positions in order to save the pending PTAs. A Democratic priority still lay on the strengthening of labor and environmental provisions by linking them to ILO standards and MEAs respectively and making them subject to regular dispute settlement procedures and remedies. USTR Schwab signaled her willingness to address these Democratic concerns from early on. However, she argued that additional obligations in these issue areas should be added through side letters to the agreements in order to avoid re-opening the text of the PTAs. Leading Democrats, however, insisted that the changes to labor and environmental obligations would have to be incorporated in the main body of the agreements. Sander Levin (D-MI), for instance, opined: 'I don't see how there can be legally enforceable changes without renegotiation' (Inside US Trade 2007).

But congressional Republicans continued to oppose stronger labor and environmental provisions on the grounds that strictly worded social standards could also open U.S. laws to litigation under PTAs, which was labelled the 'boomerang' problem. Deputy USTR Veroneau therefore warned that 'if we go too far in one direction, we could undermine our efforts to broaden support' (Inside US Trade 2007). Republicans were well aware that the discussions could lead to a new template for social standards that would also apply to other ongoing PTA negotiations (Interview record #11, 2015). As a consequence, efforts by staff members of the House Ways and Means Committee to develop a compromise failed. Moderate proposals for changes to the labor and environmental provisions by the USTR on the other hand were rejected as insufficient by leading House Democrats. Instead, Ways and Means Committee Chairman Charles Rangel (D-NY) presented the Bush administration on March 27th 2007 the 'Democratic Trade Policy Principles' that contained Democratic priorities in five key areas (Inside US Trade 2007).

With regard to labor and the environment, the document called the U.S. executive to 'require countries to adopt, maintain and enforce basic international labor standards in their domestic laws and practices—not merely enforce their own laws.' On top of that, congressional Democrats called for further measures to address specific environmental challenges in partner countries. As demanded by the AFL-CIO and environmental groups (The Economist 2007)[33], they requested the U.S. administration to 'promote sustainable development and combat global warming by requiring countries to implement and enforce common multilateral environmental agreements and address illegal logging of mahogany in Peru.'[34]

After extensive consultations between the Bush administration and the Democratic and Republican leadership in Congress, 'A New Trade Policy for America' was announced on May 10th 2007 (Weisman 2007). The so-called 'May 10th agreement' or 'Bipartisan Trade Deal' stipulated that labor commitments in trade agreements referred to the principles of the 1998 ILO Declaration – but not to the more specific language of the eight ILO core conventions – and the environmental provisions to seven MEAs which the US had already ratified. This shielded U.S. labor and environmental laws from litigation and was therefore acceptable to Republicans. Apart from that, the 'May 10th agreement' reflected almost entirely the Democrats' trade principles from March (Callan and Molony 2007). Labor and environmental standards should make reference to international rules – not only domestic laws - and be equally enforceable as commercial obligations. Even the required annex on illegal logging for the US-Peru PTA made it into the inter-branch arrangement. The disproportional attention for this issue in the US-Peru PTA can be traced back to the ability of envi-

---

33 The AFL-CIO and environmental NGOs considered this to be a labor and human rights issue as well, since indigenous people would be forced to work in illegal logging camps in Peru.

34 The other three Democratic principles called the USTR to 'reestablish a fair balance between promoting access to medicines in developing countries and protecting pharmaceutical innovation'; 'promote US national security by protecting operations at US ports'; and to ensure that a trade agreement accords 'no greater rights' to foreign investors in the United States than to US.'

ronmentalists to draw on an already existing coalition with labor unions and the U.S. timber lobby that had emerged around the passage of a separate law against illegal logging of timber in 2007 (Condon 2015: 143). Environmental groups again could successfully offset their relative lack of resources in trade politics and push their interests by skillful coalition building.

AFL-CIO President John Sweeny welcomed the 'May 10th agreement' in a press statement as a 'substantial progress made in improving workers' rights and environmental standards'. However, he doubted the Bush administration's willingness to really enforce these new standards and enumerated a number of issues the 'Bipartisan Trade Deal' left unaddressed (AFL-CIO 2007). U.S. environmental groups equally cautiously praised the improvements to the environmental chapters even though they insisted on further modifications (Defenders of Wildlife et al. 2007). Even business groups such as the U.S. Council for International Business and the U.S. Chamber of Commerce supported the 'May 10th agreement' even though they had long been fighting strict social standards in PTAs. They understood that a settlement of the social standards issue was a precondition for moving forward with the pending trade agreements (Interview record #15, 2015). However, they were satisfied, as the Chamber wrote in a press statement, that at least 'the labor provisions cannot be read to require compliance with ILO Conventions' (U.S. Chamber of Commerce 2007; USCIB 2007).

Peru accepted the required changes to the social standards in late June 2007 without demanding any concessions in the hope of a rapid ratification of the agreement (Interview record #16, 2015). President Garcia equally accepted to add an 'Annex on Forest Sector Governance' to the PTA that should govern the implementation and enforcement of the Convention on International Trade in Endangered Species of Wild Flora and Fauna (CITES). The annex was made subject to the regular dispute settlement procedure and outlined steps that Peru had to take in order to combat the illegal logging of timber in detail. These measures included adopting new regulations on illegal logging, establishing export quotas on mahogany, and increasing criminal penalties for violation of forestry laws (**Condon 2015: 112**).

Leading congressional Democrats, however, demanded that Peru should equally modify its domestic labor code to bring it in line with ILO standards before the congressional consideration of the PTA. But USTR Susan Schwab considered 'unilaterally requiring another sovereign country to change its domestic laws' a 'fundamental break with U.S. law, policy and practice' (Weisman 2007). The Peruvian government was equally cautious not to create the impression its labor law reforms were dictated by the US. The U.S. administration and the Peruvian government agreed that the country should under no circumstances be obligated to change its labor code through an act of Parliament. In order to address labor issues, however, Peruvian President Alan Garcia pledged to issue several presidential decrees to clarify the country's labor laws in five areas that were identified in close cooperation with House Democrats.

Peru was equally required to change environmental laws within eighteen months after ratification in order to come into compliance with the trade agreements obligations. President Alan Garcia therefore enacted nearly one hundred new laws by decree in mid-2008 (Jinnah and Kennedy 2011: 105; Condon 2015: 113) which were drafted with the help of U.S. government lawyers and USTR officials (Inside US Trade 2008). President Garcia even drove forth the creation of an Environment Ministry. He explained that 'the free trade agreement has brought a fundamental call to attention, that we owe to our Democrat friends in the U.S. Congress, to strengthen labor rights and the defense of the environment' (Peruvian Times 2007). The U.S. administration supported Garcia's efforts by providing millions of dollars for environmental capacity buildings projects (GAO 2014).[35]

U.S. environmental NGOs welcomed these efforts and lauded especially the 'Annex on Forest Sector Governance'. Yet, they also identified a series of shortcomings in other areas such as investment protection. Therefore, they neither endorsed nor opposed the agreement (Inside US Trade 2007). The AFL – CIO criticized the actions taken as insufficient to 'improve conditions on the ground in a meaningful way'. However, the AFL–CIO assumed a neutral position regarding the US-Peru PTA, since its member unions were split over the agreement (Swanson 2007). The neutral stance of these key constituencies gave many Democrats enough leeway to vote in favor of the Peru PTA. The agreement passed the House with a comfortable 285 to 132 majority in November 2007, with roughly half of Democrats giving their consent. The Senate approved the trade accord with an even broader majority of 77 to 18 votes in December the same year (Villareal 2008).

The Colombian government had equally accepted the required changes to the agreement's social standards in June 2007. However, domestic opposition in the US to the ratification of the agreement was much more pro-

---

35 Peru received nearly $49 million from 2009 to 2013 in funding for environmental cooperation activities related to the US – Peru free trade agreement from the United States Agency for Development (USAID).

nounced than in the case of the US-Peru PTA. The AFL-CIO vigorously opposed the US-Colombia PTA on the grounds of the high levels of violence against unionists in the country (AFL-CIO 2007). Major U.S. environmental NGOs equally rejected the agreement, since they considered workers' rights, human rights and environmental rights to be inextricably linked (Sierra Club and Friends of the Earth 2008). Hence, U.S. labor and environmental groups again took a joint position on a trade policy issue which gave their respective demands greater impact on congressional Democrats. As a consequence, leading House Democrats considered even the adjustments stipulated by the 'May 10th agreement' inadequate to address the problems of the persistent anti-union violence and the impunity of perpetrators in the country. Before the agreement should be presented to Congress for a vote, they required evidence of real improvements of the actual situation in Colombia (Inside US Trade 2007). The U.S. administration therefore led various congressional delegations to the country in order to convince Democratic lawmakers of the achieved progress on the ground.

For President Bush, however, the foreign policy implications of the PTA clearly outweighed all other issues. He repeatedly casted the trade pact as leverage against the 'hostile and anti-American regime' of Venezuelan President Hugo Chávez and pressed for its swift ratification (Eggen 2008; Lerer and McGrane 2008; Weisman 2007). But since the Bush administration declined to impose any further labor obligations on the Colombian government, Democrats continued to object congressional consideration of the agreement. Therefore, President Bush decided in April 2008 to send the implementing bill for the agreement to Congress without the consent of congressional Democrats (Politi, Ward, and Luce 2008; Stout 2008; Eggen 2008). As a response to this unprecedented step, the democratic controlled House enacted a rule change for the Colombia PTA. This removed the obligation for the House to vote on the PTA within 60 legislative days as specified under the trade promotion law. Instead, it was in the hands of the Democratic House leadership to schedule a vote at any time of its choosing (Eggen 2008). This spared House Democrats a though vote on the controversial trade deal before the elections in November 2008 that potentially could have alienated their labor and environmental constituencies (Hulse 2008). Hence, even though the Bush administration sought to rapidly pass the agreement through Congress for strategic reasons, he was not able to override congressional Democrats. It exemplified the tight control Congress has over the trade policy processes in the US during all stages of negotiations.

The U.S. administration ultimately failed to get the agreement passed before the end of Bush's presidency. With Barack Obama assuming the office of U.S. President in January 2009, Democrats now again controlled both Congress and the White House. Like President Clinton before him, Obama had to perform a delicate balancing act between the interests of trade sceptical Democratic constituencies and the strategic and economic imperatives of the U.S. Presidency (Wall Street Journal 2010). Obama therefore took a carefully balanced position on trade. During his presidential campaign he opposed the ratification of the pending agreements with Colombia and South Korea, at least in their 'current form', to gain the support of labor unions and environmental groups. Even though social standards had already been upgraded through the 'May 10th agreement', he insisted on improved labor and environmental protections. In addition, he advocated broadening the Trade Adjustment Assistance (TAA) program for displaced U.S. workers (The Economist 2009).

After assuming office, the Obama administration first announced a comprehensive review of U.S. trade policies in order to have time to plan his next moves (Barfield 2009: 232). In 2010, however, he made trade a key aspect of his economic recovery measures after the financial crisis of 2008. In the 2010 State of the Union address, he launched the 'National Export Initiative', a plan to double U.S. exports over the next five years. In addition, he intended to strengthen ties with Colombia as an important political ally in South America, where he feared the US would lose ground to economic competitors like China. Therefore, he sought ways to move forward with the pending trade agreement.

Consequently, he reached out to union leaders and engaged in several efforts to win over labor's support for the Colombia and other PTAs (Williamson and Trottman 2010). The social standards of the PTAs in limbo had already been strengthened under President Bush. Therefore, he had to resort to other measures in order to set himself apart from the previous administration and proof his commitment to labor and environmental concerns. Again, the effective implementation of social standards was a core issue, since congressional Democrats and labor and environmental groups increasingly doubted the willingness of the USTR to use the existing enforcement mechanisms. Already in April 2008, the AFL-CIO and a coalition of Guatemalan trade unions had filed a complaint with the U.S. Department of Labor, claiming that Guatemala had failed to meet the labor requirements of DR-CAFTA. At the time, Thea Lee, policy director of the AFL-CIO clarified: 'We would like to see some evidence that our government is willing to enforce the labor provisions in any existing free-trade agreement before entering into new ones' (Dickerson 2008).

The Bush administration, however, took no steps to start the dispute settlement process. The Obama administration, equally remained inactive on the issue in its first 18 months in office. In August 2010, however, the Obama administration requested formal consultations with the Guatemalan government over labor rights in the country. This marked the first time a U.S. administration initiated the dispute settlement process under a PTA's labor chapter. The timing and circumstances of the decision, however, suggested that it mainly constituted an attempt to demonstrate democratic lawmakers and their constituencies the new administration's seriousness regarding the enforcement of social standards. The move was intended to satisfy critics and broaden the congressional support for the Colombia and other PTAs (Chan 2010; COHA 2010; Williamson and Trottman 2010). President Obama's USTR Ron Kirk declared to that effect:

> 'With this case, we are sending a strong message that our trading partners must protect their own workers, that the Obama administration will not tolerate labor violations that place U.S. workers at a disadvantage, and that we are prepared to enforce the full spectrum of American trade rights from labor to the environment' (cited in Chan 2010).

In addition, President Obama and Colombian President Santos presented a 'Labor Action Plan' in April 2011 that aimed at improving Colombian labor legislation, prevent violence against labor leaders, and prosecute the perpetrators of such violence. The plan listed nine issue areas to strengthen labor rights that Colombia was required to address before the PTA could receive congressional approval.[36] The initiative, however, generally failed to convince firm critics of the PTA. U.S. unions, environmental groups and various democratic lawmakers criticized the plan as unenforceable and therefore inadequate for dealing with the country's massive labor and human rights violations (Cooper and Greenhouse 2011; Sierra Club 2011).

---

36 The nine areas that Colombia agreed to address under the Labor Action Plan were (1) creation of a specialized Ministry of Labor; (2) criminal code reform; (3) prohibiting the misuse of cooperatives; (4) preventing the use of temporary service agencies to circumvent labor rights; (5) criminalizing the use of collective pacts to undermine the right to organize and bargain collectively; (6) collecting and disseminating information on the definition of essential services; (7) seeking the ILO's assistance in implementing the Labor Action Plan and working with the ILO to strengthen its presence, capacity, and role in Colombia; (8) reforming protection programs; and (9) criminal justice reforms.

But the plan enabled the Obama administration to fend off criticism it would ignore the labor rights situation in Colombia. Therefore, it allowed President Obama to move forward with the ratification process. In another attempt to broaden congressional support for the agreement, TAA, a program designed to help displaced U.S. workers, was renewed and extended. Like labor standards, TAA was intended to appease U.S. labor unions and thereby to enable more Democratic legislators to give their consent to the agreement (Goldfarb and Montgomery 2011; Williamson 2011; Rowland 2011).

Since environmental issues were not equally controversial, the Obama administration made no similar concentrated efforts in this field. This furthermore demonstrates that environmental groups alone have less clout than unions in U.S. trade politics. In contrast to environmental NGOs, labor unions are often crucial for Democrats in terms of financial contributions and organizational support during election campaigns. In the run-up to the mid-term elections of 2010 unions spend as much as $100 million and were heavily involved in grass roots campaigns. In addition, trade union members comprised a voting bloc of more than 17 million voters and 23% of the entire electorate were from union households (Trottman 2010). Hence, the Democratic administration was careful not to repel its labor constituency at that time. Environmentalists, by contrasts, are a much more diverse constituency that cannot provide the same amount of financial and organizational support.

The measures taken by the Obama administration to tackle labor rights problems in Colombia, however, failed to bring the AFL-CIO around. As a consequence, House Democrats overwhelmingly continued to reject the agreement. Therefore, President Obama had to rely largely on congressional Republicans to deliver the necessary votes for the PTA. Republicans regained control of the House in the mid-term election of 2010 and strongly supported the agreement. Consequently, the Colombia PTA passed the House with a relatively comfortable majority of 262 to 167 votes in October 2011. As expected, the PTA received almost unanimous support from congressional Republicans but only 31 yes-votes from Democrats (Appelbaum and Steinhauer 2011). The same day, the Colombia trade accord also passed the democratic-controlled Senate with 66 to 33 votes, again with almost unanimous support from Republicans. But also 21 of 51 Democrats gave the agreement their approval.[37] For many Senators, including Democrats, the strategic importance of ratifying an agreement with a crucial U.S. ally in the region outweighed all other concerns (Wall Street Journal 2011).

Hence, the requirement of congressional ratification for negotiated trade agreements provided Congress with an effective *ex-post* control mechanism that enabled the respective congressional majority to dictate the executive branch in detail how to design the labor and environmental provisions of PTAs. As House Speaker Nancy Pelosi (D – CA) put it bluntly after the mid-term election victory of Democrats in 2008: 'It's all a question of who has the leverage. We have taken the leverage from the executive office, and we have put it back in the hands of the American working families' (Barfield 2008).

The US – Korea Free Trade Agreement (KORUS FTA)

On February 2nd 2006, the US and South Korea officially announced their intention to negotiate a comprehensive PTA (Cooper and Manyin 2006: 1). The U.S. administration particularly aimed at strengthening a critical foreign policy and national security alliance in East Asia against North Korea. Furthermore, the PTA should serve as a counterweight to the rising economic and political clout of China in the region (Williams et al. 2014: 7). Hence, again strategic objectives played a significant role in President Bush's rationale for a PTA. But this time, the U.S. government had also a profound economic interest in the agreement. The value of two-way trade between the two countries totaled already impressive $75.5 billion in 2006. Korea constituted the seventh-largest trading partner of the US and a major export market for semiconductors, machinery, aircraft, and agricultural products (Manyin 2007: 2). Thus, in contrast to the Latin American PTAs, the agreement with Korea promised to yield significant commercial gains for the U.S. economy. Hence, the U.S. executive had every interest in concluding the agreement as soon as possible and to brush aside any issue that could run counter to that overall objective.

---

37 For a detailed overview for voting behavior on the US-Colombia PTA in the House see http://politics.nytimes.com/congress/votes/112/senate/1/163; and for voting behavior in the Senate see http://politics.nytimes.com/congress/votes/112/house/1/781.

Labor and environmental problems in Korea were generally considered less severe than in Central America or the Andean nations by outside observers (Williams et al. 2014: 43). South Korea had already ratified all major MEAs and had taken several steps over the last decades to transform its industrial and energy structure to become more environmentally friendly (Yoon 2003). In the area of labor, however, Korea's record of convention ratification was worse. Above all, the country had not ratified several core conventions, including ILO Convention No. 87 on freedom of association and the right to organize and ILO Convention No. 98 on the right to organize and collective bargaining. As a consequence, the Korean government was anxious not to enter into commitments that would force it to ratify these ILO conventions or change domestic labor laws. Like in the US-Andean PTA negotiations, the Bush administration initially aimed at including only the 'enforce-your-own-laws' language for social standards into the PTA. This approach avoided imposing additional labor or environmental obligations on Korea.

The Korean government was equally keen to reach an agreement since the US was Korea's third-largest trading partner, second-largest export market, third-largest source of imports, and its second largest supplier of foreign direct investment (FDI) in 2006 (Manyin 2007: 2). Therefore, the Korean government was ready to make certain concessions in order to facilitate the conclusion of negotiations. As a consequence, Korea reluctantly agreed to incorporate the 'enforce-your-own-laws' language as the price it had to pay to get the agreement from the outset of negotiations. (Interview record #6, 2015).

Negotiations for KORUS began in Washington, D.C. on June 5th 2006. The talks were held under immense time pressure from the outset since TPA was to expire at the end of June 2007. Therefore, negotiations were set to be concluded in March 2007 within only five formal rounds (Fifield 2006). The major hurdles during negotiations were genuine economic issues such as agricultural products, automobiles, pharmaceutical products and beef. The AFL-CIO, however, identified a number of serious problems with South Korean labor laws, including the absence of trade union rights for public servants, excessive limitation on strike activity and widespread intervention in internal trade union affairs by the state. Consequently, the AFL-CIO demanded that Korean labor laws must be brought into full compliance with international standards of freedom of association and collective bargaining rights (Lee 2006). Moreover, the AFL-CIO along with major U.S. environmental groups again demanded fully enforceable labor and environmental standards for the PTA.

South Korean President Roh Moo-hyun created further uproar in the US, when he insisted to grant preferential treatment also to products made in the Kaesong industrial complex (KIC) (Hitt 2006). In the Kaesong industrial complex South Korean firms operate on North Korean territory, employing North Koreans in the production of labor-intensive manufactures. The U.S. administration vigorously opposed the inclusion of the KIC in KORUS on the one hand since it provided a source of revenue for the North Korean regime, which receives a share from the salaries paid to the North Korean workers (Cooper et al. 2011: 40). On the other hand, an inclusion of the KIC in the agreement would have intensified opposition to the agreement from U.S. labor and environmental groups (Schott, Bradford, and Moll 2006: 12).

The KIC is on North Korean territory which is why North Korean labor and environmental legislation apply to the zone that does not meet international standards by far (Manyin and Nanto 2011; Human Rights Watch 2007). North Korea is neither a member of the ILO nor a signatory of any major MEA. Since the North Korean regime generally restricted access to the Kaesong zone to third-party observers, the involvement of international bodies such as the ILO in monitoring conditions in the zone and certifying compliance with agreed standards was no viable solution. In short, South Korea could not ensure the enforcement of the labor and environmental chapters' obligations of KORUS in Kaesong (Schott, Bradford, and Moll 2006: 13). Several Democrats warned therefore that adding Kaesong to the agreement would sink the PTA's chances in Congress (Hitt 2006).

Additional frictions over the contentious issue of market access for agricultural products and automobiles protracted talks until April 2007 when negotiations were concluded after eight rounds (Olsen 2007). In the end, the US and Korea had reached a compromise on the KIC. The industrial complex was not to be mentioned in KORUS and KIC products were not made eligible for the agreement's special treatment provisions. However, a binational committee was formed to study the possibility of eventually incorporating products from 'Outward Processing Zones' (OPZs) like the KIC. If products from an OPZ should be incorporated in the agreement this committee had to certify that the OPZ meets a number of requirements including progress regarding environmental protection and labor standards. Furthermore, the two governments had to agree that the PTA should be amended accordingly and to seek legislative approval for any such amendment (Cooper et al. 2011: 40). Hence, the U.S. administration established considerable hurdles which ensured that KIC products are not likely enter the US under KORUS in the foreseeable future.

Nevertheless, labor unions in the US continued to firmly oppose the trade pact. They feared massive job losses in the US through Korean competition. The Labor Advisory Committee (LAC) report of the KORUS PTA reflected the highly critical stance of most U.S. labor unions to the agreement. The report stated that the PTA 'will not protect the fundamental human rights of workers in either the United States or Korea' and would contain 'essentially the same flawed labor chapter found in DR-CAFTA' (Labor Advisory Committee 2007). Environmental NGOs joined forces with labor groups to oppose the KORUS PTA. They argued that the agreement would contain insufficient environmental standards but excessive investment protection provisions (Hirsch 2007).

As described above, Democrats gained the House majority in the November 2006 congressional elections. The Bush administration, therefore, entered into discussions with Democrats on how to move forward with a number of pending trade agreements. As for all PTAs in limbo, a core democratic demand was the strengthening of labor and environmental standards in the agreement. Even though the main controversies were centered on the Peru and Colombia trade deals, Democrats were determined to use the inter-branch negotiations to press for a new template for social standards that would apply to all U.S. trade agreements, including the US-Korea PTA. South Korea, however, was strongly opposed to any changes to the accord's social standards. Korea's chief negotiator Kim Jong-Hoon stated bluntly: 'The deal has been done and that's it. There will be no renegotiations' (AFX News 2007). As a result, USTR Schwab initially attempted to find case-by-case solutions for the different pending agreements in order to avoid reopening the text of the KORUS agreement. One month later, however, the 'May 10th agreement' was agreed between the U.S. administration and Congress which required the USTR to incorporate stricter social standards into all pending PTAs. Congress again proved to have considerable control over the executives' actions in U.S. trade politics. The new Democratic majority in Congress could de facto set new negotiation objectives in the area of labor and environment that the U.S. government had to comply with in order to get strategically and economically important agreements passed. Korea on the other hand was left in a take-it-or-leave-it situation since TPA was set to expire on July 1st and had no prospect for renewal. In view of this fact, the South Korean government soon backed down and agreed to strengthen the accord's social provisions (Interview record #9, 2015).

The South Korean government was aware that this was a necessary step to make the deal acceptable to the U.S. Congress but would hardly alter

Korean labor or environmental laws. During a meeting of the Korean National Assembly's trade committee in May 2007, the country's chief negotiator Kim Jong-hoon reassured lawmakers that the renegotiations would not aim 'at forcing [South Korea] to sign off on all the provisions of the ILO treaty on labor standards' (The Hankyoreh 2007). The Korean government was extremely anxious not to enter into commitments that would force it to ratify ILO conventions or to change labor (or environmental) laws. Therefore, an additional footnote was added to KORUS that reaffirmed that labor obligations of the agreement would only refer to the 1998 ILO Declaration but not to the ILO core conventions. However, the threat of trade sanctions for inadequate labor or environmental laws still was a central concern to South Korean policy-makers.

But Jong-hoon was confident that the 'U.S. will balk at doing so because it is not free from problems [...]. There have been almost no cases in which issues in areas of labor and the environment between two trading nations resulted in such retaliatory measures' (The Hankyoreh 2007). Since the U.S. administration had shown restraint in the application of trade sanctions in the context of previous PTAs, the strengthened enforcement measures in the legal text of KORUS were easier to accept for the Korean government. However, this restraint in enforcing social standards also eroded the credibility of these clauses among labor and environmental advocates. This complicated the ratification of trade accords in the US (Dickerson 2008).

The agreement was finally signed on June 30th 2007 in Washington, D.C so that it still qualified for the fast-track implementing procedures afforded by the TPA (Cooper and Manyin 2007: 1). Yet, the Bush administration continued to face stiff opposition to the ratification of the agreement from Democrats. It had refrained from renegotiating the PTA's provisions concerning automotive trade as stipulated by the May 10th agreement. South Korea's decision to reintroduce restrictions on the import of U.S. beef in October 2007 additional thwarted President Bush's efforts for a rapid ratification. Presidential and parliamentary elections and massive domestic protests in South Korea prevented a swift settlement of the dispute. When an initial agreement on the beef issue was finally found in summer 2008 it was too late for President Bush to submit the KORUS PTA to Congress before the U.S. presidential and congressional elections (Sang-Hun 2008). Subsequently, Barrack Obama emerged victorious from the 2008 presidential elections and Democrats managed to defend their majority in both Houses in the midst of a severe economic downturn in the US. Even though he had repeatedly criticized the Korea trade deal when he was candidate, he now praised the agreement. It would create jobs in the United States, which he described as his 'No. 1 priority' (Stiles 2010). The economic aspect was crucial for President Obama since the PTA promised an increase in U.S. exports of nearly $11 billion annually according to a report by the International Trade Commission (Williamson 2010).

Consequently, he made the passage of the KORUS PTA a key objective of his 'National Export Initiative' in 2010. Therefore, he started to work towards the approval of the KORUS PTA with extensive support of business groups (Semuels and Hamburger 2011). After North Korea had launched an attack on a South Korean island in November 2010, the ratification of the agreement became an even more urgent matter to President Obama for foreign policy and security reasons (Ramstad 2010). As a result, South Korea and the US aimed at quickly removing the roadblocks to the PTA's ratification. After several meetings in the fall of 2010, the US and South Korea agreed in December on changing the automobile provisions of the trade accord. This step immediately ended the opposition of U.S. car makers and automobile workers because it gave the U.S. auto industry some breathing room to prepare for the increased competition through Korean automotive imports (Williamson 2010). Consequently, the United Automobile Workers (UAW) came out in support of the Korea trade deal along with another big U.S. union, the United Food and Commercial Workers, who were pleased by modifications made on beef exports. In an attempt to gain also the support of other labor groups, the Obama administration took additional steps to address labor-related concerns.

In August 2010, the Obama administration filed the first labor rights case under a PTA against Guatemala, aimed at proving to critics that social standards were not mere 'paper tigers'. USTR Ron Kirk declared that the Obama administration was committed to use 'every option available in the trade enforcement playbook to help sustain jobs here in America' (Kirk 2010). In addition, Obama insisted that Trade Adjustment Assistance, a top priority for labor unions that was set to expire in February 2011, would be extended and expanded before he would seek congressional approval of the pending trade agreements (Williamson 2011).

Nevertheless, labor groups such as the AFL-CIO and the United Steel Workers continued to opposed the agreement. They still argued it would lack adequate provisions to protect American workers. Consequently, the labor movement in the U.S. was split since two powerful unions supported the agreement. This fact gave many congressional Democrats more leeway to support the KORUS PTA. They argued the accord was supported by a wide range of societal groups (Greenhouse 2010). In the mid-term elections of 2010 Republicans regained a majority in the House which made a rapid ratification of the KORUS PTA more likely. Yet, Republicans opposed to extend the in their view costly TAA legislation and demanded that the Korea, Colombia and Panama PTAs should be submitted jointly to Congress. They feared that President Obama might forego submitting the controversial Colombia PTA, once the KORUS PTA was ratified. Due to these disagreements the congressional consideration of the pending trade accords was delayed until October 2011. The KORUS PTA ultimately passed the Senate with astonishing 83 to 15 votes thanks to its strategic implications and expected gains to the overall economy. But also the House approved the trade deal with a comfortable majority of 278 to 151 votes (Appelbaum and Steinhauer 2011).

4.4 Concluding Remarks

The formulation of trade policy in the US is tightly controlled by the legislative branch since the institutional structure of U.S. trade policy-making gives the U.S. Congress considerable sway over the executive's actions before, during and after international trade negotiations. The shape of social standards in U.S. PTAs can therefore mainly be traced back to the preferences of the U.S. legislature and its ability to push through its demands. Even though U.S. administrations have varied over time with regard to the question if and how to address labor and environmental issues in trade agreements, U.S. Presidents from both sides of the political aisle were rather careful to seek fully enforceable social standards in PTAs. It was the U.S. Congress that obligated the U.S. administration to negotiate strong social standards.

Congress itself, however, was split between Republicans and Democrats. This is because interest groups have a strong influence on U.S. lawmakers especially in the House of Representatives. Due to the majoritarian electoral system in the US and the absence of strong party structures, narrow interests have disproportional influence on representatives. While Republicans tend to represent organized business, Democrats are susceptible to labor and environmental groups' demands. Therefore, votes on TPA and trade agreements are often very close in the US. In order to secure trade promotion authority and the congressional ratification of PTAs, the U.S. administration repeatedly had to accommodate Democratic demands with regard to social standards. Hence, a relatively small number of Democrats in the House could make a sanction-based approach a pre-condition for their consent to trade promotion authority and the ratification of PTAs. The more numerous Democrats were in Congress, the more the final shape of social standards resembled the preferences of their Democratic proponents.

Hence, the enforceable social standards that can be found in U.S. PTAs are a by-product of the U.S. administrations struggle to construct a majority for the passage of TPA and PTAs in Congress. Of all administrations, it was under President Bush that the US incorporated fully enforceable social standards in its trade agreements. This was despite the fact that the Bush administration took several initiatives to curtail trade union rights domestically (Lichtenstein 2010) and was branded as 'the most anti-environmental president in our nation's history' by U.S. environmentalists (Guber and Bosso 2010: 55). But the preferences of the incumbent U.S. administration did hardly matter for the design of U.S. social standards. Instead, the U.S. executive had to follow meticulously the instructions of Congress during negotiations in order to avoid a congressional veto. Negotiation partners of the U.S. on the other hand had to accept the labor and environmental chapters the U.S. negotiators proposed without any alterations. Therefore, the labor and environmental chapters in U.S. PTAs invariable correspond exactly to the respective template demanded by Congress at the time.

5. Social Standards in EU Preferential Trade Agreements

Europe is the region with the world's strictest labor laws. As a consequence, the EU has a natural interest to strengthen labor legislation worldwide in order to avoid 'social dumping'. In fact, the EU has progressively intensified its support for ILO standards, frameworks and initiatives in its internal and external policies and actions over the last decades. Since 2007, all member states have ratified the eight core labor standards. Most EU member states have additionally ratified the main social governance conventions and other conventions underpinning the strategic objectives of the decent work agenda. In addition, the rights and principles enshrined in many ILO conventions are also protected by the EU Charter of Fundamental Rights. Furthermore, the EU has taken various initiatives to strengthen labor standards internationally (Novitz 2009; Orbie and Babarinde 2008; Orbie and Tortell 2009; Orbie et al. 2009; Keune 2009) and has extended its cooperation with the ILO (Johnson 2009; Kissack 2011). Europe has also some of the most stringent environmental regulations of the world (Vogel 2012). Consequently, the EU has emerged as one of the global leaders in international environmental politics over the last years (Kelemen and Vogel 2010; Oberthür and Roche Kelly 2008; Kelemen 2010; Vogler and Stephan 2007).

The EU has increasingly integrated labor and environmental norms in its trade policies as well. However, the EU has eschewed to put its greatest source of power in international trade policy – the access to its large internal market – behind the promotion of labor and environmental norms. Only at the unilateral level does the EU apply a form of conditionality to promote social objectives. In bilateral and bi-regional PTAs, by contrast, the EU solely relies on dialogue and cooperation procedures (González Garibay and Adriaensen 2013). The following sections seeks to demonstrate that this approach resulted from the EU's institutional setting in trade policy which disadvantaged actors during PTA negotiations that advocated enforceable social standards. Therefore, I will first outline the institutional framework of EU trade policy. Then, I explore the preferences of societal interest groups with regard to social standards and to what extent EU policy-makers' preferences in the legislative and executive branch were influenced by them. Finally, the chapter examines how the institutional design of EU trade policy-making structured the interaction of EU institutions with interest groups and among themselves during international trade negotiations and led to the specific shape of social standards in EU PTAs.

5.1. Institutional Structure of EU Trade Politics

Foreign trade policy has been among the first policy areas in the process of European integration that were completely transferred to the European level. The early establishment of a custom union with a common external tariff made a coherent representation in the international system indispensable. The 1957 Treaty of Rome established the European Economic Community and stipulated a two-tier delegation in the EU's so-called Common Commercial Policy (CCP). The first level of delegation concerned transferring the competence for international trade policy from the individual member states to the Council of the European Union. In a second delegation step, the European Commission was charged with conducting trade negotiations with third states and defending the collective interest of the union internationally (Meunier 2005: 21-22).

The pooling of external representation as the core feature of the CCP has never been seriously challenged by member states. However, during the 1990s and early 2000s increasing tensions emerged between the principle of national sovereignty and the need to amplify the Community competences in trade in light of the changed nature of trade policy (ibid.: 22-26). The 2009 Treaty of Lisbon dissolved much of the inconsistencies by bringing all key aspects of external trade, including services, investment and trade-related aspects of intellectual property under exclusive EU competence (Woolcock 2010: 9). The institutional setting in EU trade politics can therefore be modeled as a Principal-Agent relationship between the Council as an institution that represents the diverse interests of the Member states and the Commission which is the most centralized level of government in the EU system (Clark, Duchesne, and Meunier 2000; Dür and Elsig 2011).

In order to open trade negotiations, the Commission needs to obtain a separate negotiation mandate from the Council for each individual negotiation process. The Commission's DG Trade is in charge of elaborating draft proposals for the initiation and content of these negotiations. Therefore, it possesses considerable agenda-setting power. Subsequently, member states can influence DG Trade's proposals through a special advisory committee, the Trade Policy Committee (TPC, formerly Committee 133). As

Meunier (2005: 35) points out: 'The Commission almost always follows the advice of the Committee 133, since its members reflect the wishes of the ministers who ultimately can refuse to conclude the agreement negotiated by the Commission.' Once the Committee has scrutinized the proposals, they are transmitted to the Committee of Permanent Representatives (COREPER) which is composed of the member states' ambassadors to the EU. COREPER then submits the negotiating proposals to the General Affairs and External Relations Council (GAERC) which is the Council of the European Union, meeting in composition of the national Foreign Ministers. GAERC establishes the final bargaining objectives for the Commission through the negotiation mandate. Since the Council is composed of ministers from each government, it represents the pooled national interests of the member states (Meunier 2000: 107).

Hence, the Council possesses a central *ex-ante* control mechanism through the specification of the negotiation mandate. Formally, negotiating guidelines are approved under qualified majority voting rules; in practice, however, the Council decides on negotiation mandates by consensus. The unanimity voting rule in the Council grants each individual member state veto power on trade policy issues. As a consequence, when there is disagreement in the Council the common position reached often reflects the lowest common denominator (Meunier 2000: 109-110). Thus, the negotiation mandates awarded by the Council to the Commission are usually very broad and merely define the general negotiating guidelines. In addition, the mandates are not legally binding 'negotiation directives.' These discretion-based delegation mandates leave the Commission a high degree of leeway regarding how to translate them into the content of trade agreements. The pro-active role of the Commission in the elaborating of negotiating objectives stands in stark contrasts to the U.S. executive during the fast-track process, where the USTR receives a rule-based delegation mandate that is defined by Congress (da Conceição-Heldt 2013: 28).

The actual conduct of international negotiations is carried out by the Commission's DG Trade. Member states, however, can exert *ad locum* control over the Commission's conduct of negotiations through the TPC. The Committee provides member states with a police-patrol oversight mechanism that allows them to keep track of the negotiations and inform the Commission about their views from early on. Lastly, any agreement negotiated by the Commission needs to receive the support of the Council, which also votes on the adoption of trade agreements de facto per consensus. The threat of a possible rejection of a negotiated agreement provides the Council with a powerful *ex-post* control mechanism (da Conceição

2010). Consequently, over decades the conduct of EU trade negotiations was almost exclusively determined by the complex interplay of the Council and the Commission.

With the entry into force of the Treaty of Lisbon in 2009, however, the EP emerged as an additional institutional actor in EU trade politics. Ever since, the Commission is obliged to regularly report to the EP's International Trade Committee (INTA) about the progress in trade negotiations. This gives the EP an effective *ad locum* control mechanism. Most notably, however, the Lisbon Treaty formally established that the ratification of negotiated trade agreements requires not only the approval of the Council but also the consent of the EP. As a result, the EP obtained de facto veto power over trade agreements and thereby a strong *ex-post* control mechanism. The possible rejection of PTAs by the EP at the ratification stage forces the Commission to keep the demands of the EP in view during all phases of negotiations. However, even after the Lisbon Treaty the EP remains completely excluded from drafting the negotiation mandates. As a result, the Parliament has no formal *ex-ante* control mechanism at its disposal but can merely express its views through non-binding recommendations and resolutions (Van den Putte, De Ville, and Orbie 2015). Furthermore, the EP has no powers to modify individual PTA provisions *post-hoc* since it can only vote on agreements as a whole by a simple up-or-down vote after the international negotiations have been completed.

Most trade agreements additionally require the ratification by each national parliament in the EU. National parliaments, however, have few insights into decision-making processes since discussions within the TPC and the Council are in general opaque. In addition, investing time and resources in EU trade politics does not promise significant electoral rewards for national law-makers. As a result, most national parliaments don't concern themselves much with EU trade policy.[38] Moreover, member state governments in the EU usually can rely on stable majorities in parliament due to the parliamentary system prevalent in Europe. As a consequence, the national ratification of EU trade agreements is mostly a mere formality (Woolcock 2010: 8-9). Consequently, the following empirical section does not cover the national ratification processes in order to maintain the clarity of the argument. Figure 5 summarizes the most important institutional rules of the EU trade policy-making process.

---

38 This is somewhat different with the current CETA and TTIP negotiations which draw much public attention.

Figure 5: Trade Policy Process in the EU

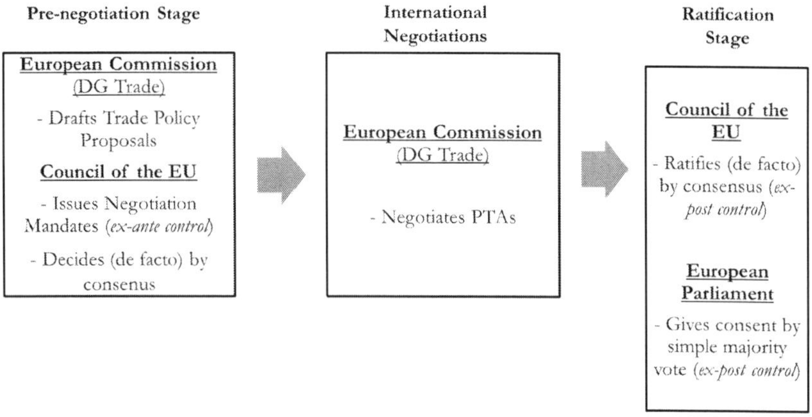

Pre-negotiation Stage	International Negotiations	Ratification Stage
European Commission (DG Trade) - Drafts Trade Policy Proposals **Council of the EU** - Issues Negotiation Mandates *(ex-ante control)* - Decides (de facto) by consenus	**European Commission** (DG Trade) - Negotiates PTAs	**Council of the EU** - Ratifies (de facto) by consensus *(ex-post control)* **European Parliament** - Gives consent by simple majority vote *(ex-post control)*

Source: Author's own compilation.

The institutional rules described above are decisive for the formulation of EU trade policy. In the EU's multi-level system, several institutional actors compete for influence. They possess different competences before, during and after the negotiation of trade agreements. Therefore, they are not equally able to determine the content of PTAs. This is important, since policy-makers in the different EU institutions often hold diverging preferences over trade policy mainly due to their different electoral incentives. In order to trace the causes for the EU's chosen approach to social standards, the next section first analyzes the preferences of interest groups in the EU and how they are translated into the policy positions of different EU institutions.

5.2 Preferences of EU Actors

The trade policy preferences of societal actors can be traced back to the effects of a policy decision on their fundamental policy objectives. The preferences of policy-makers, by contrast, are mainly influenced by re-election considerations. As rational actors they take positions that help them to stay in office. Therefore, the institutional rules that govern their relation with interest groups and voters are crucial. The more dependent a policy-makers is on particular interest groups, the more influence they have on his political stances. The more autonomy policy-makers enjoy from interest group pressures, by contrast, the more leeway they have to set policy on their own. Ultimately, the final position of EU institutions is shaped by their respective decision-making rules.

Business Groups, Labor Unions and Environmental NGOs

Societal actors in Europe have long understood that the effective exertion of influence on the EU policy-making process requires a direct representation before the EU institutions. As a result, innumerable European umbrella associations are based in Brussels where they strive to shape EU policies on behalf of their national member organizations (Coen 2007). In the field of trade policy primarily business organizations, trade unions and environmental groups compete for influence. Major European business associations include EuroCommerce, the European Service Forum (ESF) and BusinessEurope (formerly UNICE). These groups expect considerable economic gains for them from increasing international economic integration. As a consequence, they fully back the aim of liberalizing trade internationally and have long been firm supporters of trade negotiations inside the WTO framework (Dür 2008). In light of the Doha round's stalemate and America's simultaneous pursuit of PTAs , however, they urged EU policymakers to seek alternative paths (Dür 2007). Accordingly, they all welcomed the Commission's 2006 decision to strive for greater market access to emerging economies through bilateral and regional agreements (Bounds 2006; UNICE 2006; ESF 2007).

EU business groups, however, have early on voiced their strong opposition to the entanglement of trade agreements with social or environmental issues. At the sight of the almost unanimous rejection of developing countries, EU business organizations feared their inclusion would jeopardize the conclusion of lucrative trade agreements. As a result, they clearly objected the idea of introducing an enforceable 'social clause' to the WTO (Burgoon 2004: 202). BusinessEurope, the umbrella organization of national employers' federations, for instance, stated that it rejects the use of 'trade policy to achieve social policy objectives by the possible use of trade sanctions' (UNICE 1998). This view was widely shared among major EU business groups throughout the late 1990s and early 2000s (UNICE 1999, 2001; EuroCommerce 2001). In the wake of the EU's push for PTAs in 2006/2007, EU business groups renewed their opposition towards enforceable social standards. EuroCommerce, an association representing traders and retailers, stated that 'trade policy should not be linked with social or environmental standards' (EuroCommerce 2007). The European Service Forum generally warned 'that the rapid conclusion of ambitious FTAs may be hampered if their negotiations are overloaded with wider political issues' (ESF 2007). BusinessEurope did not even mention labor or environmental issues in its 2006 position paper on EU PTAs and, hence, seemed to attach little importance to them (UNICE 2006).

Overall, EU business groups agreed that labor and environmental matters should, if at all, be addressed in trade agreements in a 'cooperative and voluntary manner' (Burgoon 2009: 647). This should prevent social standards from becoming potential pitfalls in PTA negotiations. For the dispute settlement provisions of the commercial aspects of PTAs, however, EU business groups considered a different approach appropriate. With regard to the dispute settlement mechanism in the EU-Korea PTA, for instance, BusinessEurope opined: 'Precise deadlines and retaliation as a means of last resort are key' (BusinessEurope 2007). EU business organizations were less concerned about the consequences of social standards in PTAs on domestic legislation than their American counterparts. Since EU member states have a better record of ratifying ILO conventions and MEAs, the fear of a 'boomerang effect' was largely absent among EU business groups (Interview record #20, 2015).

In contrast to business groups, EU labor unions have become increasingly skeptical towards further trade liberalization especially with developing countries. As a scarce factor of production in the industrialized world, labor expects to loose from and therefore opposes trade agreements with countries that have a large supply of cheap labor. The European Trade Union Conference (ETUC), an umbrella body representing 85 national and 10 industry trade union confederations with about 60 million members in total, represents the interests of European labor before the EU institutions (Hilary 2014: 48). The ETUC cooperates also closely with the International Trade Union Confederation (ITUC), the world's largest trade union federation. Both organizations have long been advocating for the inclusion of enforceable social standards into the multilateral trading regime (O'Brien 2000; Burgoon 2004).

The ETUC responded very critical to the publication of the Commission's 'Global Europe' strategy paper that foresaw the negotiation of PTAs with emerging economies. In a position paper, the ETUC expressed its 'disagreement with the proposed general reorientation of European trade policy in favour of an extremely aggressive liberalisation agenda in the developing countries, without consideration for possible social and ecological implications'. The ETUC demanded fundamental changes to the EU's strategy in order to 'align its trade policy with the principles it promotes in its policies and Treaties, in particular the Charter of Fundamental Rights, namely the primacy of fundamental human rights - the social, health, environmental and cultural rights of peoples - over trade competition rules'. Overall, the new strategy would be in 'flagrant contradiction' of the European Commission's supposed commitment to improving coherence between the EU's trade policy and its developmental, social, and environmental objectives (ETUC 2006).

Subsequently, the ETUC repeatedly criticized the Commission's proposals for labor and environmental standards as insufficient. In July 2007, the ETUC and ITUC jointly submitted a list with detailed demands regarding the key elements of the prospective 'sustainable development chapters' in EU trade agreements. The trade union organizations demanded *inter alia* that parties to EU PTAs should be required to 'commit themselves to the effective implementation of core labour standards and other basic decent work components'. With regard to enforcement, EU trade unions called on the Commission to ensure that the 'sustainable development chapter' would be 'subject to the same dispute settlement treatment as all other components' of PTAs and would provide for sanctions at least in the form of fines. Hence, trade unions in Europe advocated coercive enforcement mechanisms for social standards in PTAs. In addition, they called for a 'Trade and Sustainable Development Forum providing for consultation with workers' organisations, employers' organisations and NGOs'. Furthermore, the list included the call for 'strong clauses concerning respect for multilateral environmental agreements' (ETUC/ITUC 2007).

Environmental NGOs in Europe were equally critical towards EU free trade policies. They focused their criticism particularly on the effects of strict trade rules on environmental protection. Especially the World Wildlife Fund (WWF) and Friends of the Earth Europe (FoEE) have been long engaged in lobbying for environmental matters in EU trade policy. Fouad Hamdan, director of FoEE, summarized the concerns of European environmentalists as follows:

> 'Trade liberalisation policies aim at reducing or eliminating all 'barriers' to trade. 'Free trade agreements' therefore introduce new rules to enforce trade liberalisation commitments, and the notion of 'trade barriers' has expanded over the years. As an effect, trade liberalisation disciplines and provisions have often contributed to water down or prevent regulatory measures in the environmental and social fields. By restricting 'policy space', trade policy has ultimately a negative impact on world governance and democracy' (Hamdan 2006).

Hence, environmental groups advocated a fundamental change of the EU trade policy model. The WWF, for instance, demanded 'that trade policy should be shaped with sustainable development at its heart.' Therefore, the WWF proposed *inter alia* to include social and environmental protocols in EU trade agreements 'addressing the most pressing environmental problems and opportunities' which should 'strengthen the institutional and regulatory capacity of the parties to improve the quality of their environments, and to harmonise, insofar as possible, environmental standards.' In addition, EU negotiators should ensure a greater environmental integration 'in the economic, trade and investment chapters of the agreements by identifying and including environmental provisions and safeguards' (WWF 2001).

FoEE, alongside numerous NGOs, equally demanded 'meaningful and enforceable environmental provisions' for the prospective agreement with the Andean Community that 'require the contracting parties to maintain and effectively enforce a set of basic environmental laws and regulations' (11.11.11 et al. 2007). These provisions should be subject to enforceable dispute resolution and violations should lead to fines. In general, however, EU environmental NGOs were rather vague regarding the enforcement mechanism they considered adequate for environmental standards. In their view, the current model of EU trade policy suffered from a series of flaws that could not be corrected by adding an isolated environmental chapter. Instead, all sections of a trade agreement should be shaped along sustainable development principles. Therefore, the WWF called for a reform of the EU trade policy-making process to hold EU trade officials more accountable to the general public. In their opinion, a small group of influential trade specialists would dominate policy making which would result in a neglect of environmental and other non-economic concerns in policy formulation (WWF 2003). In sum, the constellation of societal preferences on trade and social standards in the EU largely mirrored the situation in the US.

The Council and the European Parliament

In the political system of the EU, the Council of the European Union and the EP share legislative functions. Both institutions face a European public that has long been concerned about the possible effects of economic globalization on their economies. A 2007 Financial Times/Harris poll, for instance, found that the majority of Europeans surveyed in Britain, France,

Italy, and Spain believe that globalization hurts their countries.[39] Only in Germany, with its large export base, people seemed to consider globalization somewhat less threatening. But even there only 36% explicitly supported it. Accordingly, 94% of respondents in Spain, 93% in Italy, 89% in France and Germany, and 64% in Great Britain thought the EU should 'do more to protect people from the adverse effects of globalization' (FT/Harris 2007)[40]. In a similar vein, Europeans have long been supporting the integration of social objectives into EU external economic policies. A Eurobarometer survey, for instance, found already in 1996 that in the then 15 member states on average 70% support the restrictions of imports from countries with unacceptable working conditions (Eurobarometer 1996).[41] As outlined above, however, voters' preferences do not directly and uniformly translate into the political positions of policy-makers.

The preferences of the Council and the EP differ considerably due to their different compositions. The Council is the representation of Member States' governments which have large, national constituencies. National governments are able to balance the interests of various interest groups and take trade policy decisions that are supposed to be in the national economic or strategic interest. Member states' governments, however, are not deaf to the demands of their key constituencies. Therefore, EU member states have long varied in their position on addressing labor and environmental issues in trade agreements. Conservative and liberal governments for the most part echoed the stance of business groups that social standards are obstructive to the ultimate goal of trade liberalization. They argued that free trade itself was the best way to generate economic growth leading to improvements of labor conditions and environmental protection. Left-leaning governments, by contrast, were more responsive to labor and environmental groups. Therefore, they supported linking trade policy with social standards in principle (Hafner-Burton 2009: 70-83).

---

39 In fact, the Financial Times/Harris poll found that the share of respondents in these countries that think globalization hurts their countries is higher than in the US.

40 According to the same poll, merely 18% of Americans believe their government should do to protect people from the effects of globalization. This stands in stark contrast to the thesis, that the greater emphasis on social standards in U.S. trade agreements is the result of greater protectionist sentiments in the US compared to Europe.

41 More recent data are unfortunately not available.

During the debate about the inclusion of a 'social clause' in the WTO framework in the 1990s, the governments of France[42], Spain, Luxembourg and Belgium came out in favor of such a step. The right-leaning governments of Britain, the Netherlands and Germany, by contrast, vigorously opposed it (Waer 1996: 26; Zarocostas 1994).[43] Germany's Economy Minister Rexrodt, for instance, declared in 1995: 'We will oppose any attempt to link issues like the social clause with trade in the World Trade Organization and within the EU' (Burgoon 2009: 647). Germany and Britain viewed the WTO as 'a trade organization, not a social organization' and hence saw no place for social standards in it (Orbie and Tortell 2009: 6). The disagreement among EU member states resulted in only very vague statements by the Council regarding the relationship between trade and social standards in the run up to the 1994 Marrakesh ministerial conference. The EU even failed to present a clear 'EU position' on social standards to the 1996 Singapore ministerial conference despite efforts of the French Council Presidency to find a compromise (Orbie, Vos, and Taverniers 2005: 165). The Council merely emphasized 'the importance that WTO members attach to the efforts of the ILO to promote better definition and universal observance of core labor standards' (cited in Burgoon 2009: 650).

During Council discussions on the possible inclusion of labor standards in EU PTAs in 1995, member state governments were equally divided along ideological lines. Conservative governments, like the British Tory and the German conservative-liberal coalition government, continued to oppose such efforts. The left-leaning governments of France, Ireland, the Netherlands, and Portugal, by contrast, supported the idea (Hafner-Burton 2009: 79). However, linkage advocates among EU member states eschewed formulating a detailed position regarding their preferences for the design of such labor standards. No linkage-advocate explicitly called for a trade sanction approach for social standards. The consensus requirement in the Council obviously discouraged governments to adopt well-defined stances. Since economic and strategic objectives outweighed labor or environmental matters in trade for executives, member states governments were not

---

42 France is a notable exception to the general rule that only left-leaning governments support social standards. The country supported social standards continually over the years regardless of the political orientation of its government.

43 Belgium and the Netherlands were governed by a coalition of Christian Democrats and Social Democrats at the time which is why their governments are harder to classify clearly as right or left during that period.

willing to risk a deadlock in the Council and jeopardize the EU's ability to act in trade by pressing for strict social standards.

In preparation of the 1999 WTO ministerial conference in Seattle, the EU finally managed to reach a common position. By this time, the Council had become dominated by center-left governments. Social-democratic parties formed at least part of 13 out of the 15 EU member state executives. Most importantly, the coming to power of a Labour government in the UK (1997) and a social-democratic/green coalition government in Germany (1998) had considerably reduced the resistance in the Council to link trade with social objectives (Van den Putte and Orbie 2015: 273). Nevertheless, the UK along with the Netherlands, Ireland, Spain and Greece opposed an early Commission proposal for the creation of a working group on labor and trade in the WTO. As Orbie et al. (2005: 174-179) point out, some member states were anxious about a possible competence creep in the area of labor by the EU trough the introduction of a social clause in trade policy. They feared that an external EU competence to promote labor standards could also result in a strengthened role of the Commission regarding labor issues inside the EU. This concern of EU member states mirrored in a certain way the anxieties of the US about a possible 'boomerang effect' of labor standards in trade – a possible loss of autonomy over domestic labor legislation.

As a result of the continued disagreement in the Council, the Commission only received the mandate to advocate a 'Joint ILO/WTO Standing Forum on Trade, Globalization and Labour' at Seattle. In contrast to a working party on labor standards, this forum should not become a permanent component of the WTO's institutional framework. It was merely intended to seek 'a better understanding of the issues involved through a substantive dialogue between all interested parties.' The Council conclusion before Seattle explicitly expressed the Council's 'firm opposition to any sanctions-based approaches' to labor standards and proclaimed that 'the EU will oppose and reject any initiative to use labour rights for protectionist purposes.' In addition, the Council made clear that 'the comparative advantage of countries, particularly low-wage developing countries, must in no way be put into question' (Council of the European Union 1999). Since the emphasis lay on dialogue and on the avoidance of protectionist misuse, this extremely modest approach managed to get the consent of all member states in the Council (Orbie, Vos, and Taverniers 2005: 165).

The attempt to launch a new WTO negotiation round at Seattle, however, failed spectacularly at least partly because of U.S. President Clinton's remarks on possible trade sanctions for countries that don't abide to labor standards. This experience reinforced fears among EU member states that the entanglement of social issues with trade policy would stall international trade liberalization. As a consequence, EU member states did not protest when the Commission abandoned the demand for an ILO-WTO forum in the run-up to the launch of the Doha Development Round in 2001 as a concession to developing countries (Van den Hoven 2004: 265-267). Hence, member states clearly prioritized economic objectives of the Doha Round over the discussion of labor matters in trade fora.

EU member states have shown somewhat more enthusiasm for the discussion of environmental matters inside the international trade regime than for labor issues (Poletti and Sicurelli 2012). This can be explained as a response to the twofold pressure exerted by domestic and international institutional factors. The consensual decision-making procedures of the EU has led to very stringent environmental and food safety regulations in Europe over time that are very resistant to change. These high regulatory standards, however, have increasingly run into conflict with the negative integration obligations undertaken under the WTO (Poletti and Sicurelli 2012; Kelemen 2010). They were repeatedly challenged by powerful trade powers such as the US before the WTO's dispute settlement body (Young 2004).

As a consequence, in the run up to the Doha Round EU member states like Italy, France and Britain pressed the Commission to seek a clarification of the relationship between international trade and environmental rules in order 'to prevent disputes arising in the future' (Poletti and Sicurelli 2012: 924). Hence, EU member states sought to immunize EU rules against WTO legal challenges by increasing the scope of 'environmental exceptions' to the WTO's negative integration approach. The EU's activism for an environmental agenda in the WTO and later in PTAs, thus, was largely motivated by a defensive logic and did not aim at establishing trade measures as enforcement mechanism for international environmental rules (Poletti and Sicurelli 2016; Kelemen 2010; Kelemen and Vogel 2010; Falkner 2007).

The second supranational legislative EU institutions involved in trade politics is the European Parliament. MEPs are directly elected by European voters which is why the EP 'more closely resembles a domestic parliament or chamber in a federal system than a parliamentary assembly of an international organization' (Rittberger 2012: 18). Consequently, MEPs do not organize themselves in national delegations but in European political groups. The divide between MEPs on most subjects therefore arises rather from different ideological standpoints or constituencies' interests than from the national affiliations of representatives (Corbett, Jacobs, and

Shackleton 2011: 7). Hence, the main dimension of voting behavior both within and between the transnational political parties in the EP is the classic left-right dimension of democratic politics (Hix and Noury 2009). Votes on international trade agreements in the EP usually follow this left-right division as well and display a remarkable high intra-group voting cohesion (Hix 2013).

The political groups of the EP on the right side of the ideological spectrum, namely the European People's Party Group (EPP), the Alliance of Liberals and Democrats for Europe Group (ALDE/ADLE) and the European Conservatives and Reformists Group (ECR), generally support trade liberalization without reservation. The leftist Greens/European Free Alliance (Greens/EFA) and the European United Left/Nordic Green Left (GUE/NGL), by contrast, vote unanimously against trade liberalization in most cases. Remarkably, however, the center-left Progressive Alliance of Socialists and Democrats (S&D) mostly aligns with the center-right groups on trade issues (Van den Putte, De Ville, and Orbie 2015: 61). As firm supporters of the European integration project, social democratic parties in Europe have long made peace with market integration and free trade policies (Ross 2011).

With regard to social standards in trade agreements, however, the political groups of the EP have been split over the years according to the traditional left-right divide. In line with the preferences of European labor and environmental groups, the S&D Group, the Greens/EFA Group and the GUE/NGL Group have been generally supportive of social standards. The EPP and the ALDE/ADLE Group, by contrast, shared business groups' reservations about bringing labor and environmental issues into the international trade system (Van den Putte 2015). Despite these disagreements, the EP has long been the most vocal supporter of social standards in trade agreements among EU institutions (Orbie, Vos, and Taverniers 2005: 161-164; Bossuyt 2009: 714; Van den Putte and Orbie 2015; Bender 2002).

Already in 1994, the EP adopted a resolution calling for the introduction of a social clause in the unilateral and multilateral trading system (European Parliament 1994). In a 1996 Resolution on the WTO, the EP reiterated its support for social standards stating that it 'condemns distortions of competition caused by social and environmental dumping and calls for such dumping to be curbed by the introduction of environmental and social clauses' that allow for 'a minimum of import restrictions in the case of infringements' (European Parliament 1996). Support for social standards remained strong inside the EP over the years, even though less outspoken after the electoral victory of the European People's Party in 1999 ended the center-left dominance in the EP (Orbie, Vos, and Taverniers 2005: 173).

As Van den Putte (2015) has pointed out, this multipartisan support for social standards in the EP over time and regardless of political majorities was made possible through the vagueness with which the issue of social standards was usually dealt with in the EP. The exclusion of the EP from the formulation of negotiation mandates never forced the MEPs to elaborate and agree on a precise model of social standards in trade agreements. Therefore, right-leaning MEPs could join their left-leaning colleagues in calling for universally accepted social objectives without the risk of hampering trade negotiations. Hence, the recurring resolutions that deal with social standards in trade vary in their ambition regarding the design features of these provisions.

The European Commission (DG Trade)

In the political system of the EU, the European Commission represents the executive branch. As such the Commission, more specifically DG Trade, is in charge of negotiating trade agreements on behalf of the EU. In contrast to national governments, the Commission is not determined by elections. As a consequence, electoral incentives are absent in the Commission's rather technocratic approach towards trade policy. Officials in the Commission don't have to woo for the support of voters and interest groups to secure their re-election like members of parliament or national governments. EU trade officials rather need to ensure that their trade policy proposals are able to gain the consent of the Council and, when necessary, of the EP. Besides, DG Trade has more leeway to design trade policies according to its own preferences than elected executives. As the EU's representative in international trade policy, the Commission has a bureaucratic interest in the continuation of trade liberalization. Trade policy-making authority, in fact, was intentionally delegated to the Commission by the member states in order to insulate the process from protectionist pressures and facilitate liberalizing trade (Meunier 2005: 8-9). In addition, the Commission as the custodian of the EU's single market is generally wary of protectionist tendencies. Hence, EU trade officials in DG Trade, like their colleagues of the USTR, view themselves mandated to promote the goal of trade liberalization (Siles-Brügge 2013).

Since electoral politics do not play a role for the bureaucrats in the Commission, their relations with interest groups is different to that of policy-makers in national politics. As they don't dependent on the support of interest groups to remain in power, the Commission can select the interest groups it prefers to work with and ignore others. This form of 'top-down lobbying' leads to a situation where certain interests can exert greater influence than others (Woll 2009: 277). For lobbying the Commission, the provision of information is the key to success (Broscheid and Coen 2003: 170). Demand for policy-relevant information is high in the Commission, since its directorate-generals are often understaffed, under-resourced and pressed for time (van Schendelen 2005; Bouwen 2004: 346). Lobby groups representing exporters' interests are crucial for the formulation of EU trade policy, since they possess detailed technical expertise about trade barriers in third states that EU officials need to develop policy proposals. In addition, the Commission uses this expertise to elaborate pan-European solutions in order to prevent disputes among member states (Shaffer 2003: 78-79). Therefore, DG Trade holds close contacts with groups representing EU exporters (Dür 2008).

Since import-competing industries can't provide such critical information, DG Trade shows little compassion for declining industries in Europe as long as they are not able to convince member state governments to act on their behalf. Labor unions and environmental NGOs equally cannot generate relevant technical and expert information on core business issues in trade policy. As a consequence, the Commission's cooperation with societal actors in trade is biased in favor of business organizations (Dür and De Biévre 2007: 83). DG Trade regularly also consults the Directorates-General for Environment (DG Environment) and for Employment, Social Affairs and Inclusion (DG Employment) on sustainable development issues in trade. These DGs have close working relationships with environmental NGOs and labor unions respectively (Interview record #25, 2015; Interview record #27, 2015).

However, their influence on EU trade policy remains limited since DG Trade is charge in this policy field. In reaction to the perceived lack of civil society engagement in EU trade politics, DG Trade established the Civil Society Dialogue (CSD) in the late 1990s in order to give a greater variety of societal stakeholders an opportunity to present their views on trade policy to the Commission. However, the creation of this merely consultative forum did not fundamentally change the relationship between the Commission and non-business stakeholders. Since the Commission is still not dependent on labor and environmental groups' resources or expertize it has few incentives to engage seriously with them. Consequently, these groups continue to exert little influence on the formulation of DG Trade's trade policy proposals (Dür and De Biévre 2007).

As a consequence, just like business groups, DG Trade views strict social standards first and foremost as potential roadblocks to the objective of trade liberalization. Already in 1994, then EU Trade Commissioner Brittan explicitly opposed enforceable labor standards arguing that protectionists should not be given 'another weapon' to brandish against developing countries (Islam 1994). When several EU member states and the EP began to push for addressing social issues in the international trading system in the 1990s, however, EU trade officials were under pressure to formulate a common EU position on the role of labor standards in trade policy. In light of the disagreement within the Council and the vigorous rejection of developing countries, the Commission was in search for a compromise. EU officials speculated in 1994 that 'some kind of watered-down language could do the trick' and overcome the disunity in the Council (Zarocostas 1994). Trade Commissioner Brittan consequently described the Commission's initial stance in 1994 towards labor standards as follows:

> 'This issue is a legitimate global concern, and cannot be taboo among participants in the world economy. The WTO must be actively involved on this issue, working with the International Labour Office and other organizations. (…) There must be of course fully adequate safeguards against unilateralism or protectionist misuse and developing countries must be able to benefit from their natural advantages, to exercise their right to economic development and to maintain domestic policies appropriate to their level of development' (European Commission 1994).

In a similar vein, the Commission rejected the inclusion of punitive environmental provisions in the WTO's legal framework. Trade Commissioner Brittan predicted that such unilateral trade actions – meaning the imposition of trade sanctions – 'will drown the solution to environmental problems in a confusion of tit-for-tat measures, mutual recrimination and misunderstanding' (Mann 1996). The Commission preferred instead the clarification of the compatibility of trade and environmental rules through further discussions in the WTO's CTE. Thus, economic objectives clearly outranked environmental goals for the Commission inside the international trading regime. As one senior Commission official put it: 'We don't want the WTO to become the world environmental agency' (ibid.).

Hence, the Commission was open to discussion of social issues inside the trade sphere. However, it viewed sanction-based social standards as 'protectionist misuse' and ruled out such models from early on (Buerkle 1994). Yet, the Commission had hardly any other options as became evident in the run up to the 1996 Singapore ministerial. Trade Commissioner Brittan explained that the Commission again had to bridge 'considerably divergent views' in the Council on labor standards and that reaching 'agreement unanimously inevitably requires compromise' (Fox 1996). Thus, the Council produced only very vague statements on labor standards before Singapore. This lowest common dominator of member states' stances became the official position of the Commission at the WTO ministerial.

In the run up of the 1999 Seattle ministerial the Commission consequently advocated a WTO working group that should merely 'investigate the relationship between labor standards and trade.' But even this modest proposal was again watered down before the ministerial due to the opposition of member states such as the UK in the Council (Orbie, Vos, and Taverniers 2005: 164; Barnard 1996). The Commission merely managed to receive a mandate for a Joint ILO/WTO forum from the Council. Nevertheless, the Commission apparently agreed with the Council on the question of punitive enforcement procedures, the most controversial aspect of the 'social clause.' As trade commissioner Lamy explained at Seattle: '(…) we have to make it crystal clear: for us, sanctions are out' (Lamy 1999).

After U.S. President Clinton's comments on labor standards at the Seattle ministerial in 1999, the Commission started to emphasize mechanisms outside the trade regime for promoting social objectives. Trade commissioner Pascal Lamy revealed to U.S. business groups in 2001 that he personally opposed labor and environmental standards in the WTO since they had the potential of halting the launch of the Doha Round (Yerkey 2001). The Commission equally noted in a 2001 communication on 'Promoting CLS and improving social governance in the context of globalization' that 'it is fair to say that the issue of trade and labour and the apparent desire of at least one major WTO Member to linking labour standards to trade sanctions contributed to the failure of that Conference' and acknowledged the 'great sensitivity of the issue for virtually all developing countries.' Progress should therefore be achieved through international dialogue; the participation of the ILO, WTO, UNCTAD, World Bank, governments and civil society; the undertaking of analysis and the exchange of experience; and a clear rejection of any sanction-based approach (European Commission 2001). In 2003 the Commission even dropped its demand for a Joint ILO/WTO forum inside the WTO (Zimmermann 2008: 269-70) and 'cleverly adapted' its 'strategy to what was feasible at multilateral level, developing credible alternative tracks and policies' (European Commission 2004: 40). It focused its efforts instead on non-binding mechanisms outside the trade regime like development assistance, corporate social responsibility and an increased cooperation with the ILO (Orbie, Gistelinck, and Kerremans 2009: 159-160).

The Commission was equally cautious to address social and environmental issues in its bilateral trade relations during the early 2000s. Few PTA negotiations were under way at this time since the incoming Trade Commissioner Lamy had informally imposed a moratorium on initiating negotiations for new PTAs in 1999. Negotiations for bilateral agreements already under way, however, continued which led to the PTAs with Mexico (2000), Chile (2003) and South Africa (2004) (Meunier 2007: 912). These PTAs contained merely declaratory articles on labor and the environment. These clauses included no implementation mechanisms at all and were tailored to the respective trading partner. Hence, social standards in trade policy did not seem to have a great importance to the Commission at that time.

Instead, the Commission increasingly made the classic liberal argument that trade liberalization itself will lead to economic growth and as a consequence thereof to improved social and environmental conditions in developing countries (European Commission 2004). The apparent restraint of the Commission with regard to social standards during the early 2000s may appear surprising given the fact that the office of Trade Commissioner was held by the French socialist Pascal Lamy from 1999 to 2004. On taking office, Lamy had announced his intention to install a doctrine called 'managed globalization' which subordinated trade policy to a series of principles like multilateralism, social justice and sustainable development (Meunier 2007: 906). Nevertheless, it was only under his successor Peter Mandelson, a British liberal, that the Commission began to develop a coherent chapter for labor and environmental standards and to include it systematically in EU PTAs.

5.3 Negotiation Processes

As the previous section has shown, EU institutions differed considerably regarding the importance they attached to the inclusion of enforceable labor and environmental standards in the world trading regime. This is because the more distanced members of an EU institution are from interest groups pressures, the more autonomous they can design policies. Labor and environmental groups can only exert influence where policy-makers' re-election directly depend on their support. The shape social standards ultimately take in PTAs depends on which institutional players have the necessary competences to carry through their preferences during the different stages of the negotiation process. The following section aims to demonstrate that the institutional structure of the EU strongly favors the Commission and the Council over the EP in establishing negotiation objectives and conducting negotiations and hence, produced a template for social standards that mirrored the preferences of the former institutions. In order to test these suppositions I consider the cases of the EU- South Korea, EU-Peru/Colombia and EU-Central America PTA negotiations. Just like in the US cases, the initial proposals for social standards were developed independently of individual negotiation processes. Therefore, I discuss the developments during the pre-negotiation stages for the three cases again in one single section.

5.3.1 Pre-negotiation Stage

In October 2006, the Commission published the communication 'Global Europe: Competing in the World.' The document was the result of a redefinition of EU trade policy objectives by the incoming Trade Commissioner Paul Mandelson towards a more offensive approach to open markets for European exporters. It marked a profound shift in the EU's trade strategy since - while affirming the primacy of multilateralism - it ended the de facto moratorium on PTAs (Meunier 2007: 917). The prolonged deadlock of the Doha Development Round and the 'competitive liberalization' strategy of the US had fueled fears among business groups and policy-makers in Europe that the EU could fall behind its competitors especially in emerging markets (Bounds 2006; Sbragia 2010). DG Trade therefore emphasized in the new strategy the need to negotiate PTAs in order to increase European investment opportunities and market access in key emerging and developing economies in Asia and Latin America (Bossuyt 2009: 706).

Even though economic interests were the driving force behind 'Global Europe', DG Trade also announced that it would use the prospective negotiations to make 'a step change' in how the EU integrates its decent work and sustainable development agenda into bilateral and bi-regional trade agreements (Mandelson 2006). However, the Commission still stuck to its cooperative approach towards social standards. As Trade Commissioner Mandelson explained in 2005:

> 'Of course in our trade policies we should press the case for core labour standards and greater environmental responsibility around the world. But we must be careful that these issues are not a cover for disguised protectionism harming our ability to engage positively with our trading partners to secure our goals and interests' (Mandelson 2005).

Thus, the change principally consisted in a considerable broadening of the scope of labor and environmental standards and their integration into a homogenous 'sustainable development chapter' for all prospective PTAs. Since DG Trade was in charge of developing proposals for the upcoming trade negotiations it could strategically design the social standards. This was crucial since DG Trade needed to receive a mandate from the Council for each PTA negotiation it intended to start. Member states continued to disagree about the appropriate role of social standards in trade agreements. Countries such as France, Belgium, Denmark and the UK favored their inclusion into PTAs, while Spain and others warned not to overload commercial deals with 'non-trade issues' (Bossuyt 2009: 713-714).

As a consequence, DG Trade wooed the supporters of social standards by proposing a rather ambitious chapter in terms of scope. Since all EU member states had ratified the vast majority of ILO conventions and all the major MEAs, the reference to a wide range of international labor and environmental rules in a trade agreement was little controversial in the Council. Unlike U.S. legislators, EU member states feared no additional obligations through such a step (Interview record #22, 2015). On the other hand, DG Trade avoided causing controversy among member states by continuing to waive trade sanctions as enforcement mechanism. Since standards based on dialogue and cooperation were less likely to hamper trade negotiations, this approach was also acceptable for the sceptics among member states. As the level of preference intensity for social standards was relatively low among all member states compared to economic and strategic objectives, no government objected the soft model proposed by DG Trade. Commissioner Mandelson was therefore confident that he enjoyed the 'firm backing of the business world and the member states' for his bilateral strategy (European Report 2006).

The cooperative approach also corresponded to the Commission's own preferences. The Commission acted as a champion of international labor and environmental rules in various fora and therefore was eager to address these issues also in EU trade policies (Orbie and Babarinde 2008; Kelemen and Vogel 2010). However, DG Trade was equally concerned that the entanglement of these issues with trade could impede the conclusion of PTAs. Trade Commissioner Mandelson warned against the 'veiled protectionism advocated by some in Europe who confuse low social standards with low labour costs' and urged to 'keep things in perspective' with regard to social standards (European Report 2006). A less threatening approach for the enforcement of the broad package of social standards promised to make it more acceptable to negotiating partners. As one EU trade official explained:

> 'It was our assessment that we could arrive at a better substantive result if we have a cooperative approach. If you have a sanction approach, countries get much more worried about engaging because they see in engaging there is a risk of sanctions. With a cooperative approach we have had a very good experience in the engagement with our negotiating partners because they could see, the risk was smaller' (Interview record #22, 2015).

In April 2007, the Commission managed to receive the necessary negotiation mandates from the General Affairs and External Relations Council (GAERC) without complications. GAERC conferred the mandates for PTA negotiations with Central America, the Andean Nations, South Korea, India and ASEAN to the Commission without even holding a debate. Hence, the authority to negotiate was delegated to the executive in the EU in a very consensual manner (Interview record #22, 2015). This reflected the high concurrence of the Commission's and the national government's preferences for the economic and strategic objectives in the upcoming PTA negotiations. In its conclusion on DG Trade's proposal, GAERC specifically stressed the urgent need to increase the market access for EU exporters in the growing markets of Asia and Latin America through bilateral and bi-regional trade agreements. Apart from that, the *de facto* unanimity requirement in GAERC enhanced the readiness to compromise among member states in areas of friction. GAERC therefore conferred the Commission very vague negotiation mandates that gave the Commission considerable leeway to find compromise solutions – on social standards as well as on national economic sensitivities – that were acceptable to all member states.

In contrast to the Council, the EP was rather critical towards the Commission's push for PTAs. In its 2007 resolution on the 'Global Europe' strategy, the EP made clear that it regarded 'bilateral and regional FTAs as a sub-optimal solution' and recalled that 'such agreements lead to trade diversion, are often unbalanced, contribute to introducing discrimination in international trade relations, and tend to reduce the level of engagement of participating countries in the WTO: Therefore, the EP urged that 'new bilateral or regional free trade initiatives should only be launched when necessary to improve the competitive position of EU exporters on crucial foreign markets, especially in cases where other major trading powers have already concluded or are in the process of negotiating such agreements with the countries or regions concerned' (European Parliament 2007). Hence, the activism of the US on the bilateral level most likely convinced many MEPs of the EU's need to swiftly conclude its own PTAs. Apart from these general comments, however, the EP could not formulate detailed negotiation objectives for the executive before the start of negotiations. Since the EP is not formally involved in awarding negotiating mandates to the Commission it lacks any formal *ex ante* control mechanisms. Therefore, it could merely express its views via non-binding resolutions.

As a consequence, MEPs from different political groups were not forced to agree on a specified model for social standards. The statements it produced on the importance and shape of social standards therefore were rather vague and inconclusive. On the one hand, the EP clearly welcomed DG Trade's proposals on promoting sustainable development issues through trade. The Parliament even urged the Commission to 'pursue social goals even more vigorously in trade policy than before. The EU's biggest challenge would be to uphold the functioning of the European social model 'despite existing pressure, in increasingly competitive global markets, to further lower the social and environmental costs of production' (European Parliament 2007). However, the same resolution stated that while 'trade negotiations, at multilateral, bilateral or regional level, must strive to qualify international trade in terms of global social, environmental and human rights commitments and hence contribute to efforts made in other frameworks, [the Parliament] insists that progress on such issues should be weighed against the EU's trade interests, as foreign trade is only one, though an important, aspect of sustainable economic development in the EU' (European Parliament 2007).

Since the Commission was in charge of developing proposals for the design of social standards, the EP could not determine a model for social standards but only call on the Commission 'to clarify its understanding of the character of social and environmental rules and standards in international trade policy, to lay down the principles and content of the envisaged social and environmental chapter of new FTA and Association Agreements, and to draw up a convincing strategy on how to promote acceptance of such chapters with EU trade partners' (European Parliament

2007). The ambiguity of the EP towards social standards left the Commission significant room for maneuver to design these provisions according to its preferences.

In sum, social standards in the EU played not the same critical role in the executive's efforts to receive the negotiation authority as in the US. The Commission did not need to woo for votes in order to win a majority in the Council, the only EU legislative body responsible for delegating negotiation mandates. Instead, the Commission's proposals had to attain the unanimous support of all member states in the Council. The Commission therefore acted as a 'policy entrepreneur', designing proactively social standards and other aspects of the trade agenda in a way that it considered most viable (Bossuyt 2009). The result was a compromise between proponents and opponents in the Council that renounced the most controversial point of social standards: their enforcement through trade sanctions (González Garibay and Adriaensen 2013).

The general relatively low preference intensity of these issues in trade policy among national governments prevented that individual member states felt compelled to veto this approach. The impact of the EP on the design of social standards was very limited since it had only a consultative role and no formal competences in awarding the negotiation mandates. Even though, it was foreseeable that negotiated agreements would need the consent of the EP due to the changes brought by the entry into force of the Lisbon Treaty, the cautious stance of the EP clearly did not exert pressure on the Commission to change its approach towards social standards. In addition, the Commission had considerable leeway in formulating the PTAs' concrete sustainable development chapters' text since the negotiation mandates were very broad (Postnikov 2014: 541)

5.3.2 International Negotiations and Ratification

During the pre-negotiation stage, the Commission drafted social standards that exclusively relied on soft enforcement mechanisms. The Commission chose this approach to facilitate the upcoming negotiations on the international level and avoid frictions among Member States in the Council. However, the final shape of social standards still had to be negotiated with third countries and receive the approval of both the Council and the EP. Therefore, the following section traces the negotiation and ratification process in three cases in order to identify how the institutional dynamics shaped the final design of social standards.

The EU-South Korea Free Trade Agreement

In May 2007, the EU and South Korea announced the launch of formal negotiations for a comprehensive trade agreement, just days before the *May 10th Agreement* was reached in the US and just one month after the initial completion of the KORUS PTA talks (Olsen 2007). Hence, the successful conclusion of an EU-South Korea PTA was a top priority for the Commission in order to guarantee equal access for EU exports to the Korean market as for U.S. goods and services (Elsig and Dupont 2012: 500-501; Siles-Brügge 2014: 104). The economic potential of expanded trade with Korea itself was enormous for the EU. Two-way trade between the EU and South Korea already amounted for about $80 billion in 2006 and was expected to grow substantially through the further dismantling of tariff and non-tariff barriers. As a consequence, the Commission could rely on the support of major EU business groups from the outset of negotiations (BusinessEurope 2007; Eurochambers 2007; ESF 2009).

The EU member states supported the Commission's ambition to complete negotiations as soon as possible. Only minor frictions over negotiation objectives arose at the beginning of negotiations among EU member states in the Council due to certain national economic sensitivities (Beatty 2007). In view of the economic and strategic objectives of these institutional players, the cooperative approach for social standards promised to offer the most feasible option for the Commission to address social standards in the agreement. The Korean government had already made clear in negotiations with the US that it was not willing to sign up to any trade agreement that would force it to ratify international conventions on labor or the environment or change domestic legislation in these issue areas (The Hankyoreh 2007).

Given that the scope of the prospective labor and environmental provisions in the EU's 'sustainable development chapter' was broader than the corresponding chapters of KORUS, reservations on the Korean side were even more pronounced. Therefore, EU trade negotiators spent the first negotiating rounds explaining the differences between the U.S. and EU models of social standards and trying to allay fears of the Korean government of having to take up exuberant obligations (Interview record #29, 2015). As a result, Korean negotiators were satisfied with the EU's less challenging proposals in the fields of environment and labor. As one anonymous Korean negotiator put it: 'The EU is less harsh on this case. The American administration is showing itself to be more demanding, especially since the Democrats have been dominating Congress' (European Report 2007).

However, the Commission's proposals for the 'sustainable development chapter' in the EU-Korea PTA were heavily criticized by European labor and environmental organizations. Tom Jenkins, a representative of the ETUC, complained: 'There is no binding mechanism. We would like something more concrete. A text which mentions fines, something substantial in the event of the non-respect of the principles specified in the agreement.' The EU-Korea PTA was considered especially important by the ETUC since it was expected to serve as a precedent for social standards in future EU PTAs (European Report 2007).

As a consequence of the skepticism uttered by many civil society organizations towards the agreement, the EP placed special emphasis on the social and environmental framework of the prospective PTA. The Parliament supported the negotiations with Korea in principal but pointed out in its 2007 resolution on the PTA negotiations with Korea that a 'mutual beneficial content' of the agreement would be 'far more important than a rapid timeline' (European Parliament 2007). Consequently, the EP advocated a series of changes to the Commission's negotiating position. In a report released at the beginning of negotiations the EP's INTA Committee complained especially about the lack of enforcement of social standards in the agreement and referred to the US-Korea PTA's social standards as a model. It stated that

'effective enforcement also requires that the Sustainable Development chapter is subject to the same dispute settlement treatment as other components of the agreement. The US Administration and Congress having agreed that "all of our FTA environmental obligations will be enforced on the same basis as the commercial provisions of our agreements – same remedies, procedures, and sanctions", it is hard to see why Europe should settle for less' (European Parliament 2007).

The EP as a whole took a more unambiguous position than ever before on social standards in PTAs as well. It explicitly welcomed 'the introduction of stronger social and environmental clauses in the recently concluded US-Korea FTA as the result of pressure from the US Congress' (European Parliament 2007) indicating that it viewed the American punitive approach as an appropriate role model for the EU's 'sustainable development chapter.' Therefore, it also considered an

'ambitious sustainable development chapter to be an essential part of any agreement but recalls that the ultimate objective is the enforcement of agreed standards; takes the view that this requires the chapter to be subject to the standard dispute settlement mechanism' (ibid.).

Trade Commissioner Mandelson, however, sought to lower expectations of MEPs regarding a stricter enforcement mechanism from the outset. In the 2007 parliamentary debate on the South Korea PTA, he explained:

'The recognition and promotion of the social and environmental aspects of trade, sustainable development will be an integral part of the Free-Trade Agreement with South Korea. I agree that effective enforcement of standards is key for securing an ambitious and effective result on sustainable development in this agreement. But a cooperative tone can achieve much more in this area than the appearance of coercion. We expect to cover a greater number of Multilateral Environmental agreements, and to include issues such as decent work and a stronger commitment to ILO core conventions – and we expect to go beyond other recent agreements than those, for instance, that the Korea-US FTA includes' (European Parliament 2007).

Hence, the Commission pressed forward with its soft model of social standards in the negotiations despite the EP's criticism. The absence of coercive elements in the 'sustainable development chapter' made labor and environmental issues far less controversial than in the KORUS PTA negotiations (Interview record #26, 2015). As a consequence, the essential parts of the 'sustainable development chapter' were already agreed between the two parties at the third round of negotiations held in September 2007 in Brussels (European Report 2007). The most important issues in the negotiations between the EU and Korea were pure economic matters like tariffs, services and non-tariff barriers (Elsig and Dupont 2012: 497). During the first year negotiations progressed quickly but came to a standstill after the seventh round in May 2008 due to disagreements over the most sensitive issues, including the automotive sector and rules of origin.

The demand of South Korea to include goods produced in the Kaesong industrial complex on North Korean territory in the agreement caused further irritations in Europe. EU business organizations feared unfair competition due to lower production costs, while unionists and human rights activists protested the inacceptable human and labor rights in the North Korean enclave (Bounds and Fifield 2007; Human Rights Watch 2010). As a consequence, DG Trade insisted on the exclusion of Kaesong products from the PTA during negotiations in order to avoid creating political difficulties for the overall agreement. After another round in March 2009 and additional efforts in summer the same year, the EU and Korea could proclaim the successful conclusion of the negotiations on July 13th, 2009 (Sang-Hun 2009; Bridges 2009; Ramstad and Miller 2010). With regard to

KIC products, the EU took a similar approach as the US by excluding them from the agreement but establishing procedures for future consideration of trade preferences to apply to goods produced in the KIC (Song 2011).

The final agreement also included a 'sustainable development chapter' modeled according to the Commission's preferences. Since the labor and environmental obligations of the chapter had a rather broad scope Trade Commissioner Karel de Gucht argued that the agreement would 'break new ground in promoting the protection of the environment and respect for labour rights, containing comprehensive commitments on a range of social and environmental standards. The scope of these commitments is broader than that of any comparable agreement' (European Parliament 2010). These obligations, however, were not subject to the general dispute settlement mechanism. Instead the agreement stipulated the establishment of Domestic Advisory Groups (DAG) on sustainable development in the EU and Korea consisting of union, NGO and business representatives and the holding of regular Civil Society Forums (CSF) in which civil society actors of both parties could meet. Disputes over sustainable development issues could at the worst result in non-binding recommendations issued by a panel of experts (Van den Putte 2015). The trade pact was ultimately initialed by both sides in October 2009 (Bridges 2009).

Surprisingly, the reaction of the European labor movement to the agreement was overall positive. ETUC General Secretary John Monk called the EU-Korea PTA 'on balance a good deal' (ETUC 2010). This was despite the fact that the agreement's social standards lacked a punitive enforcement mechanism and therefore fell short of what the ETUC had initially demanded. But the European union umbrella organization assessed the PTA as economically advantageous for the majority of its members and therefore supported the overall agreement. The first-time inclusion of a 'sustainable development chapter' in a trade agreement was seen per se as positive - even if expendable – progress (ETUC 2010). The broad coverage of the chapter and the extensive inclusion of labor unions in the implementation of the commitments seemed to compensate the unions for the lack of a punitive enforcement mechanism.

The less categorical opposition of European labor unions to PTAs in comparison to their American counterparts can be also traced back to their location in smaller, more trade-dependent economies and their prior experience with market integration in Europe. Furthermore, the different membership base of unions in Europe and America also led to different economic interests. While union membership rates in Europe are relatively high and widely spread across sectors (Visser 2006), the private-sector union membership rate in the US stood at merely 6.9% in 2011 when the KORUS PTA was ratified. Since many members of U.S. unions work in import-threatened industries such as steel, textile and clothing (U.S. Department of Labor 2012), U.S. labor unions are invariably trade skeptical. As European trade unions represent a wider spectrum of the work-force, they were more likely to represent also winners from increased trade with Korea.

Even though the EP had initially also demanded sanction-based social standards, the Parliament showed itself satisfied with the agreement's provisions. In a November 2010 resolution on 'Human rights and social and environmental standards in International Trade Agreements' adopted just months before the ratification of the EU-Korea PTA, the Parliament reaffirmed its commitment to the inclusion of social standards in bilateral trade agreements. The resolution stressed that 'other countries have set positive examples for including social standards in trade agreements' in an obvious reference to the US (European Parliament 2010). The EP further recognized

> 'that the chapter on sustainable development in the bilateral agreements currently under negotiation is binding but could be strengthened by providing for: (a) a complaints procedure open to the social partners, (b) appeals to an independent body to settle disputes relating to social and environmental problems speedily and effectively (...), (c) recourse to a dispute settlement mechanism on an equal footing with the other parts of the agreement, with provision for fines to improve the situation in the sectors concerned, or at least a temporary suspension of certain trade benefits provided for under the agreement, in the event of an aggravated breach of these standards' (European Parliament 2010).

The paragraph suggested continued support by the EP for sanction-based social standards in PTAs. However, the formulation 'the chapter on sustainable development (...) *could* be strengthened' reveals that such changes were not a prerequisite for the majority in the EP to support the ratification of PTAs. Hence, even though the EU-Korea PTA constituted the first bilateral trade agreement that required the formal consent from the EP for ratification, the Parliament renounced from flexing its muscles to press for stricter social standards. In view of the supportive stance of the ETUC, even MEPs from the S&D group were not willing to jeopardize the overall agreement on the grounds that the social standards were not subject to the standard dispute settlement mechanism as demanded in the EP's 2007 EU-South Korea PTA resolution. As David Martin pointed out on behalf of the S&D group during the final plenary debate on the agreement:

'We asked as a Parliament for improved social and environmental standards. Well, Korea, since the negotiations have been initialed, has signed four ILO Conventions and their trade and sustainable development forum is going to be established as a result of this agreement allowing the civil partners in Korea to ensure that greater market opening is accompanied by labour and environmental standards improvements. All of these things, Parliament asked for. It would be ludicrous and perverse for us to turn our back on them, having achieved them' (European Parliament 2010).

Consequently, the Commission was not under pressure from the Parliament to change the social standards of the PTA. The EU member states in turn showed little interests in the details of the PTA's social provisions and, hence, placed no obstacles in the way of the Commission. The Commission, however, came under attack from EU car producers due to the treaty's automotive trade provisions. EU negotiators had largely bypassed the European car industry during negotiations since it had come out against the liberalization of automobile trade. Thanks to the autonomy the Commission enjoys vis-à-vis interest groups, EU negotiators could afford to press ahead with the agreement. The European car manufacturers, however, managed to convert their nationwide economic importance into political influence with national governments. After all, the automobile industry is by far the most important industry sector in several member states. Germany, Italy, France and others repeatedly voiced concerns in the Trade Policy Committee (TPC) on behalf of their automobile producers (Elsig and Dupont 2012: 501; Siles-Brügge 2014: 115; Goldirova 2009). Consequently, the ratification process took longer than expected. Only after all member states had dropped their resistance, the Council could approve the PTA in September 2010. On October 6th 2010 the agreement could be officially signed.

Following the entry into force of the Lisbon Treaty, the ratification of the PTA additionally required the consent of the EP. Since the ETUC was generally supportive of the trade agreement, the lines of conflict run different than expected from the Stolper-Samuelson-theorem. While most major EU business groups advocated for the agreement, the European Automobile Manufacturers' Association (ACEA) tried to induce MEPs to oppose the deal at least in its current form. As Joe Higgins (GUE/NGL), member of the EP's INTA committee pointed out: 'We usually have a conflict in this committee between capital and labour, but today its businesses who are at each other throats' (Willis 2010). Under intense pressure from European car producers, especially MEPs from countries producing small-cars pressed for and managed to secure stronger safeguard measures for the European automotive sector against increasing competition through Korean car imports (Euractive 2011).

The EP even supported efforts by several member states to induce the Korean government to relax regulations aiming at reducing CO_2 emissions of automobiles. The demand - which was ultimately accepted by Korea - was intended to facilitate the export of large European cars. This development immediately prompted concerns among EU environmental groups of setting a precedent that would make environmental laws vulnerable to accusations of protectionism between trading partners. A Greenpeace spokesperson pointed out: 'The EU is and will be involved in free trade agreements with many countries around the world. It should be careful not to class these countries' climate legislation as a non-tariff barrier since this could expose it to similar pressures with regards to the EU's own laws' (Euractive 2011).

Yet, the criticism of environmental NGOs fell on deaf ears with most MEPs. The incident illustrates that in EU trade policy most MEPs prioritized important economic objectives over environmental objectives in case they clashed. Only MEPs with an explicit 'green' constituency spoke out against the agreement. Yannick Jadot (GUE/NGL), for instance, lambasted the agreement for breaking 'new ground because, for the first time, an environmental derogation will be called for' (European Parliament 2010). This is all the more surprising since the EP had called in a 2010 resolution regarding 'international trade policy in the context of climate change imperatives' for consistency between the European Union's trade and climate policies. The resolution urged the Commission furthermore to systematically 'include environmental clauses in trade agreements concluded with non-EU countries, with particular regard to reducing CO_2 emissions and the transfer of low-emission technology' (European Parliament 2010).

Given the broad support for the overall agreement in the EP, however, the Commission was in no need to woo MEPs in opposition to the deal with stricter social standards. On February 17th 2011 the agreement passed the Parliament with a broad majority of 465 votes in favor, 128 against and 19 abstentions (Euractive 2011). While the 79 votes from the far-left and 'green' GUE/NGL and Green/EFA groups were unanimously against the trade deal, the conservative and liberal EPP, ECR and ALDE groups voted en bloc in favor. The strong voting cohesion within these latter groups is highlighted by the fact that from 315 votes casted from these groups only one MEP dissented and voted against the trade pact. The agreement also received a strong backing from the social democratic S&D group, where 133 of 158 votes were casted in favor of ratification. Dissidents in the S&D group came exclusively from France and Italy.

Like the governments of these countries before, these MEPs aimed to defend the interests of their national auto industries whose supra-regional economic importance secured them considerable influence over policymakers. As a consequence, all French S&D MEPs (13 members) and two third of Italian S&D MEPs (12 members) voted against the PTA.[44] Since the European labor movement did not oppose the deal, however, other center-left MEPs felt no pressure to reject the agreement. Hence, unlike in the KORUS negotiations the tightening of social standards became no necessary side-payment of the executive to secure the passage of the PTA in the legislature.

The EU-Peru/Colombia Preferential Trade Agreement

In May 2007, the EU officially launched negotiations for a comprehensive region-to-region Association Agreement (AA) with the Andean Community (CAN) (European Commission 2007). The economic value of the prospective agreement was very limited for the EU. In 2007, imports and exports from and to the CAN region accounted for mere 0.7% and 0.5% respectively of the total EU goods trade with the world (European Commission 2013). At the time, imports from the countries of the Andean Community already enjoyed preferential access to the EU's common market through the General System of Preferences Plus scheme (GSP+) that required compliance with a number of labor- and environment-related conditions. Peru and Colombia, however, had urged the EU to launch negotiations for a PTA. Both intended to put the trade relations with Europe on a more stable basis and achieve better access to the EU market for their most competitive exports which were largely excluded from the GSP+ scheme (Buck 2004). The left-leaning governments of Ecuador and Bolivia, by contrast, objected the further opening of their markets to EU imports and entered only reluctantly into the trade talks (Bridges 2007).

---

44 A detailed overview for voting behavior on the EU-South Korea PTA in the EP is available at the website www.votewatch.eu.

The central objective of the Commission in turn was initially rather strategic than economic. Through a region-to-region Association Agreement, including all Andean nations, the Commission aimed at fostering the regional integration process, strengthening the ties between the EU and the CAN and stabilizing the region politically and economically (Woolcock 2014). Simultaneously with the start of negotiations, the Commission also announced a large aid package of €713 million in order to demonstrate the EU's commitment to the economic development of the region (European Commission 2007). The trade accord itself was planned to go beyond a pure commercial deal and encompass three pillars instead: development co-operation, political dialogue and trade liberalization.

After Peru and Colombia had reached trade deals with the US in 2006, however, the negotiations also gained economic urgency for the EU. In order to prevent European exporters from being disadvantaged compared to U.S. companies in the Andean markets, the Commission began to accelerate the preparations for negotiations in early 2006 (Bounds 2006). EU business groups pressed the Commission to leave politically controversial aspects out of the agreement and to focus negotiations on issues that promised direct economic gains. BusinessEurope, for instance, opined that trade treaties should not be linked to 'parallel political cooperation accords' to 'ensure that the EU approaches commercial negotiations with as strong a hand as possible' (UNICE 2006).

The EP, by contrast, insisted in its 2007 resolution on the EU-CAN negotiation mandate that the EU should aim at the establishment of an '(…) advanced free trade area, the pursuit of political dialogue and cooperation and, in addition, the promotion of sustainable human development, social cohesion, consolidation of democracy and the rule of law and full respect for human, civil, political, economic, and social rights, without neglecting the cultural and environmental dimension' (European Parliament 2007). The EP specifically demanded that the agreement must include a

> '(…) 'democracy clause' and other social clauses (in connection with the labour rights incorporated in the ILO conventions, with particular reference to Convention 169 concerning Indigenous and Tribal Peoples in independent countries, the protection of decent working conditions, non-discrimination, equality of work between men and women and the eradication of child labour), and environmental clauses' (European Parliament 2007).

During the plenary debate on the initiation of the EU-CAN and EU-Central America negotiations, Trade Commissioner Mandelson reassured the

MEPs that the Commission equally opined the Association Agreements '(…) should pay particular attention to the effective implementation of internationally-agreed standards in the human rights, social, core labour and environmental fields in order to enhance sustainable development' (European Parliament 2007). Accordingly, the Commission began the negotiations with CAN aiming at a broad region-to-region Association Agreement incorporating a wide-range of non-economic issues. The bloc-to-bloc negotiations, however, stalled already after the first rounds due to profound internal disagreements within the Andean Community (Reuters 2008). The CAN governments repeatedly failed to bring a common position to the negotiation table in areas such as services, intellectual property rights and sustainable development (Correa 2008).

As a result, the Commission surprisingly cancelled the planned fourth round of negotiations in June 2008 and put the talks on hold. In November the same year, the Commission announced its intention to continue negotiations only with Peru, Colombia and Ecuador which had signaled their willingness to enter a trade agreement (Agence France Press 2008). When negotiations were relaunched in January 2009, the development cooperation and political dialogue pillars were dropped. The Commission now merely aimed at concluding a pure trade accord instead of an Association Agreement. Bolivia who had been most critical to the agreement's overall approach did not continue the negotiations. When Ecuador also withdrew from the talks in July 2009 due to the ongoing banana dispute with the EU at the WTO, negotiations boiled down to a trade deal between the EU on the one side and Peru and Colombia on the other (Fritz 2010: 4-5).

European labor and environmental groups responded very critical to the negotiation's new form. The ETUC, for instance, deplored the Commission's decision to drop the political and developmental pillars of the agreement. In addition, the ETUC criticized that the absence of Bolivia and Ecuador from the prospective agreement would impair the Andean integration process (ETUC 2009). With regard to the remaining negotiation partners, the ETUC accused the Commission of ignoring the alarming situation of trade unionists especially in Colombia. European trade unionists claimed that Colombia would not even fulfill the labor requirements necessary for its GSP+ status. Therefore, they urged the Commission to make the renewal of trade preferences for Colombia conditional on progress in terms of its compliance with ILO labor standards (ETUC 2008). Notwithstanding, the Commission extended the GSP+ preferences for Peru,

Colombia and Ecuador (and others) for additional two years in December 2008 (Cronin 2008).

The governments of Colombia and Peru, however, remained under severe criticism for failing to tackle human and labor rights' violations as well as environmental degradations in their countries (Cronin 2008; Banchón 2012; Phillips 2009, 2009). Nevertheless, the Commission aimed at the standard cooperative 'sustainable development chapter' in the agreement which it considered sufficient to deal with labor rights problems in the two partner countries (Interview record #22, 2015). Consequently, the ETUC declared:

> 'The ETUC is concerned in particular that the Sustainable Development Chapter being negotiated as part of the trade agreements will not provide the solid basis required to ensure that human and trade union rights are respected' (ETUC 2009).

EU environmental NGOs were equally critical towards the trade accord. Environmentalists were particularly concerned about the extraction of raw materials from the region and the effects of the agreement on indigenous populations. The agreement's prospective chapter on sustainable development was considered political window dressing with no moderating effect on the alleged environmental derogation caused by the trade accord (Willis 2009).

As a result of the unanimous rejection of the agreement by unionists and environmentalists, left-leaning and 'green' MEPs came out in opposition to the agreement. In view of the sustained high level of trade unionists' murders in Colombia, a group of MEPs called on the Commission to launch a formal investigation on human rights abuses in Colombia before the signing of the PTA (Phillips 2009). In addition, left MEPs explicitly requested the Commission to use the trade agreement as leverage to press for improvements in labor rights as it is practice in trade negotiations of the US. MEP Michael Cashman (S&D) explained: 'I see the fact that we have not signed the agreement as a great way to push for increased changes' (Willis 2010). Yet, the Commission rejected calls for an inquiry on human rights violations just like demands to put labor-related conditions on the signing of the agreement. The Commission considered its soft approach on social issues sufficient to achieve progress in Colombia. EU chief negotiator Rupert Schlegelmilch pointed out: 'The Colombian government is taking on board [our] recommendations. It is certainly still a bad situation, but it is improving' (Phillips 2009). Besides, the Commission presented the classic liberal argument that the best way to improve labor and environmental conditions is to create growth. Therefore, the economic benefits of the prospective agreement would itself help to tackle Colombia's problems.

The governments of Peru and Colombia in turn viewed even the envisaged cooperative monitoring of the agreements' social standards with suspicion (Mincetur 2009). They were particularly unwilling to involve civil society organizations through the creation of specialized Domestic Advisory Groups. Such fora, they feared, would provide a platform to a wide range of opposition groups to protest government policies (Interview record #26, 2015). In the end, Peru and Colombia successfully pressured the Commission to renounce stipulating the creation of such a specialized forum in the agreement. The final PTA text merely prescribed parties to the PTA to 'consult domestic labour and environment or sustainable development committees or groups, or create such committees or groups when they do not exist'.[45] Hence, the treaty's text explicitly left it up to Peru and Colombia whether to set up new fora a for the civil society dialogue or to use already existing domestic mechanisms for civil society involvement.[46] Therefore, the stipulations on the domestic monitoring mechanisms were even weaker than in the EU-Korea PTA text. In this form, Peru and Colombia accepted the social standards' monitoring mechanisms as a necessary evil to strengthen political support for the agreement inside the EU (Filipovic 2010; Banchón 2012).

Hence, the Commission deviated from its initial template for the 'sustainable development chapter' in order to facilitate the conclusion of the negotiations. Despite criticism of several MEPs, the Commission was in no need to strengthen the 'sustainable development chapter's enforcement mechanism or setting any additional labor or environment-related requirements (Willis 2010). Instead, it could afford making concessions towards Peru and Colombia without risking the rejection of the PTA (Phillips 2009). This was because it enjoyed the support of the member states and could rely on a broad majority in the EP in favor of the overall agreement (Deutsche Welle 2008). Consequently, the Commission concluded the talks with Peru and Colombia in March 2010 after nine negotiation

---

45 EU-Peru/Colombia Free Trade Agreement, Title IX, Article 281.

46 Both the Peruvian and Colombian government have opted not to create new groups but instead to use existing committees. In the case of Peru this was inter alia the General Council of Labor and Promotion of Employment and in the case of Colombia the Permanent Commission on Salaries and Labor.

rounds. The final PTA was initialed in March and signed by all parties in April 2011 in Brussels (Willis 2011).

The European labor movement fiercely opposed the signing of the EU-Peru/Colombia PTA and launched a large-scale campaign to stop the ratification of the agreement (Gregson 2010). On the margins of the EU-Latin America Summit in May 2011 in Madrid, the ETUC, in collaboration with the ITUC and the Trade Union Confederation of the Americas (TUCA), adopted a declaration against the implementation of the agreement with Peru and Colombia (ETUC/ITUC/TUCA 2010). The ETUC justified its discontent inter alia with the fact that the 'provisions of the Sustainable Development Chapter are not effectively enforceable, as the Chapter is not subject to the same dispute settlement procedures as the rest of the FTA but rather provide merely for consultations' (ETUC/ITUC/TUCA 2012). Environmental groups as well as developmental and human rights NGOs joined forces with the ETUC and equally opposed the ratification of the trade pact with Peru and Colombia in its current form (Olivet and Novo 2011).

Member states' governments, however, were not susceptible to the criticism of labor and environmental groups and hence unwilling to change the agreement's social standards. The strategic importance as well as economic gains of the prospective agreement outweighed other considerations for national governments in the EU. Countries such as Germany, Britain and Spain viewed the PTA as a tool for economic growth for both regions in the aftermath of the financial crisis. Therefore, they pressed for a rapid conclusion and entry into force of the agreement (Agence France Press 2012; Usi 2012; Vinagre 2009; Deutsche Welle 2008). Spain even made the conclusion of the trade agreements with Peru, Colombia and Central America a priority of its Council Presidency in the first half of 2010 due to its strong economic interests in Latin America (Willis 2010). As a consequence, member states' governments pressed ahead with the ratification process despite calls from ETUC and other opponents to wait with the ratification until improvements in Colombia's human and labor rights' record would become perceptible (Euractive 2012). In March 2012, the Council reached a political agreement on a draft decision approving the signing and provisional application of the trade pact with Colombia and Peru (Bridges 2012). In May, the EU trade ministers approved the trade pact officially in the Council without any further requirements (Bridges 2012).

In the EP, however, the issue of labor rights' violations provoked concern among many MEPs. Many opined that the 'sustainable development chapter' included in the agreement was insufficient to deal with the problems in these countries (Interview record #21, 2015). In its final resolution on the Peru/Colombia PTA, the EP stated that it

'regrets that, although the chapter on trade and sustainable development includes legally binding provisions, there is no binding dispute settlement mechanism for this chapter in the Trade Agreement, and that the use of the measures and sanctions foreseen in the Trade Agreement's binding general dispute settlement mechanism is excluded in the case of violations of the standards set forth in the chapter on trade and sustainable development, constituting a weakening of the current binding conditions under the EU's GSP+ scheme' (European Parliament 2012).

In the parliamentary debate before ratification, Trade Commissioner Karel de Gucht defended the Commission's chosen soft approach towards social standards:

'I consider this system more, rather than less, effective than the general dispute settlement mechanism which applies to other parts of the agreement. True, it does not provide for the usual retaliatory mechanisms, like raising tariffs, but these would be counterproductive. They do not encourage permanent changes in a country's policies, and too often they end up harming those they are intended to protect' (European Parliament 2012).

Especially left-leaning MEPs, however, were under pressure from their constituencies to take additional steps to fight labor rights' abuses and environmental derogations in Peru and Colombia (Vogel 2012). As a result, in the same resolution the EP called on the Peruvian and Colombian governments to establish 'a transparent and binding roadmap to protect trade unionists, human rights and the environment' (European Parliament 2012). Trade Commissioner Karel de Gucht initially rejected such calls since he worried that if the EU imposed unilaterally 'additional binding mechanisms ex post, our partners could question the good faith of our negotiating positions' (European Parliament 2012). Due to persistent pressure by the Parliament, however, the Commission agreed with Peru and Colombia on a roadmap in autumn 2012 that was heavily inspired by the 'Labor Action Plan' developed in the context of the US-Colombia PTA. For the Commission, the roadmap offered the advantage of addressing these issues without having to reopen the agreement and contained neither benchmarks for evaluating the achievement of objectives nor punitive elements for violations (Vogt 2015: 853-854).

The support for the overall agreement among MEPs, however, was so strong that the Commission could present the trade agreement devoid of enforceable social standards to the Parliament without risking the rejection of the deal. In December 2012, the EP overwhelmingly endorsed the EU-Peru/Colombia PTA with 486 votes in favor to 147 against with 41 abstentions (Emmott 2012; Gardner 2012). MEPs from the far-left and 'green' GUE/NGL and Green/EFA groups voted almost unanimously against the trade deal. The MEPs from these groups justified their opposition inter alia with the agreement's failure to adequately address the labor- and environment-related challenges in Peru and Colombia. Speaking on behalf of the Green/EFA group, Ana Miranda complained: 'If we consider the sustainable development chapter, it looks extremely weak and is not binding' (European Parliament 2012). The roadmap was equally dismissed by the far-left groups. As Paul Murphy (GUE/NGL) stated: 'The roadmap is being used as a fig leaf to pretend that the issue of human rights is dealt with' (European United Left/Nordic Green Left 2012).

The conservative and liberal EPP, ECR and ALDE groups, by contrast, voted en bloc in favor of the agreement. Their allies in the European business community were satisfied with the agreement's 'clear rules towards the respect of fundamental human and labour rights' and consequently had urged the deputies to approve the agreement (ACEA et al. 2012). MEPs from the center-right groups therefore accepted the Commission's chosen soft approach for social standards and praised the additional efforts undertaken by the Peruvian and Colombian government to address labor and environmental problems. The fact that from the 353 votes casted by these groups only 2 were against the trade deal demonstrates the close business ties of liberal and conservative parties and the strong party discipline they could achieve within these groups.

The social democratic S&D group, by contrast, was divided in the vote on the Peru/Colombia PTA since their MEPs were subject of conflicting pressures. On the one hand national delegations in the S&D group urged them to approve the trade deal (Interview record #21, 2015) as well as some national governments (Willis 2010). On the other hand, labor unions as the key constituency of S&D MEPs pressed them to oppose the PTA. In the end, however, only 37 of 170 votes casted by the S&D group were against the agreement.[47] This points to the fact that delegates in the EP are more willing to vote according to their party leaderships' instructions than to

---

47 A detailed overview for voting behavior on the EU-Peru/Colombia PTA in the EP is available at the website www.votewatch.eu.

their constituencies' preferences. National party delegations in the EP are ultimately more important for a MEPs' re-election chances than financial or organizational support from constituencies in the electoral district (Hix, Abdul, and Roland 2007: 133-135). This explains the usually extremely high voting cohesion the EP groups achieve in votes on trade agreements (Van den Putte, De Ville, and Orbie 2015). Hence, despite the strong resistance of the European labor movement to the Peru/Colombia PTA most S&D were not willing to jeopardize the overall agreement in order to press for stricter social standards. Instead, they settled for soft social standards and the unenforceable roadmap as a way to prove their commitment to labor rights.

The reluctance of the EP to press for stricter social standards in PTAs was therefore not merely a result of the current centre-right majority in the EP but of the greater insulation MEPs enjoy from interest group pressures compared with their colleagues in the U.S. Congress. Thus, even if a left majority in the EP would have emerged from an election during the ratification stage - like it was the case in the US - it is likely that the agreement would have passed without modifications of the social standards. In view of the broad support for the agreement among all major parliamentary groups in the EP, the rejection of the agreement by the EP was never a credible threat for the Commission (Interview record #26, 2015). As a consequence, the tightening of social standards was not necessary in order to construct a parliamentary majority. The impact of the EP's most important *ex post* control mechanism – the requirement of parliamentary approval – on the design of social standards was therefore limited. The Commission did not have to change course on social standards during the negotiation or ratification process.

The EU-Central America Association Agreement

Before the start of negotiations for a comprehensive Association Agreement in 2007, the Central American states of Costa Rica, El Salvador, Guatemala, Honduras and Nicaragua already profited from the EU's unilateral GSP+ scheme. In order to maintain the preferential access for their products to the EU's internal market granted under GSP+, the Central American states had to comply with a number of conditions, inter alia certain labor and environmental requirements. The Central American governments, however, had long called for a bi-regional PTA with the EU. Since the EU constituted Central America's second biggest trading partner after the US, the region's governments aspired to stabilize the trade relationship with Europe and achieve better market access for the region's key agricultural exports (Buck 2004; Bridges 2008). For the EU, by contrast, the economic importance of the small Central American markets was negligible. In 2007, for instance, the trade in goods with the region totaled only 0.3% of EU imports and 0.4% of EU exports (European Commission 2013).[48]

However, the EU had repeatedly stressed at biennial EU–Latin America/ Caribbean Summits since 2002 that the conclusion of a comprehensive bi- regional Association Agreement was a strategic objective for the EU. The Commission viewed the prospective treaty not only as a commercial deal but laid particular emphasize on the agreements' contribution to regional integration and sustainable development (Interview record #15, 2015). The opening of negotiations was repeatedly postponed by the EU, in order to press for more progress in Central America's regional integration efforts. After the conclusion of DR-CAFTA in 2005, however, the Commission came under increasing pressure from EU exporters to promptly initiate trade talks with Central America. European exporters demanded from the EU to sign a commercial deal with Central America as soon as possible that would restore the level-playing field with U.S. competitors in the re- gion (Woolcock 2007: 11).

As in the case of the EU-Andean Community negotiations, European business groups urged the Commission to aim at pure trade agreements and forgo controversial political agreements (UNICE 2006). The EP, how- ever, insisted on a comprehensive Association Agreement containing polit- ical dialogue, development cooperation as well as human rights, labor and environmental provisions (European Parliament 2007). As a consequence, when the negotiations between the EU and Central America were launched in Brussels in June 2007, the Commission declared it would aim at a comprehensive region-to-region Association Agreement that compro- mised a political dialogue and a cooperation pillar besides the trade com- ponent. In addition, the Commission tied the launch of negotiations to a large aid package of €840 million for the region for the period of 2007-2013 in order to address the most pressing political and social prob- lems in the region (European Commission 2007).

In October 2007, the EU and the countries of Central America held the first round of negotiations in San José, Costa Rica (Krupa 2007). As expect- ed by EU business groups, many of the political pre-conditions set by the

---

48 The statistic includes trade with the five original Central American negotiating partners and Panama that later joined the negotiations.

EU for the agreement complicated the progress of talks from the outset (Bridges 2008; Barquero S. 2008). The Commission, for instance, initially required the Central American countries to join the International Criminal Court (ICC), a demand that encountered fierce opposition from some Central American governments. In order to facilitate the continuation of the talks, the issue slowly vanished from the negotiation agenda after the third round (Carlos Nino 2008; Murillo 2008).[49] Equally, the Commission's insistence on further integration steps inside the Central American Integration System (SICA) and on provisions regarding the non-proliferation on nuclear arms caused problems with the region's governments (Murillo 2007, 2008). Nicaragua particularly was concerned that the political conditions attached to the accord's political dialogue and cooperation pillars would intervene too much into the domestic legislation of the Central American states. Nicaraguan negotiators therefore opposed any punitive political clauses on human rights, governance or the fight against terrorism (Barquero S. 2008). As a consequence, the Commission embarked on a negotiation strategy after the third round that was intended to minimize the impact of controversial political issues on the progress of negotiations as much as possible (Barquero S. 2008).

The Commission's intention to include social standards in the commercial pillar of the agreement faced less resistance from the Central American negotiators (Interview record #26, 2015). However, they insisted that no trade sanctions should be available as enforcement mechanism in the area of labor and environment (La Nación 2009; Céspedez Vargas 2009: 30). Consequently, the Commission's renunciation of penalties in the proposed 'sustainable development chapter' was received positively. The Central Americans viewed the EU approach as less intrusive than the punitive enforcement mechanism for social standards in DR-CAFTA (Interview record #26, 2015). This fact proofed to be of particular importance since the broad scope of the sustainable development chapter concerned the Central American governments (Interview record #30, 2015).

In April 2008, the Commission threatened to strip El Salvador of its GSP + benefits if it failed to fully implement the ILO conventions on freedom of association by December 2008 (Barquero S. 2008). Even though the Central American states had an overall good record of ratification of ILO conventions and MEAs, the region's governments were wary of committing themselves to additional obligations in the area of labor and the envi-

---

49 The countries that refused to recognize the International Criminal Court were Guatemala, Nicaragua and El Salvador.

ronment through the PTA. Overall, the Central American negotiators sought to restrict the scope of the 'sustainable development chapter' to the ILO core conventions and to MEAs already ratified by the Central American states (Céspedez Vargas 2009: 30). The Commission in turn viewed the ILO core conventions as fundamental pillars of the 'sustainable development chapter' but was not willing to restrict the agreement's labor obligations to them (Interview record #26, 2015).

The Central Americans, however, feared too great interference of external actors in the region's labor and environmental legislation. Therefore, they opposed the inclusion of international entities such as the ILO in the monitoring of the agreement's social standards (Céspedez Vargas 2009: 30). They equally eyed the planned involvement of domestic civil society actors in the implementation of the sustainable development provisions with concern. The Central Americans insisted that the monitoring of the labor and environmental standards should remain the exclusive competence of governments (Céspedez Vargas 2009: 33), since they feared that the opening of the enforcement mechanism to societal actors would enable these groups to challenge government policies in the region (Interview record #26, 2015). Hence, from the start of negotiations EU negotiators attempted to dispel such fears from Central American governments by thoroughly explaining the cooperative nature of civil society involvement (Interview record #29, 2015).

Labor and environmental groups in the EU casted doubt on the agreement's alleged positive effect for Central America and found particular fault with the treaty's social standards (Willis 2009). The cooperative nature of the prospective accord's social standards which facilitated negotiations on the international level for the Commission, were at the center of criticism. For labor and environmental groups in Europe, the chosen approach was proof of the Commission's lukewarm treatment of non-commercial objectives in the negotiations. Charly Poppe, spokesperson for Friends of the Earth Europe, for instance, complained:

> 'The EU has promised to include a chapter on 'Sustainable Development' in the Agreement but its position in previous bilateral negotiations and at the World Trade Organization (WTO) has always been to put market access and 'competitiveness' interests above all other concerns. With these negotiations, we are confronted with the same tactics: at best, they are political schizophrenia, at worst pure greenwashing' (Friends of the Earth Europe 2007).

The ETUC was equally dissatisfied with the agreement's labor and environmental provisions. As a result, the ETUC elaborated with the Central American trade union organization a draft social chapter for the prospective agreement that reflected the labor unions' priorities for labor and environmental standards. The draft chapter explicitly called for the possibility to apply sanctions on parties to the agreement that fail to meet the accord's labor or environmental obligations (ETUC, CCT, and CSACC 2008). This draft chapter was presented in May 2008 to the Central American and in June 2008 to the European negotiators. In March 2009, however, the trade union organizations complained that 'no progress has been made in incorporating our proposals into the documents being negotiated' and that they 'received only a few vague promises, but no real response to our positions from negotiators' (ETUC, CCT, and CSACC 2009). Hence, labor and environmental groups again were not able to significantly influence the Commission's negotiation position on social standards.

The talks proceeded swiftly until March 2009, when Nicaragua demanded to establish a 'Structural Compensation Fund' of 60 million euro (with 90% of the means coming from the EU and 10% from Central America) to compensate for the economic inequalities between the two regions. The Nicaraguan clamor triggered the suspension of the 7th round of the negotiations in April 2009. Only after the EU had agreed to review the Nicaraguan proposal negotiations could proceed (La Nación 2010). In June 2009, however, the Commission stopped negotiations completely after a coup d'état in Honduras forced acting President Manuel Zelaya to flee the country (Willis 2009). EU member states with strong economic or strategic interest in the agreement, however, subsequently pressed for a fast resumption of negotiations. Especially Spain, which held the EU Council presidency and has strong economic ties to the region, urged the Commission to resume talks as soon as possible (Gomez Arana 2014: 52-54). The Commission ultimately restarted negotiations in February 2010 after a new President had been elected in Honduras. At that time, Panama decided to fully join the negotiations after it had only participated as an observer in the preceding negotiation rounds (Tico Times 2010).

At the 8th round of negotiations in March 2010, only access for certain Central American agricultural products to the EU market and the enforcement mechanism of the 'sustainable development chapter' remained as sticking points. The Central Americans continued to insist that labor and environmental legislation is the exclusive competence of governments and therefore demanded the exclusion of civil society actors of the monitoring of social standards (La Nación 2009). Instead of the civil society mechanism proposed by the EU, Central American governments sought increased cooperation from the EU to reinforce their capacity to apply environmental and labor legislation (Tico Times 2010). The final agreement, however, stipulated each party to 'convene new or consult existing Advisory Groups on trade and sustainable development'. In addition, the parties agreed to organize once a year a bi-regional 'Civil Society Dialogue Forum, with a balanced representation of environmental, economic and social stakeholders'.

Hence, the provisions replicated largely the EU-Peru/Colombia PTA text. The Commission again had made concessions to negotiation partners on the shape of the 'sustainable development chapter' in order to eliminate stumbling blocks to the agreement. The requirement to establish new domestic civil society dialogue mechanisms was dropped. Instead, each party of the PTA could also make use of existing domestic advisory groups. In this form, the Central Americans accepted the civil society involvement in the monitoring as well as the broad scope of social standards. Central Americans were satisfied that no penalties could be imposed on them in the area of labor and the environment and that they were not obliged to ratify further international conventions (Bermúdez Mora 2010).

In May 2010, the EU and the Central American states officially closed the negotiations for the trade pillar of the Association Agreement at the 6th EU-Latin America Summit in Madrid (Bridges 2010). The ETUC immediately rejected the negotiated agreement on the grounds that negotiators had 'not taken on board reiterated proposals by the ETUC and the sub-regional Central American CSACC and CCT based on fair trade, the correcting of asymmetries by means of promoting development in Central America and on a Social Chapter' (ETUC/ITUC/TUCA 2010). Friends of the Earth Europe along with several developmental NGOs equally came out in opposition of the agreement (ALOP et al. 2012). Nevertheless, EU member states with Spain leading the way were in full support of the final agreement given the economic and strategic importance several EU governments attached to the deal (Gomez Arana 2014). As a consequence, in June 2012 the Council authorized the signing and provisional application of the agreement without any objections. The complete deal was signed by all parties later that month in Tegucigalpa, Honduras (Bridges 2012). However, the agreement still required the consent of the EP in order to become fully operational.

In the EP, merely MEPs from the GUE/NGL and Green/EFA groups were susceptible to the concerns of labor and environmental groups and voted almost unanimously against the agreement. In the parliamentary debate preceding the ratification of the AA, representatives from these groups deplored the agreement for intensifying the economic asymmetries between the two regions and claimed that the agreement made 'no reference to social and environmental standards whatsoever' (European Parliament 2012). But Trade Commissioner Karel de Gucht defended the final agreement against the substantial criticism regarding the accord's labor and environmental provisions. De Gucht declared satisfied: 'Through the trade pillar we help implement internationally recognised core labour standards and key multilateral environment agreements in Central America, and we strengthen the role of civil society' (ibid.).

The conservative and liberal EPP, ECR and ALDE groups equally praised the treaty for strengthening the commercial relations between the two regions and simultaneously supporting the Central American integration process as well as improving political and developmental cooperation (ibid.). Thus, MEPs from these latter groups voted en bloc in favor of the agreement. Despite the considerable opposition of labor and environmental groups to the Association Agreement with Central America, even the S&D group voted almost unanimously in favor of the treaty. In fact, only one single S&D MEP voted against the agreement.[50] Therefore, the EP approved the Association Agreement with an overwhelming majority of 557 to 100 votes with 21 abstentions in December 2012 (Gardner 2012; Euractive 2012; Emmott 2012).

Hence, European labor and environmental groups again failed to get center-left MEPs to vote against a trade agreement they opposed. As a consequence, throughout the negotiation process the Commission could count on the support of an overwhelming parliamentary majority and of the EU member states in the Council. Unlike the U.S. executive, the Commission did not have to respond to demands by trade skeptical legislators in order to secure ratification. Quite the contrary, the strong support for the agreement even enabled the Commission to concede on certain aspects of the social standards' design in order to iron out obstacles during the international negotiation process. In sum, the final agreement contained social standards since they were demanded by the EP. But the design of these standards corresponded largely to the Commission's preference for provisions that caused as less controversy as possible during the international bargaining process.

---

50 A detailed overview for voting behavior on the EU-Central America AA in the EP is available at the website www.votewatch.eu.

5.4 Concluding Remarks

EU trade politics is an executive-dominated process in which the Commission and the member states' governments largely set the tone together. Therefore, they also had the leading role in establishing the EU's approach for social standards. National governments in the EU are generally strong supporters of trade liberalizations independent of their political orientation (Milner and Judkins 2004: 110). Therefore, they were reluctant to introduce labor and environmental issues into trade policy in a way which could have complicated or even jeopardized the conclusion of trade agreements. Center-left governments, however, were under pressure from their labor and environmental constituencies to address worker rights and ecological matters in trade. Therefore, they advocated including some form of social standards in PTAs. The Commission, however, was concerned about the viability of negotiating sensitive labor and environmental issues in trade negotiations.

As an unelected body, the Commission is largely insulated form societal pressure groups and therefore has a technocratic approach towards trade policy. But in order to initiate PTA negotiations the Commission has to receive negotiation mandates from the Council. Due to the de facto consensus requirement in the Council, the Commission was in need to develop policy proposal that were acceptable to all member states. Therefore, the Commission opted for 'soft' social standards that satisfied left-leaning governments due to their relatively broad scope but were still acceptable to center-right governments in the Council. Thanks to the lack of punitive enforcement mechanisms, this approach promised not to hamper the signing of trade agreements.

As described above, even the cooperative approach for social standards was mostly met with reservations at the international level. Thanks to the strong support for the overall agreements in the Council and the EP, however, the Commission could even afford to make concessions on the design of the social standards and drop the most controversial requirements when necessary. Surprisingly, in the cases examined above the Commission was more inclined to make concessions with the economically weaker negotiating partners of Central America as well as Peru and Colombia than with South Korea. This hints to the fact that not the relative bargaining power of the negotiation partners mattered for the Commission's negotiation stance with regard to social standards but rather the degree of rejection the EU experienced from the trading partner.

The role of the EP as the only directly elected body of the EU was only marginal during negotiations since it was institutionally excluded from the setting of negotiation objectives beforehand. Even though the EP had repeatedly advocated for stronger, sanction-based social standards before and during the negotiation processes, the strong control of national delegations over the re-election chances of individual MEPs secured large majorities in favor of the PTAs in the EP. Hence, despite being 'one of the most left-leaning and environmentally conscious legislative bodies in the world' (Sachs 2006: 87), most MEPs settled for the 'soft' social standards when the PTAs was presented for ratification in the EP.

In sum, the electoral incentives of policy-makers and the institutional structure of EU trade politics allowed the executive branch to design social standards largely according to its own preferences. Since social standards did not promise economic gains but were often fiercely rejected by negotiation partners at the international level, the Commission drafted social standards that were easier to accept for them. The findings of this chapter support the view that trade officials in the Commission are quite autonomous from societal pressures and only constrained by the member states (Zimmermann 2007; Meunier 2005; Woolcock 2005). When member states are split over an issue - like it was the case with social standards -, however, the Commission enjoys additional leeway to formulate policy since it is in charge of developing compromise proposals (Elsig 2010). In this sense, the soft character of the social standards in EU PTAs can be seen as the lowest common denominator of the member states and the desire of the Commission to make labor and environmental clauses as acceptable as possible for third countries.

6. Conclusion

Why did the US enshrine stricter social standards in its PTAs than the EU? Neither the US nor the EU is a unitary actor that chooses deliberately the most effective enforcement mechanism for social standards. Instead, the design of labor and environmental provisions is - just like the shape of any other feature of PTAs - the result of domestic political dynamics and their effect on the international bargaining process. Since the constellation of societal preferences with regard to the right model for social standards were quite similar in the US and Europe, the differences in their final design can be traced back to the institutional structures that channel these societal demands. The final chapter of this book will first provide a comparative summary of the major empirical findings from the previous two chapters. Then possible alternative explanations for the different models of U.S. and EU social standards are considered. The chapter concludes with a preliminary assessment of the functioning of U.S. and EU social standards in practice.

6.1 Key Insights and Broader Implications

Economists, political scientists and policy commentators agree that economic globalization has profound impacts on the societies of the United States and Europe. Optimists stress the opportunities unrestricted trade yields for economic growth and the general welfare (Wolf 2005; Irwin 2015). Pessimistic voices fear that the dismantling of trade barriers with cheap-labor countries and the increasing competition among workers across borders leads to wage cuts and job losses in industrialized countries. Simultaneously, the increasing legalization of international commercial rules would entail a privileging of commercial goals over other public policy objectives such as environmental protection. In the worst case, free trade would lead to a global 'race-to-the-bottom' where countries undercut each other in labor and environmental regulations in order to compete for increasingly footloose capital (Collingsworth, Goold, and Harvey 1994; Rodrik 1997; Wallach and Sforza 1999). Even though the empirical evidence for the 'race-to-the-bottom' argument is rather thin, its influence on trade policy debates has been considerable (Drezner 2001).

Thus, hypothesis 1 of this study predicted that the expected distributional effects of trade liberalization in industrialized economies will pit capital and labor against each other in the debate over PTAs. In addition, environmental groups were assumed to join forces with labor to fight the assumed negative consequences of increased economic exchange and strict commercial rules for environmental protection. Accordingly, an alliance of unions and environmental NGOs should have pressed for enforceable provisions to protect workers and control pollution. Business groups, by contrast, should prefer keeping such controversial issues out of trade agreements in order to facilitate negotiations. As the empirical chapters have shown, this pattern was in fact observable for the constellation of societal preferences both in the US and the EU. The large export-oriented American and European Business groups invariably supported the push for bilateral and regional trade agreements regardless of the economic importance of the respective negotiation partner. They were equally vocal in their rejection of enforceable labor and environmental provisions. American business groups seemed to have been even more insistent in their opposition to social standards than their European counterparts. American businesses feared the effects of enforceable provisions on domestic U.S. labor and environmental legislation which in several instances is not in line with the requirements of international rules.

Labor unions on both sides of the Atlantic, by contrast, rejected PTAs in most cases and demanded inter alia fully enforceable provisions for the protection of workers (and the environment). In the US, the big umbrella organization AFL-CIO opposed all but one trade agreement out of the four PTAs examined in this study. Only with regard to the US-Peru PTA took the AFL-CIO a neutral position due to internal disagreements among its members and at least partly thanks to the strengthening of social standards through the May 10th Agreement shortly before the vote on the PTA. U.S. labor unions vigorously opposed, however, the earlier DR-CAFTA agreement partly to the PTA's weaker social standards, which followed the 'enforce-your-own-laws' principle. They equally rejected both the US-Colombia PTA and the KORUS PTA, despite the stricter social standards of these agreements.

In Europe, the ETUC equally opposed the EU-Central America Association Agreement and the EU-Peru/Colombia PTA, citing inter alia the agreements' inadequate social standards as reason for their position. In the case of the EU-Korea PTA, however, the ETUC supported a PTA due to its economic benefits for European workers despite the fact that the agreement's social standards showed the same deficiencies as in the other two cases. However, just like their American counterparts, European trade unions demanded sanction-based social standards for all PTA without exception, even when they assessed the economic effects of a PTA for their members positively.

As expected, the major environmental groups in the US and the EU overwhelmingly objected PTAs as well. In the US, 'green' NGOs opposed all PTAs analyzed for this study except the US-Peru PTA due to their lack of sufficient environmental safeguards. The U.S. agreement with Peru contained strict environmental standards and additionally unique and extensive provisions for the fight against illegal logging which induced many American environmentalists to take a neutral stance with regard to this particular PTA. European environmental organizations, by contrast, rejected all of the three PTAs covered by this study owing to the believed negative environmental impact of the agreements and the ineffectiveness of the PTA's environmental clauses. Hence, as expected by Hypothesis 1 both in the US and the EU the political cleavages in trade politics run largely between business on the one side and labor and environmental groups on the other side.

Hypothesis 2 of this study was only partially confirmed. It expected that especially policy-makers who equally depend on business, labor and environmental organizations for reelection would promote enforceable social standards as a way to balance these conflicting interests. While this seems to hold true for the US, things were different in the EU. In the US, Republican congressman mainly represented export-oriented business interests in trade politics. As the main beneficiaries of business campaign contributions, they voted overwhelmingly in favor of the 2002 Trade Promotion Authority and the ratification of all PTAs examined in this study. At the same time, they tried to keep social standards as unenforceable as possible or to leave them out of PTAs altogether. Congressional Democrats, by contrast, heavily depend on the support of unions and – to a lesser extent – environmental groups for their re-election. As a result, Democrats voted mostly 'nay' in trade votes.

Hostility towards trade liberalization, however, was more pronounced among Democrats in the House than in the Senate. Thanks to longer terms of office and larger constituencies, members of the Senate are less frequently exposed to electoral politics and less dependent on narrow interest groups during election campaigns. The call for enforceable social standards in U.S. PTAs consequently has been led by two long-serving Democratic House Representatives, namely Sander Levin (D-MI) and Charles Rangel (D-NY). Both held leading positions in the House Ways and Means Committee, which is responsible for trade. In this function they struggled on the one hand not to alienate business donors and on the other hand to mollify Democrats' labor and environmental constituencies with strict PTA social standards.

In Europe, by contrast, all centrist political groups supported the conclusion of PTAs. The strong voting cohesion within all groups points to the fact that the voting behavior of legislators in the EP is more determined by the instructions of their party than the demands of constituencies. The proportional representation and the power of political parties to set the order of candidates on the electoral list for EP elections, guarantees them strong control over the voting behavior of their representatives. The voting results of the center-left S&D group in the votes on the EU-Central America and EU-Peru/Colombia is a clear indication of this. Despite the fact that their labor and environmental constituencies vigorously opposed these agreements, MEPs from the S&D group overwhelmingly voted in favor of ratification. Only MEPs from far-left, green and partly from far-right groups came out overwhelmingly against the PTAs and appeared to be the most vigorous supporters of enforceable social standards. Hence, not policy-makers that tried to balance conflicting interests were the strongest advocates of social standards, but MEPs from the left and 'green' fringes of the EP who have little or no ties to the business community. However, it is highly questionable if stronger social standards would have changed their voting behavior given their fundamental critic of many aspects of the EU's trade policy.

In any case, social standards never emerged as a crucial instrument to construct a legislative majority like in the US due to the large support of PTAs in the EP resulting from the electoral incentives of MEPs. Hence, even though the major political groups in the EP all welcomed some sort of social provisions, these groups were not willing to press for enforceable standards wholeheartedly. The Member States in the Council, the other part of the EU's legislative branch, differed with regard to social standards. Unsurprisingly, left-leaning governments showed more enthusiasm than conservative and liberal ones. However, due to their large, national constituencies and foreign policy priorities, none of the EU member states governments was willing to jeopardize a PTA in order to achieve stricter social standards.

The negotiating executives of the US and the EU were both keen to conclude PTAs and concerned that enforceable social standards might impede that objective. In the US, both U.S. Presidents that held office during the investigation period were committed to promote free trade regardless of their party affiliation. Republican President George W. Bush initiated America's reinforced steering towards bilateral PTAs in the early 2000s but initially forcefully rejected any form of social standards in trade agreements. Only the difficulty to receive TPA from Congress and get already negotiated PTAs ratified, led the Bush administration to embrace enforceable social standards as an inevitable concession to congressional Democrats. Bush's Democratic successor in the White House President Barack Obama continued America's efforts for trade liberalization despite certain attacks on free trade during his presidential campaign. Even though he rhetorically laid more emphasis on labor and environmental issues in trade policy, he basically followed meticulously Congress's stipulations regarding the shape of social standards just like his predecessor. In Europe, the Commission as the EU's executive in trade policy equally promoted trade liberalization through PTAs. In the absence of re-election considerations, the Commission viewed enforceable social standards technocratically as potential stumbling blocks to the rapid conclusion of trade agreements. Hence, the Commission invariably opted for cooperative standards that minimized the danger that labor or environmental issues could derail trade talks.

Finally, hypothesis 3 of this study expected that the more the institutional structure of trade policy-making favors proponents of strict social standards, the stronger such provisions will be in the final PTA text. In the US, the institutional form of delegation ensured that Congress retained firm control over the executive during international trade negotiations. The provisions of the 2002 Trade Promotion Authority Act enabled the American legislative branch to lay down *ex ante* detailed negotiating objectives with regard to the shape of social standards. The majority voting rules and the the low party discipline in the House gave swaying representatives disproportionate influence over the specifics of the bargaining goals. Thus, a relatively small group of Democrats promoted enforceable social standards in PTAs as a way to serve simultaneously business as well as labor and environmental interests. The need to seek ratification for negotiated agreements and the existing narrow majorities in the House forced the U.S. administration to follow minutely TPA's stipulations regarding social standards. Hence, the credible threat of a veto provided the U.S. legislature with an effective *ex post* control mechanism.

In the EU, by contrast, the Commission was confronted with the Council where member states were divided largely along party affiliations over the issue of social standards in PTAs before negotiations started. The de facto consensus decision-making in the Council forced the Commission to draft social standards that managed to obtain the acceptance of all member states. Thus, in the context of the 2006 'Global Europe'-strategy that marked a general reorientation of EU trade policy towards bilateral and bi-regional trade agreements, the Commission came up with proposals for a 'sustainable development chapter' that contained relatively broad, but un-enforceable labor and environmental provisions. The negotiation mandates for the three PTAs examined for this study containing this approach were smoothly accepted by the Council in 2007.

The EP as the EU institution most supportive of strict social standards was excluded from defining negotiation objectives including the shape of social standards. Hence, the Commission could enter negotiations with its preferred model of soft social standards. The Council and a large majority in the EP supported the overall negotiations in all three examined cases. Hence, the rejection of the agreements by the Council or the EP never emerged as a credible threat for the Commission. Since the PTAs had a se-cure majority, proponents of stricter social standards in the EP never had the chance to push through their demands. Quite the contrary, the over-whelming support of the PTAs gave the Commission the leeway to even make concessions to trading partners on the wording of the social stan-dards that helped to facilitate the conclusion of negotiations. Hence, the shape of the 'sustainable development chapters' in EU trade agreements re-sembles more closely executives' preference for social standards which don't threaten to become hurdles in trade negotiations.

Besides answering the empirical puzzle of why the US and the EU re-sponded to the same international challenge in diametrical opposed ways, the results of this study equally provide valuable insights for broader theo-retical questions. The study contributes to the growing literature that com-pares the foreign economic policy-making of the US and the EU and focus-es on the effects of their respective institutional setting on the political pro-cess and outcomes (De Biévre and Dür 2005; Zimmermann 2007; Clark, Duchesne, and Meunier 2000; Leeg 2018). The findings of the empirical chapters provide strong evidence for the so-called 'collusive delegation ar-gument' according to which greater insulation from societal pressures fa-cilitates promoting trade liberalization. Both the US and the EU have dele-gated powers to the most centralized level of government in their respec-tive political systems. However, the Commission as the executive in charge of trade negotiation in the EU is considerable more shielded from societal pressures than the U.S. administration. This is because the Commission, in contrast to the U.S. executive, is not subject to general elections and there-fore does not depend on voters and interest group resources.

As evidenced in chapter 5, the lack of electoral pressure and the ensuing discretion allows the Commission to largely ignore stakeholders that do not help them to advance on their objectives and to conduct trade policy in an apolitical and technocratic way (Woll 2012). The results of this study confirm the notion suggested by Dür and De Biévre (2007) that non-commercial NGOs are particularly incapable of influencing the Commission's conduct of trade policy. Moreover, the findings of the process-tracing exercised in three different cases of EU trade negotiation suggest that labor unions are equally unable to make their voices heard with the Commission. Instead, the Commission collaborates closely with export-oriented business groups that can provide crucial information regarding barriers to trade in third countries.

The U.S. executive seems to be equally committed to trade liberalization regardless of political affiliation of the incumbent government. However, both Republican and Democratic administrations regularly deviate from this general line and make concessions to key constituencies that are crucial for their re-election. Hence, the conduct of trade policy by the executive branch is far more politicized in the US than in the EU. As the traditional allies of labor and environmental groups, Democrats in the office of U.S. President are of course more inclined to address the concerns of these constituencies. Still, the empirical chapter on U.S. trade negotiations found strong evidence that apart from political posturing, U.S. Presidents of both political camps consistently promote free trade policies.[51] The importance the issue of social standards gained in trade policy debates in the US can be traced back to the attempt of Democrats to advance trade liberalization without heeding the concerns of labor and environmental groups. Since the electoral system induces U.S. legislators to advance primarily the interests of their relatively small electoral districts, the delegation of negotiation authority to the President ensures that the US remains capable to act in international trade politics at all. However, the far-reaching control mechanisms established under the fast-track procedure and the narrow majority in the House give the U.S. legislative branch much sway in U.S. trade politics.

The results of this study echo Peter Katzenstein's (1977) observation that the institutional features of the American state make it a 'weak state' vis-à-vis the American society in foreign economic policy-making. This means that the policy-making process in the U.S. is poorly insulated from societal

---

51 This widely held notion might now be challenged with the election of Donald Trump as U.S. President.

interests. Since all branches of government are highly accessible to interest groups and the policy process is fragmented, societal actors in the US possess multiple channels through which they can exercise influence. In comparison, the institutional setting of the EU's political system in trade policy make it resemble more a 'strong state' where public policy-making is much more shielded from societal pressures. Even though the policy-making process is fragmented as well through the multilevel nature of EU politics, political institutions in EU trade policy have more leeway to set policy unaffected from particular interest groups.

6.2 Alternative Explanations

This study argued that the shape of labor and environmental provisions in PTAs are the result of the interaction of domestic politics and international negotiations. The different design of social standards in U.S. and EU PTAs is mainly attributable to the particular institutional features of the U.S. and EU system of trade policy-making. The study furthermore departed from the assumption that the coercive approach of the U.S. is stricter and ultimately more effective than the cooperative approach of the EU, since trading partners can be compelled to follow their obligations, while the EU approach depends on the long-term cooperativeness of trading partners for success. However, several factors could provide an alternative explanation for the question why the US and the EU decided to apply a different logic to the enforcement of social provisions.

First, the US never actually imposed sanctions for violations of labor or environmental obligations of PTAs. Since the US was first to include social standards in PTAs, the EU may have just learned from the U.S. experience. EU policy-makers might have chosen a 'soft' approach because they considered the U.S. approach inapplicable in practice. However, this perspective misapprehends how sanctions in reality influence state behavior. As pointed out by Drezner (2003), it is usually the threat rather than the actual sanction that leads to compliance. This notion was confirmed by empirical research that showed that the imposition of sanctions almost never led to the desired behavior change, but that the threat of sanctions was successful in 57% of the investigated cases (Elliott 2000). Hence, the number of cases of sanction imposition is not a good indicator of effectiveness. Moreover, the US and the EU are equally reluctant to apply sanctions to enforce the commercial aspects of PTAs. Both prefer amicable means for the settlement of disputes like governmental consultation and cooperation activities instead (Interview record #16, 2015; Interview record #29, 2015). Nevertheless, the existence of a punitive enforcement mechanism as a last resort is viewed by both as crucial to guarantee the compliance of the parties with the commercial obligations of a PTA. The puzzle is therefore, why the EU should consider a sanction mechanism superfluous when it comes to social standards.

Second, societal interest groups and policy-makers in the US and the EU might have had different ideas about the effectiveness and appropriateness of the respective enforcement mechanisms. However, as the empirical sections have shown, the respective actors on both sides of the Atlantic held very similar views. U.S. as well as EU labor and environmental groups almost unanimously viewed sanction-based standards as more effective. American and European business groups, by contrast, were concerned that strict social standards would jeopardize the conclusion of PTAs. Therefore, they agreed that social standards should either not be part of PTAs at all or at least be non-binding. The relevant legislative bodies in the US and Europe were both internally divided about the right enforcement mechanism. And policy-makers in the executive branch of the US and the EU initially both declared that they viewed cooperative clauses as more expedient. Hence, it cannot be maintained that there existed fundamentally different views and assessments of the right enforcement mechanism in the US and the EU. Actors that advocated sanction-based standards were merely more successful in the US than in the EU in determining the final design of PTAs' social standards.

Ultimately, the diverging approaches to social standards might be the result of the specific regional, social and economic characteristics of the US and EU PTA partners. Yet, as the empirical sections of this study have shown, the US and the EU unalterably used their respective approach for social standards regardless of the regional and economic particularities of trading partners. Hence, neither the relative bargaining power nor the initial levels of labor and environmental protections in third countries had an effect on the respective approach of the US and the EU. This confirms the basic assumption of this study, that the design of social standards can be basically traced back to domestic factors in the US and the EU and not the characteristics of the respective international negotiation partner.

6.3 The Functioning of U.S. and EU Social Standards in practice

This study has shown that the inclusion of social standards in U.S. and EU PTAs and their particular shape are largely the result of political struggles in the U.S. and EU domestic arenas. However, this does not mean that social standards in PTAs cannot actually lead to the improvement of labor and/or environmental conditions in third sates. Yet, empirical investigations of the real impact of said provisions are difficult, since social standards in PTAs are a rather new phenomenon. Nevertheless, in recent years a number of researchers have attempted to provide us with preliminary evaluations about the impact of social standards in PTAs. Kim (2012), for instance, argued that PTAs with the US systematically lead to improvements in labor protections in trade partner states. However, he argued that these improvements are not the result of the *ex post* enforcement of labor provisions after PTAs have entered into force. Rather, PTA partners are likely to pursue *ex ante* improvements in domestic labor protection prior to signing a PTA or even before negotiating a PTA with the US. Given that the U.S. Congress has increasingly placed value on strong labor protection, third states engage *ex ante* due diligence in order to increase their attractiveness as PTA partners and facilitate the ratification of a negotiated PTA in the US. This *ex ante* effect has been also described by Vogt (2015).

The present book has equally observed extensive reforms of the domestic labor and environmental codes in the cases of Central America, Peru and Colombia during, and mostly because of, the PTA negotiations with the US. In order to create the conditions for domestic ratification the U.S. has repeatedly exerted large influence on the specifics of labor and environmental legislation in PTA partners. U.S. pressure in the context of PTA negotiation even led to the creation of a Ministry of the Environment in Peru and to the establishment of a Ministry of Labor in Colombia. Once PTAs were in force, however, the US showed considerable constraint to enforce labor and environmental standards. As one interview partner indicated, the US has been generally very cautious to seek legal actions, since it is legally difficult to establish that the non-enforcement of labor and environmental laws in one country directly affects trade with another country (Interview record #3, 2015). Most likely, U.S. administrations of any party affiliation also fear a rigorous enforcement of social standards might scare off prospective negotiation partners.

Therefore, even the Democratic administration of President Obama sought to handle labor-related problems rather through cooperative means, like action plans, than through punitive measures. The only labor-related (or environmental-related) case to date that has resulted in a formal dispute settlement process was initiated by the US against Guatemala in 2010.[52] The complaint against the Central American country was already filed in April 2008 by the AFL-CIO and six Guatemalan trade unions but the U.S. government initially remained inactive (Vogt 2015: 843-844).

The political circumstances in summer 2010, however, seemed to have induced the U.S. administration to take actions. The decision to proceed against Guatemala under CAFTA-DR's labor chapter coincided with efforts of the Obama administration to secure the ratification of the pending trade agreements with Colombia, South Korea and Panama (Chan 2010). The US accused the Guatemalan government of failing to effectively enforce domestic labor laws and first invoked government consultations in July 2010 which produced no tangible results. Therefore, in June 2011 the US convened the FTA Commission, the last step before a party could request arbitration. The U.S. administration attempted to persuade the Guatemalan government to accept legal and administrative reforms to improve the enforcement of its labor law. Since Guatemala rejected the required reforms, the USTR called for the creation of an arbitration panel in August 2011 which was established at the end of 2012.

Nevertheless, the U.S. government still tried to settle the conflict amicably. The increasing likelihood of financial fines induced the Guatemalan government to agree with the US on an action plan in April 2013 that detailed steps the country had to take in order to correct the lack of labor law enforcement (Needham 2013). The US granted Guatemala six months to fulfill its commitments and even extended the deadline several times in 2014 (Needham 2014). However, in September 2014 the USTR found the efforts of Guatemala insufficient and submitted its concerns in November 2014 to the re-established arbitration panel (Needham 2014). After repeated delays, the arbitration panel finally issued its decision in June 2017. It found that Guatemala had indeed failed to enforce certain labor laws. However, the panel also ruled that the evidence presented by the US did not prove it was "sustained or recurring" and "in a manner affecting trade," and thus did not violate CAFTA's provisions. Some commentators therefore have taken a pessimistic view regarding the feasibility of the US coercive approach to PTA labor standards. However, the failure to hold Guatemala's government accountable for its apparent breaches of labor standards can be clearly contributed to critical flaws in the wording of

---

52 There have been six formal complaints against labor rights violations accepted by the USTR in total to date.

CAFTA's labor provisions (Abel 2018) which could be corrected. Critics have even argued that the US showed no particular interest in winning the case in the first place (Cross 2017).

With regard to the EU, Postnikov and Bastiaens (2014) found in a quantitative study that EU PTAs with labor provisions are able to raise the labor standards in PTA partners. However, they argued that the improvements occur not *ex ante* during the negotiation process but *ex post* as a result of learning by civil society actors during the implementation phase of labor provisions. However, it is questionable that the agreements' labor provisions itself are responsible for this positive development. As pointed out by numerous researchers (Orbie et al. 2016; Van den Putte 2015; Harrison, Barbu, Campling, Richardson, et al. 2018; Harrison, Barbu, Campling, and Ebert 2018; Ebert 2016; Marx, Lein, and Brando 2016), the EU's sustainable development chapters suffer from a whole range of shortcomings.

The case of the EU-South Korea PTA illustrates a number of problems that the EU's sole reliance on civil society mechanisms for the monitoring of sustainable development obligations entails. The agreement foresees the establishment of Domestic Advisory Groups (DAGs) in the EU and Korea as well as the organization of a joint Civil Society Forum (CSF) composed of members of the EU and Korean DAGs. The 'sustainable development chapter' stipulates that the DAGs should consist of 'independent representative organizations' of the civil society that represent economic, labor and environmental stakeholders. However, the selection of participating organizations is largely left to the governments of the respective country. The Korean government initially staffed its DAG largely with academics and members linked to the government instead of civil society representatives. Only on the insistence of the EU, the Korean government agreed to reshuffle the composition of its DAG (Van den Putte 2015: 229). However, the Korean government still seems to ban disagreeable organizations from the DAG, such as the teacher's union (ETUC 2013). In addition, to the composition of the DAGs, the low frequency and short durations of DAG meetings seem to additionally undermine the effectiveness of the EU's approach. Meetings of the DAGs usually take place four times a year and last for merely one day. The joint CSFs are even organized only once a year and last hardly longer (Interview record #23, 2015).

The experience of the EU-Peru/Colombia PTA equally does not provide grounds for optimism with regard to the viability of the EU model. Both the Peruvian and Colombian government made use of the latitude provided by the trade treaty's legal wording and declined to establish a DAG. Instead both countries made use of already existing mechanisms to monitor the implementation of the 'sustainable development chapter'. Equally, the Peruvian government failed to send civil society representatives to the first joint CSF meeting that took place from 16-17 June 2015 in Bogota, Colombia. According to the joint EU-Colombia civil society declaration neither the government of Peru nor Colombia engaged seriously in discussions. Both had not responded to correspondence from the EU DAG nor had they shared any information about their respective domestic mechanisms (Vogt 2015: 856). Hence, foreign governments often show reluctance to seriously engage in the civil society dialogue mechanisms and there is little the EU can do about it. In the case of PTAs with emerging and developing economies there additionally remains the question of funding for civil society organizations' participation in CSF meetings. The 'sustainable development chapter' is silent on the question and third states gave no indication that they are willing to provide resources for this purpose (Interview record #23, 2015). This further aggravates the problem of a balanced representation in the civil society dialogue mechanisms.

The Commission itself has been cautious to engage in labor- or environmental-related issues in third states. In January 2014, members of the EU DAG urged Trade Commissioner de Gucht in a letter to initiate formal governmental consultation under the EU-Korea PTA. The letter detailed numerous serious labor rights violations perpetrated by the Korean government in 2013. The Commission, however, rejected the request to initiate consultations and confirmed its intention to pursue the matter through other channels. Environmental issues seemed to have received even less attention. The EU DAG of the Korea PTA, for instance, contains no environmental organization at all (Vogt 2015: 857).

The problems with the EU PTA's civil society dialogue mechanisms outlined above have led to a complete disillusionment with the EU's current approach towards social standards among most civil society organizations (Interview record #28, 2015). At the center of criticism is still the EU's refusal to apply coercive measures to change the behavior of other governments. Based on its experience with PTA's civil society dialogue mechanisms, the ETUC criticized the absence of a sanctioning mechanism in a hearing before the EP's INTA committee in December 2013:

> 'This is a critical flaw in the process. The EU insists that it will not include 'sanctions' in relation to the sustainable development provisions and that it will only work through 'incentives'. This is a naïve approach which will not overcome obstructionist attitudes' (ETUC 2013).

In a similar vein, Friends of the Earth Europe, a major environmental NGO on the European level, opined on the proposed 'sustainable development chapter' for TTIP: 'The only chapter that could bring strong language to protect essential regulations to build a sustainable future is weak and unenforceable' (Friends of the Earth Europe 2015).

Criticism, however, also persists with regard to the U.S. approach. In the context of the TPP negotiations, the AFL-CIO lamented that the enforcement of labor standards to date 'relies totally on the political will of governments' (AFL-CIO 2015). Therefore, the AFL-CIO complained:

> 'Worker rights obligations have never been fully enforced under existing free trade agreements, which have provided too much discretion for worker complaints to be delayed for years or indefinitely (e.g., Honduras, Guatemala). A progressive TPP would eliminate this shortcoming, not repeat it. Given that no administration has ever self-initiated labor enforcement under a free trade agreement, any promise to "strongly enforce" the TPP should be met with skepticism' (AFL-CIO 2015).

U.S. environmental groups are equally pessimistic about the functioning of the current U.S. template for PTA environmental standards (350.org et al. 2015). The Sierra Club, for instance, criticized that

> 'the TPP environment chapter includes the same overall enforcement mechanism that the George W. Bush administration included for the environmental provisions of its last four trade deals – a mechanism that has failed to curb rampant, widely-documented environmental violations in trade partner countries' (Sierra Club 2015).

In sum, both the U.S. and EU enforcement mechanisms so far have displayed several flaws in practice that prevent a greater effectiveness. These shortcomings partly stem from the lack of experience with the handling social standards in trade agreements but partly have also been intentionally inscribed into the treaty. Since negotiation partners were overwhelmingly reluctant to allow the US or the EU to meddle in their domestic labor and environmental legislation through a trade agreement, the US and the EU drafted the legal wordings of the social standards in a way that cushioned as much as possible the disagreeable elements of the social provisions. Therefore, the US has included several terms and conditions in its trade treaty texts that have to be fulfilled to prove the infringements of labor or environmental obligations of a PTA and effectively reduce the likelihood for PTA partners to be penalized. The EU in turn kept the PTA provisions regarding the civil society dialogue mechanisms sufficiently vague to allow trading partners themselves to decide over the degree of civil society involvement. These qualifications that made the controversial provisions more acceptable to trading partners during negotiation partners are reducing *ex post* the effectiveness of the social standards once the agreements are in force.

6.4 Concluding Considerations and Outlook

Given the severe domestic political struggles that produced their respective models, both the US and the EU seem to be reluctant to make significant changes to their approach. In the context of the TTIP negotiations, for instance, the EU preferred social standards with a broad scope and soft enforcement mechanisms. The US, by contrast, opposed any incorporation of obligations under ILO conventions and MEAs it is not a party to (Inside US Trade 2015). Most controversially, however, was again the issue of the enforcement mechanism. The EU's proposal of October 2015 leaves the issue purposely open (European Commission 2015). In November 2015 Trade Commissioner Malmstroem declared: 'We have deliberately not yet addressed the issue of how those commitments would be implemented and enforced. Clearly we do need an effective system of international oversight, participation and monitoring by civil society and enforcement that gives these commitments teeth. But we want to work step by step' (Teffer 2015).

The U.S. position on the issue, however, was and is very clear. The Bipartisan Congressional Trade Priorities and Accountability Act, the current fast-track bill adopted in June 2015, stipulates as key negotiating objectives of the U.S. administration 'to ensure that enforceable labor and environment obligations are subject to the same dispute settlement and remedies as other enforceable obligations under the agreement'[53] Thus, U.S. negotiators have little leeway but to insist on the enforceable model of social standards common to all U.S. PTAs. The text of the original TPP as well as the recently concluded USMCA already resemble strongly the May 10th template. This further underlines the fact, that the U.S. model for social stan-

---

53 US Congress, "Bipartisan Congressional Trade Priorities and Accountability Act of 2015", 11 May 2015, available on the Internet at: <https://www.congress.gov/11 4/bills/s995/BILLS -114s995rs.pdf> (accessed on June 23, 2016).

dards is hardly influenced by the incumbent administration. Instead, U.S. Congress largely dictates the content of U.S. social standards.

On the other side of the Atlantic, the EP equally demanded in 2016 the

'coverage of human rights clauses and TSD chapters by the general dispute settlement on an equal footing with the other parts of the agreement (…)' and 'effective deterrent measures, including in the form of monetary remedies, in the event of serious, proven breaches of the provisions of the agreement's chapter on sustainable development; such measures could be implemented through a temporary slowing down, reduction or even suspension of certain trade benefits provided under the agreement in the event of an aggravated, continuous breach of these standards as a measure of last resort, and the introduction of action plans with our partners could help remedy non-compliance with certain commitments made in trade and investment agreements' (European Parliament 2016).

The Commission, however, has proven to be extremely reluctant to include enforceable social provisions even when dealing with countries like Colombia or Guatemala. The Commission is concerned that including systematically enforceable social standards in PTAs could be a deal breaker in negotiations with countries like India (The Economic Times 2009; Leeg 2014). Already in 2011, then Trade Commissioner Peter Mandelson urged the MEPs during an EP debate 'to remain realistic' and explained: '(…) we (…) need to be clear that a sustainable development chapter which would allow the use of trade restrictions linked to social or environmental issues will not be acceptable to India' (European Parliament 2011).

In reaction to sustained criticism of the effectiveness of the sustainable development chapters by the EP, labor unions and civil society organizations, however, in July 2017the Commission initiated a debate about the EU's approach to social standards in PTAs. The Commission published a non-paper which proposed two differing reform options for the sustainable development chapters. The first option involved enhancing the current processes of dialogue and cooperation, while the second option was to create a sanction-based mechanism. After consultations with various stakeholders, the Commission published a second non-paper in February 2018, which announced the continuation of the dialogue-based approach (Harrison, Barbu, Campling, and Ebert 2018: 13-14). The Commission argued that consultations had revealed 'divergent points of view' which is why it was 'impossible to move to such an approach'. Instead, the Commission identified 'a clear consensus that the implementation of TSD chapters should be stepped-up and improved' (European Commission 2018: 2-3). Therefore, the Commission proposed no less than fifteen measures to enhance the functioning of the current dialogue-based approach. The 15 actions are organized under four headings: Working Together; Enabling Civil Society; Delivering; and Communicating and Transparency. They include a closer cooperation between the Commission, the EP, EU Member States and international organizations such as the ILO, the identification of country-specific priorities and various actions to improve the functioning of the DAGs. Various stakeholders in the EU, however, have already declared that they view these measures as insufficient (e.g. EESC 2018). It is therefore more than likely that the discussion about the right enforcement mechanisms in EU PTAs will continue in the coming years.

References

11.11.11, ALOP, ANC, APRODEV, CNCD, FIDC, FIDH, Friends of the Earth Europe, Grupo Sur, ICCO, IEPALA, and Secours Catholique – Caritas France. 2007. Re: Recommendations on the EU-CAN negotiation directives. *Joint Letter EU-CAN Negotiations*, February 1. Available at: http://www.aprodev.eu/files/Central_America/200701_cso_letter_eu-ca_negotiation_directives.pdf

350.org, Center for International Environmental Law, Center for Biological Diversity, Earthjustice, Food & Water Watch, Friends of the Earth, Green America, Greenpeace USA, Institute for Agriculture and Trade Policy, Natural Resources Defense Council, Oil Change International, Sierra Club, and SustainUS. 2015. Environmental Provisions in the Trans-Pacific Partnership. *Letter from 13 U.S. environmental organizations to Congress*, October 29. Available at: https://www.sierraclub.org/sites/www.sierraclub.org/files/uploads-wysiwig/TPP%20letter%20FINAL%20%282%29.pdf

Aaronson, Susan, and Jamie M. Zimmerman. 2008. *Trade Imbalance. The Struggle to Weigh Human Rights Concerns in Trade Policymaking*. Cambridge: Cambridge University Press.

Abbott, Kenneth W., and Duncan Snidal. 2000. Hard and Soft Law in International Governance. *International Organization* 54 (3):401-419.

Abel, Patrick. 2018. Comparative Conclusions on Arbitral Dispute Settlement in Trade-Labour Matters Under US FTAs. In *Labour Standards in International Economic Law*, edited by H. Gött. Heidelberg: Springer.

ACEA, BusinessEurope, CEFIC, CEEV, CEPS, CEPI, DIAGEO, DIGITALEUROPE, EBCY, ESF, ETNO, EURATEX, and Pernod-Ricard. 2012. Approval of the EU-Colombia & Peru Trade Agreement. *EU business co-signed letter*, October 3. Available at: http://spirits.eu/files/32/eu-business-letter-in-favour-of-eu-colombia-agreement.pdf

Addo, Kofi. 2002. The Correlation between Labor Standards and International Trade. Which Way Forward? *Journal of World Trade* 36 (2):285-303.

———. 2015. *Core Labour Standards and International Trade*. Heidelberg: Springer Verlag.

AFL-CIO. 2002. 'Free Trade' Too Costly For Workers at Home and Abroad. *Press Release*, Washington, D.C.: American Federation of Labor and Congress of Industrial Organizations. Available at: http://www.aflcio.org/mediacenter/resources/upload/trade.pdf

———. 2002. NAFTA's Seven-Year Itch: Promised Benefits Not Delivered to Workers. *Press Release*, Washington, D.C.: American Federation of Labor and Congress of Industrial Organizations. Available at: http://www.citizenstrade.org/ctc/wp-content/uploads/2011/05/nafta_at_seven.pdf

———. 2007. Statement by AFL-CIO President John Sweeney on U.S. Trade Policy Developments. May 11. Washington, D.C.: American Federation of Labor and Congress of Industrial Organizations. Available at: http://www.aflcio.org/Press-R oom/Press-Releases/Statement-by-AFL-CIO-President-John-Sweeney-on-U.S3

———. 2015. Ten Critical Problems with the Trans-Pacific Partnership. Washington, D.C.: American Federation of Labor and Congress of Industrial Organizations.

———. 2015. The Trans-Pacific Partnership: Four Countries That Don't Comply With U.S. Trade Law. Washington, D.C.: American Federation of Labor and Congress of Industrial Organizations.

AFX News. 2007. SKorea will not renegotiate FTA with US - top negotiator. *AFX News*, April 13. Available at: http://www.finanznachrichten.de/nachrichten-2007 -04/8056877-skorea-will-not-renegotiate-fta-with-us-top-negotiator-020.htm

Agence France Press. 2008. EU to negotiate trade pact with Colombia, Peru. *Agence France Press*, November 11. Available at:

———. 2012. Merkel urges swift EU trade progress with Peru, Colombia. *Agence France Press*, June 12. Available at: https://au.finance.yahoo.com/news/merkel-urg es-eu-trade-progress-031915783.html

Aggarwal, Vinod K., and Edward A. Fogarty. 2004. Between regionalism and globalism: European Union interregional trade strategies. In *EU Trade Strategies: Between Regionalism and Globalism*, edited by V. K. Aggarwal and E. A. Fogarty. New York: Palgrave Macmillan.

Akhtar, Shayerah Ilias, and Vivian C. Jones. 2014. Transatlantic Trade and Investment Partnership (TTIP) Negotiations. In *CRS Report for Congress*. Washington, D.C.: Congressional Research Service.

Alden, Edward. 2003. Workers bar way to free trade in central America. *Financial Times*, December 4. Available at: http://www.citizenstrade.org/ctc/wp-content/up loads/2011/05/financialtimes_cafta.pdf

———. 2005. Bush likely to pay high price at home for deal on Central American trading pact. *Financial Times*, June 27. Available at: http://www.ft.com/intl/cms/s /0/40af84a8-e6a8-11d9-b6bc-00000e2511c8.html#axzz40zoqp870

Allee, Tod, and Manfred Elsig. 2014. Dispute settlement provisions in PTAs: new data and new concepts. In *Trade Cooperation: The Purpose, Design and Effects of Preferential Trade Agreements*, edited by A. Dür and M. Elsig. Cambridge: Cambridge University Press.

ALOP, APRODEV, CIFCA, CNCD, FIAN, Friends of the Earth Europe, Grupo Sur, and OIDHACO. 2012. The European Parliament prioritises trade interests over human rights and sustainable development. *Press Release*, December 11. Available at: http://www.cifcaeu.org/en/the-european-parliament-prioritises-trade-inte rests-over-human-rights-and-sustainable-development/

Alston, Phillip. 2004. 'Core Labour Standards' and the Transformation of the International Labour Rights Regime. *European Journal of International Law* 15 (3):457-521.

Alt, James E., Jeffrey Frieden, Michael J. Giligan, Dani Rodrik, and Ronald Rogowski. 1996. The International Political Economy of International Trade: Enduring Puzzles and an Agenda for Inquiry. *Comparative Political Studies* 29 (6):689-717.

Alt, James E., and Michael Gilligan. 1994. The Political Economy of Trading States: Factor Specificity, Collective Actions Problems and Domestic Political Institutions. *Journal of Political Philosophy* 2 (2):165-192.

Andrews, Edmund L. 2005. House Approves Free Trade Pact. *New York Times*, July 28. Available at: http://www.nytimes.com/2005/07/28/business/worldbusiness/house-approves-free-trade-pact.html?_r=0

———. 2005. Pleas and Promises by G.O.P. As Trade Pact Wins by 2 Votes. *New York Times*, July 29. Available at: http://query.nytimes.com/gst/fullpage.html?res=9D01E2DE113FF93AA15754C0A9639C8B63

———. 2005. Senate Approves Free Trade Pact. *New York Times*, July 1. Available at: http://www.nytimes.com/2005/07/01/politics/senate-approves-central-american-free-trade-pact.html

———. 2005. White House Makes Deals for Support of Trade Pact. *New York Times*, July 25. Available at: http://www.nytimes.com/2005/07/26/politics/white-house-makes-deals-for-support-of-trade-pact.html?_r=0

Antkiewicz, Agata, and Bessma Momani. 2009. Pursuing Geopolitical Stability through Interregional Trade: the EU's Motives for Negotiating with the Gulf Cooperation Council. *Journal of European Integration* 31 (2):217-235.

Appelbaum, Binyamin, and Jennifer Steinhauer. 2011. Congress Ends 5-Year Standoff on Trade Deals in Rare Accord. *New York Times*, October 12. Available at: http://www.nytimes.com/2011/10/13/business/trade-bills-near-final-chapter.html?pagewanted=all

Baccini, Leonardo. 2010. Explaining formation and design of EU trade agreements: The role of transparency and flexibility. *European Union Politics* 11 (2):195-217.

Baccini, Leonardo, Andreas Dür, and Manfred Elsig. 2015. The Politics of Trade Agreement Design: Revisiting the Depth–Flexibility Nexus. *International Studies Quarterly* 59 (4):765-775.

Bailey, Michael A., Judith Goldstein, and Barry R. Weingast. 1997. The Institutional Roots of American Trade Policy: Politics, Coalitions, and International Trade. *World Politics* 49 (3):309-338.

Baldwin, Matthew. 2006. Multilateralising Regionalism: Spaghetti Bowls as Building Blocs on the Path to Global Free Trade. *The World Economy* 29 (11):1451-1518.

Baldwin, Richard. 1986. *The Political Economy of US Import Policy*. Cambridge: MIT Press.

Baldwin, Richard, and Dany Jaimovich. 2012. Are Free Trade Agreements contagious? *Journal of International Economics* 88 (1):1-16.

Baldwin, Robert E. 2003. *The Decline of US Labor Unions and the Role of Trade*. Washington, D.C.: Institute for International Economics.

Balistreri, Edward J. 1997. The Performance of the Heckscher-Ohlin-Vanek Model in Predicting Endogenous Policy Forces at the Individual Level. *The Canadian Journal of Economics / Revue canadienne d'Economique* 30 (1):1-17.

Banchón, Mirra 2012. Acuerdo UE-Colombia y Perú, a discusión. *Deutsche Welle*, February 29. Available at: http://www.dw.com/es/acuerdo-ue-colombia-y-per%C3%BA-a-discusi%C3%B3n/a-15775764

Bang, Guri. 2011. Signed but Not Ratified: Limits to U.S. Participation in International Environmental Agreements. *Review of Policy Research* 28 (1):65-81.

Bardwell, Kedron 2000. The Puzzling Decline in House Support for Free Trade: Was Fast Track a Referendum on NAFTA? *Legislative Studies Quarterly* 25 (4):591-610.

Barfield, Claude. 2008. The Fast-Track Trade War. *The American*, May 7. Available at: https://www.aei.org/publication/the-fast-track-trade-war-2/

———. 2009. Politics of Trade in the USA and in the Obama Administration: Implications for Asian Regionalism. *Asian Economic Policy Review* 4 (2):227–243.

Barnard, Bruce. 1996. EU wants to discuss Wages, Labor Standards. Asia, Britain certain to oppose proposal. *Journal of Commerce*, July 25. Available at:

Barquero S., Marvin. 2008. Nicaragua objeta condiciones de Acuerdo con Unión Europea. *La Nación*, April 18. Available at: http://www.nacion.com/economia/Nicaragua-condiciones-Acuerdo-Union-Europea_0_971102995.html

———. 2008. Temas políticos obstaculizan avance de Acuerdo con UE. *La Nación*, April 19. Available at: http://www.nacion.com/economia/Temas-politicos-obstaculizan-Acuerdo-UE_0_971302941.html

———. 2008. UE anuente a acelerar Acuerdo de Asociación con el Istmo. *La Nación*, April 17. Available at: http://www.nacion.com/economia/UE-acelerar-Acuerdo-Asociacion-Istmo_0_970902920.html

Barrett, Scott. 2003. *Environment and Statecraft : The Strategy of Environmental Treaty-Making*. Oxford: Oxford University Press.

Bartels, Lorand. 2013. Human Rights and Sustainable Development Obligations in EU Free Trade Agreements. *Legal Issues of Economic Integration* 40 (4):297-313.

Beach, Derek. 2016. It's all about mechanisms - what process-tracing case studies should be tracing. *New Political Economy* 21 (5):463-472.

Beach, Derek, and Rasmus Brun Pedersen. 2013. *Process-Tracing Methods: Foundations and Guidelines*. Ann Arbor: University of Michigan Press.

Beatty, Andrew. 2007. Trade deals spark battle over services. *Politico*, April 11. Available at: http://www.politico.eu/article/trade-deals-spark-battle-over-services/

Beaulieu, Eugene. 2002. Factor or Industry Cleavages in Trade Policy? An Empirical Analysis of the Stolper–Samuelson Theorem. *Economics & Politics* 14 (2):99-131.

———. 2002. The Stolper–Samuelson Theorem Faces Congress. *Review of International Economics* 10 (2):343-360.

Becker, Elisabeth. 2003. A Pact on Central America Trade Zone, Minus One. *New York Times*, December 18. Available at: http://www.nytimes.com/2003/12/18/business/a-pact-on-central-america-trade-zone-minus-one.html

Becker, Elizabeth 2003. U.S. Begins Talks for Trade Pact With Central Americans. *New York Times*, January 9. Available at: http://www.nytimes.com/2003/01/09/bu siness/us-begins-talks-for-trade-pact-with-central-americans.html

Behrens, Maria, and Holger Janusch. 2012. Great 'Normative Power': The European and American Trade Approaches with Chile and Mexiko. *European foreign affairs review* 17 (3):367-386.

Bender, Peter. 2002. The European Parliament and the WTO. *European foreign affairs review* 7 (2):193-208.

Benedick, Richard. 2009. *Ozone Diplomacy: New Directions in Safeguarding the Planet*. Cambridge and London: Harvard University Press.

Bennett, Andrew. 2004. Case Study Methods: Design, Use, and Comparative Advantages. In *Models, Numbers, and Cases: Methods for Studying International Relations*, edited by D. F. Sprinz and Y. Wolinsky. Ann Arbor: Universtiy of Michigan Press.

Bennett, Andrew, and Jeffrey T. Checkel. 2014. *Process Tracing: From Metaphor to Analytic Tool*. Cambridge: Cambridge University Press.

Berger, Axel, Clara Brandi, and Dominique Bruhn. 2017. Environmental Provisions in Trade Agreements: Promises at the Trade and Environment Interface. *Discussion Paper: German Development Institut 16/2017*.

Bermúdez Mora, Kattia 2010. Europa no podrá tomar represalias comerciales en temas laborales y ambientales. *El Financiero*, April 21. Available at: http://wvw.elf inancierocr.com/ef_archivo/2010/abril/25/economia2343251.html

Bernhard, William, Lawrence J. Broz, and William Roberts Clark. 2003. *The Political Economy of Monetary Institutions*. Cambridge: MIT Press.

Bhagwati, Jagdish. 1995. Trade Liberalisation and 'Fair Trade' Demands: Addressing the Environmental and Labour Standards Issues. *The World Economy* 18 (6):745–759.

———. 2000. On thinking clearly about the linkage between trade and the environment. *Environment and Development Economics* 5 (4):483-529.

———. 2007. *In Defense of Globalization*. Oxford: Oxford University Press.

———. 2008. *Termites in the Trading System. How Preferential Trade Agreements Undermine Free Trade*. Oxford: Oxford University Press.

Bilby, Ethan. 2013. Europe trade action against Bangladesh would have big impact. *Reuters*, May 1. Available at: http://www.reuters.com/article/us-eu-bangladesh-tra de-idUSBRE9400JQ20130501

Blustein, Paul. 2005. U.S., Peru Strike Free-Trade Agreement. *The Washington Post*, December 8. Available at: http://www.washingtonpost.com/wp-dyn/content/arti cle/2005/12/07/AR2005120702791.html

Bolle, Mary Jane. 2013. Overview of Labor Enforcement Issues in Free Trade Agreements. In *CRS Report for Congress*. Washington, D.C.: Congressional Research Service.

Bollyky, Thomas J., and Anu Bradford. 2013. Getting to Yes on Transatlantic Trade. Consistent U.S.-EU Rules Could Remake Global Commerce. *Foreign Affairs*, July 10. Available at: https://www.foreignaffairs.com/articles/united-states/2013-07-10 /getting-yes-transatlantic-trade

Bomberg, Elizabeth. 2005. *Green Parties and Politics in the European Union*. London and New York: Routledge.

Bomberg, Elizabeth, and David Schlosberg, eds. 2013. *Environmentalism in the United States: Changing Conceptions of Activism*. New York: Routledge.

Bossuyt, Fabienne. 2009. The Social Dimension of the New Generation of EU FTAs with Asia and Latin America: Ambitious Continuation for the Sake of Policy Coherence. *European foreign affairs review* 14 (5):703-722.

Bounds, Andrew. 2006. EU trade deals will not hang on Doha. *Financial Times*, July 10. Available at: http://www.ft.com/intl/cms/s/0/abca11b4-0faf-11db-ad3d-00007 79e2340.html?siteedition=intl#axzz40zoqp870

Bounds, Andrew, and Anna Fifield. 2007. EU told to exclude N Korea enclave from pact. *Financial Times*, October 16. Available at: http://www.ft.com/intl/cms/s/0/d 7bd5ffe-7b80-11dc-8c53-0000779fd2ac.html#axzz3zZOi8qWh

Bouwen, Pieter. 2004. Exchanging access goods for access: A comparative study of business lobbying in the European Union institutions. *European Journal of Political Research* 43 (3):337-369.

Brack, Duncan. 2004. Trade and the Environment. In *Trade Politics*, edited by B. Hocking and S. McGuire. London: Routledge.

Brainard, Lael, and Hal Shapiro. 2001. Fast Track Trade Promotion Authority. In *Brookings Policy Brief*. Washington, D.C.: Brookings Institution.

Briceno Ruiz, José. 2007. Strategic Regionalism and Regional Social Policy in the FTAA Process. *Global Social Policy* 7 (3):294-315.

Bridges. 2007. EU-Andean Trade Pact Underway. *Bridges*, October 1. Available at: http://www.ictsd.org/bridges-news/bridges/news/eu-andean-trade-pact-underway

———. 2008. Little Progress In EU-Central America FTA Talks. *Bridges*, April 23. Available at: http://www.ictsd.org/bridges-news/bridges/news/little-progress-in-e u-central-america-fta-talks

———. 2009. EU, South Korea Conclude FTA Talks. *Bridges*, July 15. Available at: http://www.ictsd.org/bridges-news/bridges/news/eu-south-korea-conclude-fta-tal ks

———. 2009. EU, South Korea Sign Free Trade Accord. *Bridges*, October 21. Available at: http://www.ictsd.org/bridges-news/bridges/news/eu-south-korea-sign-free -trade-accord

———. 2010. EU Resumes Trade Talks with Mercosur, Concludes Talks with Central America. *Bridges*, May 19. Available at: http://www.ictsd.org/bridges-news/br idges/news/eu-resumes-trade-talks-with-mercosur-concludes-talks-with-central-a merica

———. 2012. EU Trade Ministers Agree to Approve Deal with Colombia, Peru. *Bridges*, March 21. Available at: http://www.ictsd.org/bridges-news/bridges/news/ eu-trade-ministers-agree-to-approve-deal-with-colombia-peru

———. 2012. EU Trade Ministers Approve Pact with Colombia, Peru. *Bridges*, June 6. Available at: http://www.ictsd.org/bridges-news/bridges/news/eu-trade-ministe rs-approve-pact-with-colombia-peru

———. 2012. EU, Central America Sign Region-to-Region Deal. *Bridges*, July 4. Available at: http://www.ictsd.org/bridges-news/bridges/news/eu-central-america -sign-region-to-region-deal

Broscheid, Andreas, and David Coen. 2003. Insider and Outsider Lobbying of the European Commission. An Informational Model of Forum Politics. *European Union Politics* 4 (2):165–189.

Brunnée, Jutta. 2004. The United States and International Environmental Law: Living with an Elephant. *European Journal of International Law* 15 (4):617-649.

Buck, Tobias. 2004. Latin Americans face EU trade talks disappointment. *Financial Times*, May 5. Available at: http://www.ft.com/intl/cms/s/0/7ed0f4b6-9e32-11d8-8 1c6-000e2511c801.html#axzz3zmPLJWQf

Buerkle, Tom 1994. Brittan Rebuffs Clinton Over Labor Standards. *New York Times*, January 18. Available at: http://www.nytimes.com/1994/01/18/business/worldbus iness/18iht-gatt_0.html

Burchell, J. 2014. *The Evolution of Green Politics: Development and Change Within European Green Parties*. Abingdon: Taylor & Francis.

Burgoon, Brian. 2004. The Rise and Stall of Labor Linkage in Globalization Politics. *International Politics* 41 (2):196-220.

———. 2009. The Distinct Politics of the European Union's 'Fair Trade' Linkage to Labour Standards *European foreign affairs review* 14 (5):643–661.

Business Round Table. 2001. The Case for U.S. Trade Leadership: the United States is Falling Behind. *Press Release*, February 9. Washington, D.C.: Business Round Table. Available at: http://www.businessroundtable.org/publications/publication .aspx?qs=2496BF807822B0F19D2

Business Week. 2001. Calming the Waters: A Talk with the U.S. Trade Rep. *Business Week*, July 23. Available at: http://www.bloomberg.com/news/articles/2001-07-22 /q-and-a-calming-the-waters-a-talk-with-the-u-dot-s-dot-trade-rep

BusinessEurope. 2007. Position on the EU-Korea Free Trade Agreement (FTA). *Position Paper*, July 18. Brussels: BusinessEurope. Available at: http://www.bilaterals. org/IMG/pdf/EU-Korea_position_BusinessEurope_180707.pdf.

Büthe, Tim, and Helen V. Milner. 2014. Foreign Direct Investment and Institutional Diversity in Trade Agreements: Credibility, Commitment, and Economic Flows in the Developing World, 1971–2007. *World Politics* 66 (1):88-122.

Callan, Eoin. 2007. Democrats to throw out Colombia trade deal. *Financial Times*, November 22. Available at: http://www.ft.com/intl/cms/s/0/84143836-799d-11db -90a6-0000779e2340.html#axzz3yuKqURup

Callan, Eoin, and Anastasia Molony. 2007. White House trades on Democrats' terms. *Financial Times*, May 13. Available at: https://www.ft.com/content/f5b199 52-0192-11dc-8b8c-000b5df10621

Carlos Nino, Luis 2008. EU Drops IPC Prerequisite from Trade Talks with Central America. *IHS Global Insight*, April 22. Available at:

Center for International Environmental Law, Defenders of Wildlife, Earthjustice, Friends of the Earth, Greenpeace, League of Conservation Voters, Mineral Policy Center, National Environmental Trust, National Wildlife Federation, Natural Resources Defense Council, Sierra Club, and U.S. Public Interest Research Group. 2002. U.S. Fast Track Conference Bill neither Reflects America's Environmental Values nor Addresses Fundamental Problems with Investment Rules. *Letter to Congress*. Available at: http://www.ciel.org/news/u-s-fast-track-conference -bill-neither-reflects-americas-environmental-values-nor-addresses-fundamental-p roblems-with-investment-rules/

Céspedez Vargas, Renzo. 2009. Negociaciones Del Acuerdo De Asociacion Centroamérica-Unión Europea, Retos Y Oportunidades Para Los Sectores Productivos De Los Países Centroamericanos. San José: Fundación Friedrich Ebert.

Chalmers, Adam William. 2013. Trading information for access: informational lobbying strategies and interest group access to the European Union. *Journal of European Public Policy* 20 (1):39–58.

Chan, Anita. 2003. Racing to the bottom: international trade without a social clause. *Third World Quaterly* 24 (6):1011-1028.

Chan, Sewell. 2010. U.S. Plans Trade Complaint Against Guatemala. *New York Times*, July 30. Available at: http://www.nytimes.com/2010/07/31/business/global /31trade.html

Charnovitz, Steve. 1987. The influence of international labour standards on the world trading regime. A historical overview. *International Labour Review* 26 (5):565-584.

———. 1992. Environmental and Labour Standards in Trade. *The World Economy* 15 (3):335-356.

———. 2005. The Labor Dimension of the Emerging Free Trade Area of the Americas. In *Labour Rights as Human Rights*, edited by P. Alston. Oxford: Oxford University Press.

Chayes, Abram, and Antonia Handler Chayes. 1995. *The New Sovereignty: compliance with international regulatory agreements*. Cambridge: Harvard University Press.

Clark, William Roberts, Erick Duchesne, and Sophie Meunier. 2000. Domestic and International Asymmetries in United States–European Union Trade Negotiations. *International Negotiation* 5 (1):69-95.

Coen, David. 2007. Empirical and theoretical studies in EU lobbying. *Journal of European Public Policy* 14 (3):333–345.

COHA. 2010. Obama's hard stance on Guatemalan labor: A monumental step for labor or mere political manoeuvring? *Council on Hemispheric Affairs*. Available at: http://www.coha.org/obama%E2%80%99s-hard-stance-on-guatemalan-labor-a-m onumental-step-for-labor-rights-or-mere-political-maneuvering

Collier, David. 2008. Understanding Process Tracing. *PS: Political Science & Politics* 44 (4):823-830.

Collingsworth, Terry, J. William Goold, and Pharis J. Harvey. 1994. Time for a Global New Deal. *Foreign Affairs* 73 (1):8-13.

Collinson, Sarah. 1999. 'Issue-systems', 'multi-level games' and the analysis of the EUs external commercial and associated policies: a research agenda. *Journal of European Public Policy* 6 (2):206-224.

Condon, Madison. 2015. The Integration of Environmental Law into International Investment Treaties and Trade Agreements: Negotiation Process and the Legalization of Commitments. *Virginia Environmental Law Journal* 33 (1):102-152.

Cooper, Helene, and Steven Greenhouse. 2011. U.S. and Colombia Near Trade Pact. *New York Times*, April 6. Available at: http://www.nytimes.com/2011/04/07/business/07trade.html

Cooper, William H., and Mark E. Manyin. 2006. The Proposed South Korea-U.S. Free Trade Agreement (KORUSFTA). In *CRS Report for Congress*. Washington, D.C.: Congressional Research Service.

———. 2007. The Proposed South Korea-U.S. Free Trade Agreement (KORUS FTA). In *CRS Report for Congress*. Washinghton, D.C.: Congressional Research Service.

Cooper, William H., Mark E. Manyin, Remy Jurenas, and Michaela D. Platzer. 2011. The Proposed U.S.-South Korea Free Trade Agreement (KORUS FTA): Provisions and Implications. In *CRS Report for Congress*. Washington, D.C.: Congressional Research Service.

Corbett, Richard, Francis Jacobs, and Michael Shackleton. 2011. *The European Parliament*. 8th ed. London: John Harper Publishing.

Correa, Jorge. 2008. Negociación en bloque, CAN y Unión Europea es inviable. *Portafolio*, April 30. Available at: http://www.portafolio.co/economia/finanzas/negociacion-bloque-can-union-europea-inviable-289698

Council of the European Union. 1999. WTO: Preparation of the Third Ministerial Conference - Council Conclusions of 26 October 1999. Luxembourg: Council of the European Union (12121/99).

Cronin, David. 2008. EU has decided to push ahead with plans to secure a free trade agreement. *Inter Press Service*, December 8. Available at:

———. 2008. Europe: EU official reverse course, give Colombia trade deal. *Inter Press Service*, December 11. Available at:

Cross, Ciaran. 2017. Focus: Failure by design: Did the US choose to lose the Guatemala labour dispute? *International Union Rights* 24 (3):23-25.

da Conceição, Eugénia. 2010. Who Controls Whom? Dynamics of Power Delegation and Agency Losses in EU Trade Politics. *Journal of Common Market Studies* 48 (4):1107–1126.

da Conceição-Heldt, Eugénia. 2011. *Negotiating Trade Liberalization at the WTO. Domestic Politics and Bargaining Dynamics*. Basingstoke: Palgrave Mcmillian.

———. 2013. Do Agents "Run Amok"? A Comparison of Agency Slack in the EU and US Trade Policy in the Doha Round. *Journal of Comparative Policy Analysis* 15 (1):21-36.

———. 2013. Two-level games and trade cooperation: What do we now know? *International Politics* 50 (4):579–599.

Dadush, Uri. 2013. Cold Water for Hot Trade Deals. *The National Interest*, May 13. Available at: http://nationalinterest.org/commentary/cold-water-hot-trade-deals-8 460?page=show

Damro, Chad. 2012. Market power Europe. *Journal of European Public Policy* 19 (5):682-699.

Dark, Taylor E. 1999. *The Unions and the Democrats. An Enduring Alliance*. Ithaca: Cornell University Press.

Davis, Bob. 2004. U.S. to Renew Trade Focus On Latin America. *Wall Street Journal*, October 11. Available at: http://www.wsj.com/articles/SB109744579434841472

Davis, Christina L. 2012. *Why Adjudicate?: Enforcing Trade Rules in the WTO*. Princeton: Princeton University Press.

De Biévre, Dirk. 2006. The EU regulatory trade agenda and the quest for WTO enforcement. *Journal of European Public Policy* 13 (6):851–866.

De Biévre, Dirk, and Andreas Dür. 2005. Constituency Interests and Delegation in European and American Trade Policy. *Comparative Political Studies* 38 (10):1271-1296.

De Biévre, Dirk, and Arlo Poletti. 2015. Judicial Politics in International Trade Relations: Introduction to the Special Issue. *World Trade Review* 14 (S1):1-11.

Defenders of Wildlife, Earthjustice, Friends of the Earth, and Sierra Club. 2007. Statement by Defenders of Wildlife, Earthjustice, Friends of the Earth, Sierra Club regarding Trade and Environment Deal. *Press Release*, May 14. Available at: http://vault.sierraclub.org/trade/downloads/peru-statement.pdf.

Destler, I.M. 1997. *Renewing Fast-Track Legislation, Policy Analyses in International Economics*. Washington, D.C.: Institute for International Economics.

———. 2005. *American Trade Politics*. 4th ed. Washington, D.C.: Institute for International Economics.

———. 2007. American Trade Politics in 2007: Building Bipartisan Compromise. Washington, D.C.: Peterson Institute for International Economics.

Destler, I.M., and Peter J. Balint. 1999. *The New Politics of American Trade: Trade, Labor, and the Environment, Policy Analyses in International Economics*. Washington, D.C.: Institute for International Economics.

Destler, I.M., and John S. Odell. 1987. *Anti-Protection: Changing Forces in United States Trade Policies*. Washington, D.C.: Institute for International Economics.

Deutsche Welle. 2008. Merkel ofrece ayuda a Colombia para aclarar violaciones de DDHH. *Deutsche Welle*, May 15. Available at: http://www.dw.com/es/merkel-ofre ce-ayuda-a-colombia-para-aclarar-violaciones-de-ddhh/a-3344780

Dickerson, Marla. 2008. CAFTA labor complaint filed. *Los Angeles Times*, April 24. Available at: http://articles.latimes.com/2008/apr/24/business/fi-labor24

Doherty, Brian. 2005. *Ideas and Actions in the Green Movement*. Abingdon: Routledge.

Donnan, Shawn, and Demetri Sevastopulo. 2015. US, Japan and 10 countries strike Pacific trade deal. *Financial Times*, October 5. Available at: https://next.ft.com/co ntent/d4a31d08-6b4c-11e5-8171-ba1968cf791a

Downs, George W., David M. Rocke, and Peter N. Barsoom. 1996. Is the good news about compliance good news about cooperation? *International Organization* 50 (3):379-406.

Draper, Peter, Khumalo Nkululeko, and Faith Tigere. 2017. Sustainability Provisions in Regional Trade Agreements: Can they be Multilateralised? In *RTA Exchange*. Geneva: International Centre for Trade and Sustainable Development (ICTSD) and Inter-American Development Bank (IDB).

Drezner, Daniel W. 2001. Globalization and Policy Convergence. *International Studies Review* 3 (1):53-78.

———. 2003. The Hidden Hand of Economic Coercion. *International Organization* 57 (3):643-659.

———. 2007. *All Politics is Global: Explaining International Regulatory Regimes*. Princeton: Princeton University Press.

Drutman, Lee. 2015. *The Business of America is Lobbying: How Corporations Became Politicized and Politics Became More Corporate*. Oxford: Oxford University Press.

Dryzek, John S., David Downes, Chrisitan Hunold, David Schlosberg, and Hans-Kristian Hernes, eds. 2003. *Green States and Social Movements: Environmentalism in the United States, United Kingdom, Germany, and Norway*. Oxford: Oxford University Press.

Duffy, Robert J. 2012. Organized Interests and Environmental Policy. In *The Oxford Handbook of U.S. Environmental Policy* edited by M. E. Kraft and S. Kamieniecki. Oxford: Oxford University Press.

Dür, Andreas. 2006. Assessing the EU's role in international trade negotiations. *European political science* 5 (4):362-376.

———. 2007. EU Trade Policy as Protection for Exporters: The Agreements with Mexico and Chile. *Journal of Common Market Studies* 45 (4):833–855.

———. 2008. Bringing Economic Interests Back into the Study of EU Trade Policy-Making. *British Journal of Politics and International Relation* 10 (1):27-45.

Dür, Andreas, Leonardo Baccini, and Manfred Elsig. 2014. The design of international trade agreements: Introducing a new dataset. *Review of International Organizations* 9 (3):353-375.

Dür, Andreas, and Dirk De Biévre. 2007. Inclusion without Influence? NGOs in European Trade Policy. *Journal of Public Policy* 27 (1):79-101.

Dür, Andreas, and Manfred Elsig. 2011. Principals, agents, and the European Union´s foreign economic policies. *Journal of European Public Policy* 18 (3):323-338.

Dür, Andreas, and Hubert Zimmermann. 2007. Introduction: The EU in International Trade Negotiations. *Journal of Common Market Studies* 45 (4):771-787.

Dymond, William A. 2001. Core labour standards and the world trade organization: Labour's love lost. *Canadian Foreign Policy Journal* 8 (3):99-114.

Dymond, William A., and Michael M. Hart. 2000. Post-Modern Trade Policy. Reflections on the Challenges to Multilateral Trade Negotiations After Seattle. *Journal of World Trade* 34 (3):21-38.

Ebert, Franz Christian. 2016. Labour Provisions in EU Trade Agreements. *International Labour Review* 155 (3):407-433.

Eckersley, Robyn. 2004. The Big Chill: The WTO and Multilateral Environmental Agreements. *Global Environmental Politics* 4 (2):24-50.

Eckhardt, Jappe, and Manfred Elsig. 2015. Support for international trade law: The US and the EU compared. *International Journal of Constitutional Law* 13 (4):966-986.

EESC. 2018. Opinion. Trade and sustainable development chapters (TSD) in EU Free Trade Agreements (FTA). Brussels: European Economic and Social Comittee.

Egan, Michelle P. 2005. *Creating a Transatlantic Marketplace: Government Policies and Business Strategies*. Manchester: Manchester University Press.

Eggen, Dan. 2008. Bush Backs New Trade Pact With Colombia. *Washington Post*, April 8. Available at: http://www.washingtonpost.com/wp-dyn/content/article/2008/04/07/AR2008040700789.html

———. 2008. Bush Concedes Defeat On Colombia Trade Pact. *Washinton Post*, April 15. Available at: http://www.washingtonpost.com/wp-dyn/content/article/2008/04/14/AR2008041400991.html

Eilperin, Juliet. 2007. How Trade Breakthrough Almost Broke Down in Congress. *Washington Post*, November 22. Available at: http://www.washingtonpost.com/wp-dyn/content/article/2007/11/21/AR2007112102333.html

Elliot, Kimberly Ann. 2011. Labor Rights. In *Preferential Trade Agreement Policies for Development. A Handbook*, edited by J.-P. Chauffour and J.-C. Maur. Washington, D.C.: The World Bank.

Elliott, Kimberly Ann. 2000. Preferences for Workers? Worker Rights and the US Generalized System of Preferences. In *Working Paper*. Washington, D.C.: Institute for International Economics.

Elliott, Kimberly Ann, and Richard B. Freeman. 2003. *Can Labor Standards Improve Under Globalization?* Washington, D.C.: Institute for International Economics.

Elsig, Manfred. 2010. European Union trade policy after enlargement: larger crowds, shifting priorities and informal decision-making. *Journal of European Public Policy* 17 (6):781-798.

Elsig, Manfred, and Cédric Dupont. 2012. European Union Meets South Korea: Bureaucratic Interests, Exporter Discrimination and the Negotiations of Trade Agreements. *Journal of Common Market Studies* 50 (3):492-507.

Elsig, Manfred, and Jappe Eckhardt. 2015. The Creation of the Multilateral Trade Court: Design and Experiential Learning. *World Trade Review* 14 (S1):13-32.

Emmott, Robin. 2012. EU approves deals to boost trade with Latin America. *Reuters*, December 11. Available at: http://www.reuters.com/article/eu-trade-latam-idUSL5E8NB8IO20121211

Epstein, David, and Sharyn O'Halloran. 1996. The partisan paradox and the U.S. tariff, 1877 - 1934. *International Organization* 50 (2):301-324.

ESF. 2007. ESF Position Paper on EU Free Trade Agreements. *Position Paper*, February 28. Available at: http://www.esf.be/new/wp-content/uploads/2009/01/esf-position-paper-on-eu-free-trade-agreements-final.pdf

———. 2009. Services Industry Calls for swift conclusion of the EU-Korea FTA. *Letter to Commission President José Manuel Barroso*, July 6. Available at: http://www.esf.be/new/wp-content/uploads/2009/01/esf-korea-letter-to-barroso-july-6-2009.pdf.

ETUC. 2006. On the communication 'Global Europe: competing in the world. Resolution adopted by the ETUC Executive Committee in their meeting held in Brussels on 7–8 December. Brussels: European Trade Union Confederation.

———. 2008. Notorious rights violations rewarded in new European Union trade preferences system *Press Release*, December 12. Available at: https://www.etuc.org/press/notorious-rights-violations-rewarded-new-european-union-trade-preferences-system#.WEWDCnoabJg

———. 2009. EU Trade negotiations with Colombia and Peru. Resolution adopted by the ETUC Executive Committee in their meeting held in Brussels held from 1-2 December 2009. *Press Release*. Available at: http://etuc.org/a/6736

———. 2010. ETUC welcomes EU Parliament decisions on trade and sustainable development *Press Release*, November 26. Available at: https://www.etuc.org/press/etuc-welcomes-eu-parliament-decisions-trade-and-sustainable-development#.VrtQg0aql_k

———. 2010. EU Trade Commissioner and ETUC's General Secretary discuss labour standards and trade policy. *Press Release*, April 13. Available at: https://www.etuc.org/press/eu-trade-commissioner-and-etucs-general-secretary-discuss-labour-standards-and-trade-policy#.VrtMa0aql_k

———. 2013. EP INTA Hearing on Sustainable Development Chapters in Trade Agreements. *Speech at the EP's INTA Committee*, November 27. Available at: https://www.etuc.org/speeches/ep-inta-hearing-sustainable-development-chapters-trade-agreements#.WEWGa3oabJg

ETUC, CCT, and CSACC. 2008. Proposed Social Chapter for an Association Agreement by and between Central America and the European Union. April 2008. Available at:

———. 2009. Open Letter from the CSACC-CCT-CES concerning the Central America-EU Association Agreement. *Letter*, March 5. Available at: http://www.ituc-csi.org/IMG/pdf/CartaAbierta-EN.pdf.

ETUC/ITUC. 2007. ETUC/ITUC statement of trade union demands relating to key social elements of 'sustainable development' chapters in European Union negotiations on free trade agreements (FTAs). *ETUC/ITUC*, October 7. Available at: https://www.ituc-csi.org/IMG/pdf/TLE_EN.pdf.

ETUC/ITUC/TUCA. 2010. Appeal to European Union, Latin American and Caribbean Heads of State and of Government. LAC-EU Trade Union Summit 4th & 5th May 2010. Available at: https://www.ituc-csi.org/appeal-to-european-union-latin

————. 2012. ETUC letter on the proposed European Union Free Trade Agreement with Colombia and Peru. *Letter to MEPs*, February 22. Available at: www.etuc.or g/sites/www.etuc.org/files/Letter.pdf

Euractive. 2011. Parliament clears EU-South Korea trade pact. *Euractive*, February 18. Available at: http://www.euractiv.com/trade/parliament-clears-eu-south-korea -news-502267

————. 2012. EU lawmakers approve trade deals with Latin America. *Euractive*, December 11. Available at: http://www.euractiv.com/trade/eu-lawmakers-approve-t rade-deals-news-516590

————. 2012. EU-Latin America trade deals in troubled water. *Euractive*, June 28. Available at: http://www.euractiv.com/global-europe/eu-latin-america-trade-deals -tro-news-513602

Eurobarometer. 1996. Standard Eurobarometer Survey: 44.2bis.

Eurochambers. 2007. The European Commission's Questionnaire on FTAs. *Position Paper*, April 2007. Available at:

EuroCommerce. 2001. Jahresbericht 2001. Aktionsplan 2002. Brussels: EuroCommerce.

————. 2007. Free Trade Negotiations. Contribution to the DG Trade Stakeholder Consultation. *Position Paper*, May 31. Available at:

European Commission. 1994. Statement by Sir Leon Brittan. *Meeting at Ministerial Level Marrakesh (Morocco)*, April 12. Available at:

————. 2001. Communication from the Commission to the Council, the European Parliament and the Economic and Social Committee - Promoting core Labour Standards and Improving Social governance in the context of globalisation, COM(2001) 416 final. Brussels: European Commission.

————. 2004. The Social Dimension of Globalisation - the EU's policy contribution on extending the benefits to all, COM(2004) 383. Available at:

————. 2004. Trade policy in the Prodi Commission 1999-2004. An assessment. Brussels: European Commission.

————. 2005. Communication from the Commission to the European Parliament: "European values in the globalised world - Contribution of the Commission to the October Meeting of Heads of State and Government", 20 October 2005, COM(2005) 525 final. Brussels: European Commission.

————. 2007. Commission Staff Working Document: The external dimension of the Single Market review. Brussels: European Commission.

————. 2007. EU and Central America start negotiations for new Association Agreement. *Press Release*, June 29. Available at: http://europa.eu/rapid/press-relea se_IP-07-981_en.pdf.

————. 2007. EU to start negotiations for Association Agreement with the Andean Community; aid package for the region of EUR 713 million. *Press Release*, April 20. Available at: http://europa.eu/rapid/pressReleasesAction.do?reference=IP/07/ 534&format=HTML&aged=0&language=EN&guiLanguage=en

————. 2008. Industrial Relations in Europe 2008. Brussels: European Commission.

————. 2013. European Union, Trade in goods with Andean community. Brussels: European Commission.

————. 2013. European Union, Trade in goods with Central America (6). Brussels: European Commission.

————. 2015. EU Textual Proposal. Trade And Sustainable Development. Brussels: European Commission.

————. 2018. Feedback and way forward on improving the implementation and enforcement of Trade and Sustainable Development chapters in EU Free Trade Agreements.

European Parliament. 1994. Resolution on the Introduction of a Social Clause in the Unilateral and Multilateral Trading System, A3-0007/94. Strasbourg: European Parliament.

————. 1996. Resolution on the World Trade Organization (WTO), A4-0320/96. Strasbourg: European Parliament.

————. 2007. Debates - Thursday, 13 December 2007: 5. Economic and trade relations with Korea. Strasbourg: European Parliament.

————. 2007. Debates - Wednesday, 14 March 2007: Negotiation of an EU-Central America Association Agreement - Negotiation of an EU-Andean Community Association Agreement. Strasbourg: European Parliament.

————. 2007. European Parliament resolution of 13 December 2007 on the trade and economic relations with Korea (2007/2186(INI)). Strasbourg: European Parliament.

————. 2007. European Parliament resolution of 22 May 2007 on Global Europe - external aspects of competitiveness (2006/2292(INI)). Strasbourg: European Parliament.

————. 2007. Negotiation of an EU-Andean Community Association Agreement European Parliament recommendation of 15 March 2007 to the Council on the negotiating mandate for an association agreement between the European Union and its Member States, of the one part, and the Andean Community and its member countries, of the other part (2006/2221(INI)). Strasbourg: European Parliament.

————. 2007. Negotiation of an EU-Central America Association Agreement. European Parliament recommendation of 15 March 2007 to the Council on the negotiating mandate for an association agreement between the European Union and its Member States, of the one part, and the countries of Central America, of the other part (2006/2222(INI)). Strasbourg: European Parliament.

————. 2007. Report on the Trade and Economic Relations with Korea (2007/2186(INI)). Strasbourg: European Parliament.

————. 2010. Debates - Wednesday, 10 February 2010: 19. EU - South Korea free trade agreement. Strasbourg: European Parliament.

————. 2010. European Parliament resolution of 25 November 2010 on human rights and social and environmental standards in international trade agreements Strasbourg: European Parliament.

―――. 2010. European Parliament resolution of 25 November 2010 on international trade policy in the context of climate change imperatives (2010/2103(INI)). Strasbourg: European Parliament.

―――. 2011. Debates - Monday, 9 May 2011: 20. Free trade agreement with India. Strasbourg: European Parliament.

―――. 2012. Debates - Monday, 10 December 2012: 15. EU-Central America association agreement. Strasbourg: European Parliament.

―――. 2012. Debates - Tuesday, 22 May 2012: EU trade agreement with Colombia and Peru. Brussels: European Parliament.

―――. 2012. European Parliament resolution of 13 June 2012 on the EU trade agreement with Colombia and Peru (2012/2628(RSP)). Strasbourg: European Parliament.

―――. 2016. European Parliament resolution on implementation of the 2010 recommendations of Parliament on social and environmental standards, human rights and corporate responsibility (2015/2038(INI)). Strasbourg: European Parliament.

European Report. 2006. Trade Strategy: Mandelson preaches ambitious and offensive bilateralism. *European Report*, October 12. Available at:

―――. 2007. Free Trade Agreements: EU less demanding than US in social matters. *European Report*, October 9. Available at:

European United Left/Nordic Green Left. 2012. Colombia/Peru trade deal - "Listen to the unions, Listen to the families of the victims: Vote No!". *Press Release*, December 12. Available at: http://www.guengl.eu/news/article/gue-ngl-news/colombia-peru-trade-deal-listen-to-the-unions-listen-to-the-families-of-the

Evans, Peter B., Harold K. Jacobson, and Robert D. Putnam. 1993. *Double-Edged Diplomacy: International Bargaining and Domestic Politics*. Berkley: University of California Press.

Evenett, Simon J., and Michael Meier. 2008. An Interim Assessment of the US Trade Policy of 'Competitive Liberalization'. *The World Economy* 31 (1):31-66.

Fabbrini, Sergio. 2007. *Compound Democracies: Why the United States and Europe Are Becoming Similar*. Oxford: Oxford University Press.

Falke, Andreas. 2005. EU–USA Trade Relations in the Doha Development Round: Market Access versus a Post-modern Trade Policy Agenda. *European foreign affairs review* 10 (3):339–357.

Falkner, Robert. 2007. The political economy of 'normative power' Europe: EU environmental leadership in international biotechnology regulation. *Journal of European Public Policy* 14 (4):507-526.

Falleti, Tulia G. 2016. Process tracing of extensive and intensive processes. *New Political Economy* 21 (5):455-462.

Feinberg, Richard E. 2003. The Political Economy of United States' Free Trade Arrangements. *The World Economy* 26 (7):1019–1040.

Fifield, Anna. 2006. S Korea 'will not rush' US trade accord. *Financial Times*, April 18. Available at: http://www.ft.com/intl/cms/s/0/8b44eb2c-ce77-11da-a032-0000779e2340.html#axzz3x1berC28

Filipovic, Christina 2010. Colombia backs rights monitoring in EU trade deal. *Colombia Reports*, October 11. Available at: http://colombiareports.com/colombi a-rights-monitoring-eu-trade-deal/

Financial Times. 2005. Partisanship on trade. *Financial Times*, July 29. Available at: https://www.ft.com/content/1d6f38c2-ff5c-11d9-86df-00000e2511c8

Fox, David. 1996. EU agrees to steer clear of labor issues/Move seen pleasing Asian partners. *Journal of Commerce*, October 29. Available at: http://www.joc.com/mar itime-news/eu-agrees-steer-clear-labor-issues-move-seen-pleasing-partners-asia_19 961029.html

Francia, Peter L. 2012. *The Future of Organized Labor in American Politics*. New York: Columbia University Press.

French, John D. 2002. From the Suites to the Streets: The Unexpected Re-emergence of the "Labor Question," 1994-1999. *Labor History* 43 (3):285-304.

———. 2006. North American Free Trade Agreement. In *Encyclopedia of US Labor and Working Class History*, edited by E. Arnesen. New York: Routledge.

Frennhoff Larsén, Magdalena. 2007. Principal–Agent Analysis with One Agent and Two Principals: European Union Trade Negotiations with South Africa. *Politics & Policy* 35 (3):440-463.

———. 2007. Trade Negotiations between the EU and South Africa: A Three-Level Game. *Journal of Common Market Studies* 45 (4):857-881.

Frieden, Jeffrey. 1988. Capital Politics: Creditors and the International Political Economy. *Journal of Public Policy* 8 (3/4):265-286.

———. 1991. *Debt, Development and Democracy*. Princeton: Princeton University Press.

———. 1999. Actors and Preferences in International Relations. In *Strategic Choice and International Relations*, edited by D. A. Lake and R. Powell. Princeton: Princeton University Press.

Frieden, Jeffrey, and Lisa L. Martin. 2003. International Political Economy: Global and Domestic Interactions. In *Political Science: The State of the Discipline*, edited by I. Katznelson and H. V. Milner. New York: W.W. Norton.

Friends of the Earth Europe. 2007. Central Americas poor and environment will be hit by free trade with the EU. *Press Release*, October 22. Available at: https://www .foeeurope.org/press/2007/Oct22_CP_CA_free_trade.htm

———. 2015. TTIP leak exposes EU's failure to protect the environment. *Press Release*, October 26. Available at: http://www.foeeurope.org/TTIP-leak-exposes-EU %E2%80%99s-failure-protect-environment-231015

Fritz, Thomas. 2010. Die zweite Eroberung. Das EU-Freihandelsabkommen mit Kolumbien und Peru. Berlin and Amsterdam: Forschungs- und Dokumentation-szentrum Chile-Lateinamerika/Transnational Institute.

FT/Harris. 2007. Poll Finds Strong Populist Mood in Europe and to a Lesser Extent in the USA. In *Press Release*: Harris Interactive.

Gallagher, Kevin P. 2008. Understanding developing country resistance to the Doha Round. *Review of International Political Economy* 15 (1):62–85.

Gantz, David A. 2011. Labor Rights and Environmental Protection Under NAFTA and Other U.S. Free Trade Agreements. *Arizona Legal Studies*. Discussion Paper No. 11-13.

GAO. 2007. International Trade: An Analysis of Free Trade Agreements and Congressional and Private Sector Consultations under Trade Promotion Authority. In *Report to Congressional Requesters*. Washington, D.C.: United States Government Accountability Office.

———. 2014. Free Trade Agreements: Office of the U.S. Trade Representative schould continue to improve its Monitoring of Environmental Commitments. In *Report to Congressional Requesters*. Washington, D.C.: United States Government Accountability Office.

———. 2014. Free Trade Agreements: U.S. Partners Are Adressing Labor Commitments, but More Monitoring and Enforcement Are Needed. In *Report to Congressional Requesters*. Washington, D.C.: United States Government Accountability Office.

Garcia Bercero, Ignacio. 2006. Dispute Settlement in European Union Free Trade Agreements: Lessons Learned? In *Regional Trade Agreements and the WTO Legal System*, edited by L. Bartels and F. Ortino. Oxford: Oxford University Press.

Gardner, Andrew. 2012. MEPs approve Latin American trade deals. *Politico*, December 12. Available at: http://www.politico.eu/article/meps-approve-latin-american-trade-deals/

Garrett, Geoffrey, and George Tsebelis. 1996. An institutional critique of intergovernmentalism. *International Organization* 50 (2):269-299.

George. 2014. Environment and Regional Trade Agreements. Emerging Trends and Policy Drivers. In *OECD Trade and Environment Working Papers*: 2014/02.

George, Alexander L., and Andrew Bennett. 2005. *Case Studies and Theory Development in the Social Sciences*. Cambridge: MIT Press.

Gilens, Martin. 2012. *Affluence and Influence: Economic Inequality and Political Power in America*. Princeton: Princeton University Press.

Goldfarb, Zachary A., and Lori Montgomery. 2011. Obama gets win as Congress passes free-trade agreements. *Washinton Post*, October 12. Available at: https://www.washingtonpost.com/business/economy/obama-gets-win-as-congress-passes-free-trade-agreements/2011/10/12/gIQAGHeFgL_story.html

Goldirova, Renata. 2009. Brussels Divided Over Korean Trade Deal. *Bloomberg Business Week*, July 22. Available at: http://www.businessweek.com/globalbiz/content/jul2009/gb20090722_028291.htm

Goldstein, Judith. 1993. *Ideas, Interests and American Trade Policy*. Ithaca and London: Cornell University Press.

Gomez Arana, Arantza. 2014. The European Union and the Central American Common Market Signs an Association Agreement: Pragmatism versus Values? *European foreign affairs review* 20 (1):43-63.

González Garibay, Montserrat. 2011. The trade-labour and trade-environment linkages: together or apart? *The Journal of International Trade Law and Policy* 10 (2):165-184.

González Garibay, Montserrat, and Johan Adriaensen. 2013. The Illusion of Choice: The European Union and the Trade-Labour Linkage. *Journal of Contemporary European Research* 9 (4):542-559.

Goodman, Peter. 2007. Democrats, White House Clash on Trade. *Washington Post*, February 15. Available at: http://www.washingtonpost.com/wp-dyn/content/arti cle/2007/02/14/AR2007021401752.html

Gourevitch, Peter. 1986. *Politics in Hard Times: Comparative Responses to International Economic Crises*. Ithaca and London: Cornell University Press.

Gourevitch, Peter A., and James Shinn. 2005. *Political Power and Corporate Control: The New Global Politics of Corporate Governance*. Princeton: Princeton University Press.

Grandi, Pablo Lazo. 2009. Trade Agreements and their Relation to Labour Standards: The Current Situation. In *ICTSD Programme on EPAs and Regionalism. Issue Paper no. 3*. Geneva: International Centre for Trade and Sustainable Development (ICTSD).

Greenhouse, Steven. 2010. U.S. Union Backing Boosts Korea Trade Pact. *New York Times*, December 10. Available at: http://www.nytimes.com/2010/12/09/business/ global/09trade.html?_r=0

———. 2013. Under Pressure, Bangladesh Adopts New Labor Law. *New York Times*, July 16. Available at: http://www.nytimes.com/2013/07/17/world/asia/under-pres sure-bangladesh-adopts-new-labor-law.html

Gregson, Julie. 2010. Rights groups slam EU free trade deal with Colombia. *Deutsche Welle*, March 11. Available at: http://www.dw.com/en/rights-groups-sla m-eu-free-trade-deal-with-colombia/a-5339801

Greven, Thomas. 2005. Die Verankerung von Arbeitnehmerrechten in bilateralen und regionalen Handels- und Investitionsabkommen. In *FES Briefing Paper*. Berlin: Friedrich Ebert Stiftung.

Grossman, Gene M., and Elhanan Helpman. 1994. Protection for Sale. *The American Economic Review* 84 (4):833-850.

Grynberg, Roman, and Veniana Qalo. 2006. Labour Standards in US and EU Preferential Trading Arrangements. *Journal of World Trade* 40 (4):619-653.

Guber, Deborah, and Christopher Bosso. 2010. Past the Tipping Point? Public Discourse and the Role of the Environmental Movement in the Post-Bush Era. In *Environmental Policy: New Directions for the Twenty-First Century*, edited by N. J. Vig and M. E. Kraft. Washington, D.C.: Congressional Quarterly Press.

Hacker, Jacob S. , and Paul Pierson. 2010. Winner-Take-All Politics: Public Policy, Political Organization, and the Precipitous Rise of Top Incomes in the United States. *Politics & Society* 38 (2):152-204.

Hacker, Jacob S., and Paul Pierson. 2010. *Winner-Take-All Politics: How Washington Made the Rich Richer - and Turned Its Back on the Middle Class*. New York: Simon & Schuster.

Hafner-Burton, Emilie. 2005. Trading Human Rights: How Preferential Trade Agreements Influence Government Repression. *International Organization* 59 (3):593–629.

———. 2009. *Forced to be good: why trade agreements boost human rights*. Ithaca and London: Cornell University Press.

Haggard, Stephan. 1988. The institutional foundations of hegemony: explaining the Reciprocal Trade Agreements Act of 1934. *International Organization* 42 (1):91-119.

Haggard, Stephan, and Robert R. Kaufman. 1995. *The Political Economy of Democratic Transitions*. Princeton: Princeton University Press.

Haggard, Stephan, and Steven B. Webb. 1994. *Voting for Reform: Democracy, Political Liberalization, and Economic Adjustment*. Oxford: Oxford University Press.

Hall, Peter A. 1998. Heterogeneous preferences and the practice of group representation in U.S. trade policy. In *Constituent interests and U.S. trade policies*, edited by A. V. Deardorff and R. M. Stern. Ann Arbor: University of Michigan Press.

———. 2013. Tracing the Progress of Process Tracing. *European political science* 12 (1):20-30.

Hamdan, Fouad. 2006. Yes to Global Trade – But Protect our Planet. In *Speech at the Conference "EU Trade on Trial" in Brussels, November 23, 2006*. Brussels: Friends of the Earth Europe.

Hamilton, Daniel S. 2014. America's Mega-Regional Trade Diplomacy: Comparing TPP and TTIP. *The International Spectator* 49 (1):81–97.

———. 2014. *The Geopolitics of TTIP: Repositioning the Transatlantic Relationship for a Changing World*. Washington, D.C.: Center for Transatlantic Relations.

Harrison, James, Mirela Barbu, Liam Campling, and Franz Christian Ebert. 2018. Labour Standards Provisions in EU Free Trade Agreements: Reflections on the European Commission's Reform Agenda. *World Trade Review*.

Harrison, James, Mirela Barbu, Liam Campling, Ben Richardson, and Adrian Smith. 2018. Governing Labour Standards through Free Trade Agreements: Limits of the European Union's Trade and Sustainable Development Chapters. *Journal of Common Market Studies*.

Haworth, Nigel, Stephen Hughes, and Rorden Wilkinson. 2005. The international labour standards regime: a case study in global regulation. *Environment and Planning* 37 (11):1939-1953.

Henisz, Witold J., and Edward D. Mansfield. 2006. Votes and Vetoes: The Political Determinants of Commercial Openness. *International Studies Quarterly* 50 (1):189-212.

Hepple, Bob. 2008. Enforcement: the law and politics of cooperation and compliance. In *Social and Labour Rights in a Global Context. International and Comparative Perspectives*, edited by B. Hepple. Cambridge: Cambridge University Press.

Heydon, Kenneth, and Stephen Woolcock. 2009. *The rise of bilateralism: Comparing American, European and Asian approaches to preferential trade agreements*. New York: United Nations University Press.

Hilary, John. 2014. European Trade Unions and Free Trade: Between International Solidarity and Perceived Self-Interest. *Globalizations* 11 (1):47-57.

Hirsch, Steve. 2007. Labor, greens denounce trade policy. *Washington Post*, February 14. Available at: http://www.citizenstrade.org/ctc/wp-content/uploads/2011/05/washtimes_laborgreensdenouncetpa_02142007.pdf

Hitt, Greg. 2006. Washington, Seoul Face a Thorny Issue. *Wall Street Journal*, July 10. Available at: http://www.wsj.com/articles/SB115248923871401893

Hix, Simon. 2013. Why the 2014 European Elections Matter: Ten Key Votes in the 2009–2013 European Parliament. *SIEPS European Policy Analysis*. September 2013: 15epa.

Hix, Simon, Noury G. Abdul, and Gérard Roland. 2007. *Democratic Politics in the European Parliament*. Cambridge: Cambridge University Press.

Hix, Simon, and Abdul Noury. 2009. After Enlargement: Voting Patterns in the Sixth European Parliament. *Legislative Studies Quarterly* 34 (2):159-174.

Hocking, Brian. 2004. Changing the terms of trade policy making: from the 'club' to the 'multistakeholder' model. *World Trade Review* 3 (1):3-26.

Hopewell, Kristen. 2015. Different paths to power: The rise of Brazil, India and China at the World Trade Organization. *Review of International Political Economy* 22 (2):311-338.

Horn, Henrik, Petros C. Mavroidis, and André Sapir. 2010. Beyond the WTO? An Anatomy of EU and US Preferential Trade Agreements. *The World Economy* 33 (11):1565-1588.

Hornbeck, J. F. 2005. The Dominican Republic-Central America-United States Free Trade Agreement (DR-CAFTA). In *CRS Report for Congress*. Washington, D.C.: Congressional Research Service.

Hornbeck, J. F., and William H. Cooper. 2013. Trade Promotion Authority (TPA) and the Role of Congress in Trade Policy. In *CRS Report for Congress*. Washington, D.C.: Congressional Research Service.

Howse, Robert, and Michael J. Trebilcock. 1996. The fair trade-free trade debate: Trade, labor, and the environment. *International Review of Law and Economics* 16 (1):61–79.

Hughes, Steve, and Rorden Wilkinson. 1998. International labour standards and world trade: No role for the world trade organization? *New Political Economy* 3 (3):375-389.

Hulse, Carl. 2008. House Votes to Put Off Trade Deal Bush Sought. *New York Times*, April 11. Available at: http://www.nytimes.com/2008/04/11/business/11trade.html?_r=0

Human Rights Watch. 2007. The US-Korea Free Trade Agreement. Annex 22-B: A Missed Opportunity on Workers' Rights in North Korea. Washington, D.C.: Human Rights Watch.

———. 2010. EU: Try to Improve Human Rights in North Korea. *Press Release*, June 14. Available at: https://www.hrw.org/news/2010/06/14/eu-try-improve-human-rights-north-korea

Ikenberry, G. John, David A. Lake, and Michael Mastanduno. 1988. Introduction: approaches to explaining American foreign economic policy. *International Organization* 42 (1):1-14.

ILO. 2017. Handbook on Assessment of Labour Provisions in Trade and Investment Arrangements. Geneva: International Labour Organisation.

ILO, and IILS. 2013. Social Dimension of Free Trade Agreements. Geneva: International Labour Organization and International Institute for Labour Studies.

Inside US Trade. 2001. Zoellick lays out deliberate approach to Jordan, Vietnam. *Inside US Trade*, February 2. Available at:

———. 2002. U.S. looks for Fines, Sanctions Mix for Chile, Singapore FTAs. *Inside US Trade*, October 25. Available at:

———. 2003. Administration faces tough fight for textile Republican votes on CAFTA. *Inside US Trade*, January 2. Available at:

———. 2003. Baucus proposes new CAFTA environment rules to bolster U.S. position. *Inside US Trade*, October 17. Available at:

———. 2003. CAFTA negotiators likely to meet on agriculture this month. *Inside US Trade*, August 8. Available at:

———. 2003. House Democrats criticize U.S. Labor Proposal in CAFTA as Inadequate. *Inside US Trade*, May 16. Available at:

———. 2003. Major CAFTA issues unresolevd as U.S., others announce conclusion. *Inside US Trade*, December 19. Available at:

———. 2003. Senators call for improved CAFTA labor, environmental standards. *Inside US Trade*, November 28. Available at:

———. 2003. U.S. tables CAFTA agriculture, industrial market access proposals. *Inside US Trade*, May 30. Available at:

———. 2003. Vargo warns CAFTA delay could threaten 2004 congressional vote. *Inside US Trade*, December 12. Available at:

———. 2004. Ecuador, Peru settle outstanding issues, will be included in FTA talks. *Inside US Trade*, May 7. Available at:

———. 2004. Peru, Ecuador could be dropped from Andean FTA over Investment. *Inside US Trade*, October 8. Available at:

———. 2004. U.S. hints at delaying sanctions decision after new promises. *Inside US Trade*, March 26. Available at:

———. 2004. U.S.-Andean FTA talks begin next week, deadline hinges on fast track. *Inside US Trade*, May 14. Available at:

———. 2004. U.S., Costa Rica settle insurance, textile issues in FTA talks. *Inside US Trade*, January 30. Available at:

———. 2004. USTR says no changes to CAFTA text on labor, as AFL-CIO gears up for fight. *Inside US Trade*, February 27. Available at:

———. 2005. CAFTA countries lay out labor enforcement plan, seek more funding. *Inside US Trade*, April 8. Available at:

———. 2005. Ecuador presses for better FTA treatment for flowers, canned tuna. *Inside US Trade*, February 11. Available at:

———. 2005. Levin sees little USTR Willingness to compromise on labor in FTAs. *Inside US Trade*, November 11. Available at:

———. 2005. No definite date set for conclusion of Andean FTA talks. *Inside US Trade*, October 28. Available at:

———. 2005. U.S. warns Ecuador of possible Andean FTA exclusion over labor. *Inside US Trade*, October 7. Available at:

———. 2005. U.S., Andean talks adjourn after achieving most progress with Peru. *Inside US Trade*, November 25. Available at:

———. 2005. U.S., Andeans agree to intensify FTA work, hope to finish by mid-November. *Inside US Trade*, September 30. Available at:

———. 2005. Unions say they will punish Democrats for supporting DR-CAFTA deal. *Inside US Trade*, July 29. Available at:

———. 2005. USTR delays preliminary decisions on Andean Trade Benefits. *Inside US Trade*, January 21. Available at:

———. 2005. Vargo says major work remains in key areas of the Andean FTA. *Inside US Trade*, March 25. Available at:

———. 2006. Portman to stick to labor provisions outlined in Fast Track. *Inside US Trade*, February 10. Available at:

———. 2006. U.S. freezes Ecuador FTA after government cancels occidental contract. *Inside US Trade*, May 19. Available at:

———. 2006. U.S., Colombia beef unresolved as notification to Congress lags. *Inside US Trade*, August 4. Available at:

———. 2007. Environmental groups laud new Peru language as first step. *Inside US Trade*, June 29. Available at:

———. 2007. Levin skeptical of FTA labor side letters in Schwab Meeting. *Inside US Trade*, January 26. Available at:

———. 2007. Rangel unveils Democratic trade policy principles to administration. *Inside US Trade*, March 27. Available at:

———. 2007. Rangel, Levin say conceptual agreement not enough for Colombia FTA. *Inside US Trade*, May 11. Available at:

———. 2007. Schwab says FTA labor talks focused on substance, not form. *Inside US Trade*, January 19. Available at:

———. 2008. New Peru FTA Decrees Anger Civil Society Over Labor, Environment. *Inside US Trade*, July 4. Available at:

———. 2015. EU pushes new environmental rules, but without enforceability. *Inside US Trade*, February 13. Available at:

———. 2016. Malmstrom Non-Committal on Enforcement for TTIP Labor, Environment Provisions. *Inside US Trade*, July 7. Available at:

Irwin, Douglas A. 1994. The Political Economy of Free Trade: Voting in the British General Election of 1906. *The Journal of Law and Economics* 37 (1):75-108.

———. 1996. Industry or class cleavages over trade policy? Evidence from the British General Election of 1923. In *The Political Economy of Trade Policy: Papers in Honor of Jagdish Bhagwati*, edited by J. N. Bhagwati, R. C. Feenstra, G. M. Grossman and D. A. Irwin. Cambridge: MIT Press.

———. 2015. *Free Trade under Fire*. Princeton: Princeton University Press.

Islam, Shada. 1994. Europe: EC Row Brewing over Trade and Labor Standards Link. *Inter Press Service*, January 27. Available at:

Jacoby, Wade, and Sophie Meunier. 2010. Europe and the management of globalization. *Journal of European Public Policy* 17 (3):299–317.

Jaffe, Adam B., Steven R. Peterson, Paul R. Portney, and Robert N. Stavins. 1995. Environmental Regulation and the Competitiveness of U.S. Manufacturing: What Does the Evidence Tell Us? *Journal of Economic Literature* 33 (1):132-163.

Janusch, Holger. 2015. Labor Standards in U.S. Trade Politics. *Journal of World Trade* 49 (6):1047-1072.

Jensen, Nathan M. 2006. *Nation-States and the Multinational Corporation: A Political Economy of Foreign Direct Investment*. Princeton: Princeton University Press.

Jinnah, Sikina, and Julia Kennedy. 2011. A New Era of Trade-Environment Politics: Learning from US Leadership and its Consequences Abroad. *The Whitehead Journal of Diplomacy and International Relations* 12 (1):95-109.

Jinnah, Sikina, and Elisa Morgera. 2013. Environmental Provisions in American and EU Free Trade Agreements: A Preliminary Comparison and Research Agenda. *Review of European Community & International Environmental Law* 22 (3):324-339.

Johnson, Ailish. 2009. EU-ILO relations. Between regional and global governance. In *The European Union and the Social Dimension of Globalization. How the EU Influences the World*, edited by J. Orbie and L. Tortell. Abingdon: Routledge.

Jones, Kent. 2010. *The Doha Blues: Institutional Crisis and Reform in the WTO*. Oxford: Oxford University Press.

Jones, Vivian C. 2015. Generalized System of Preferences: Background and Renewal Debate. In *CRS Report for Congress*. Washington, D.C.: Congressional Research Service.

Kagan, Robert A. 2003. *Adversial Legalism. The American Way of Law*. Harvard: Harvard University Press.

Kahler, Miles, and David A. Lake. 2003. *Governance in a Global Economy: Political Authority in Transition*. Princeton: Princeton University Press.

Kahn-Nisser, Sara. 2016. A Matter of Degree: Europeanization, ILO Treaty Ratification and Labour Standards in Europe. *Journal of Contemporary European Studies* 24 (3):356-374.

Karol, David. 2000. Divided Government and U.S. Trade Policy: Much Ado About Nothing? *International Organization* 54 (04):825-844.

Karp, Larry. 2011. The Environment and Trade. *Annual Review of Resource Economics* 3:397–417.

Katzenstein, P. J. 1977. *Between Power and Plenty: Foreign Economic Policies of Advanced Industrial States*. Madison: University of Wisconsin Press.

Katzenstein, Peter J. 1977. Conclusion: domestic structures and strategies of foreign economic policy. *International Organization* 31 (04):879-920.

Keech, William R., and Kyoungsan Pak. 1995. Partisanship, Institutions, and Change in American Trade Politics. *The Journal of Politics* 57 (04):1130-1142.

Kelemen, Daniel R., and Eric C. Sibbitt. 2004. The Globalization of American Law. *International Organization* 58 (1):103-136.

Kelemen, Daniel R., and David Vogel. 2010. Trading Places: The Role of the United States and the European Union in International Environmental Politics. *Comparative Political Studies* 43 (4):427–456.

Kelemen, R. Daniel. 2010. Globalizing European Union environmental policy. *Journal of European Public Policy* 17 (3):335-349.

———. 2011. *Eurolegalism. The Transformation of Law and Regulation in the European Union.* Cambridge: Harvard University Press.

Kelemen, R. Daniel, and Tim Knievel. 2015. The United States, the European Union, and international environmental law: The domestic dimensions of green diplomacy. *International Journal of Constitutional Law* 13 (4):945-965.

Kerremans, Bart. 1999. The US Debate on Trade Negotiating Authority between 1994 and 1999. *Journal of World Trade* 33 (5):49-85.

Kerremans, Bart, and Myriam Martins Gistelinck. 2009. Interest Aggregation, Political Parties, Labour Standards and Trade: Differences in the US and EU Approaches to the Inclusion of Labour Standards in International Trade Agreements. *European foreign affairs review* 14 (5):683–701.

Keune, Maarten. 2009. EU enlargement and social standards. Exporting the European social model? In *The European Union and the Social Dimension of Globalization. How the EU influences the world*, edited by J. Orbie and L. Tortell. Abingdon: Routledge.

Kim, Moonhawk. 2012. Ex Ante Due Diligence: Formation of PTAs and Protection of Labor Rights. *International Studies Quarterly* 56 (4):704-719.

Kim, Soo Yeon, Edward D. Mansfield, and Helen V. Milner. 2016. Regional Trade Governance. In *The Oxford Handbook of Comparative Regionalism*, edited by T. Börzel and T. Risse. Oxford: Oxford University Press.

King, Neil Jr. 2004. Kerry Would Seek Tighter Standards Governing CAFTA. *The Wallstreet Journal*, June 1. Available at: http://www.wsj.com/articles/SB10857763 8109124157

Kirk, Ron. 2010. Tough Trade Enforcement Supports Jobs for American Workers. *White House Blog*. Available at: https://www.whitehouse.gov/blog/2010/07/30/tough-trade-enforcement-supports-jobs-american-workers

Kissack, Robert. 2009. Writing a new normative standard? EU member states and ILO conventions. In *The European Union and the Social Dimension of Globalization: How the EU Influences the World*, edited by J. Orbie and L. Tortell. Abingdon: Routledge.

———. 2011. The Performance of the European Union in the International Labour Organization. *Journal of European Integration* 33 (6):651-665.

Klein, Rick. 2005. House Passes Free-Trade Agreement in Tight Vote. *The Boston Globe*, July 28. Available at: http://archive.boston.com/news/nation/washington/articles/2005/07/28/house_passes_free_trade_agreement_in_tight_vote/

Kohl, Tristan, Steven Brakman, and Harry Garretsen. 2016. Do Trade Agreements Stimulate International Trade Differently? Evidence from 296 Trade Agreements. *The World Economy* 39 (1):97-131.

Kotz, David M. 2015. *The Rise and Fall of Neoliberal Capitalism*. Cambridge: Harvard University Press.

Kraft, Michael E., and Sheldon Kamieniecki. 2007. *Business and Environmental Policy: Corporate Interests in the American Political System*. Cambridge: MIT Press.

Krasner, Stephen D. 1977. US Commercial and Monetary Policy: Unravelling the Paradox of External Strength and Internal Weakness. *International Organization* 31 (4):635-671.

———. 1978. *Defending the National Interest: Raw Materials Investments and U.S. Foreign Policy*. Princeton: Princeton University Press.

Krugman, Paul R. 1993. The Narrow and Broad Arguments for Free Trade. *The American Economic Review* 83 (2):362-366.

Krupa, Peter. 2007. E.U. Negotiations Launch, So Does Opposition. *Tico Times*, October 26. Available at: http://www.ticotimes.net/2007/10/26/e-u-negotiations-launch-so-does-opposition

Kucik, Jeffrey. 2012. The Domestic Politics of Institutional Design: Producer Preferences over Trade Agreement Rules. *Economics and Politics* 24 (2):95–118.

Kull, Steven. 2005. Americans on CAFTA and US Trade Policy: The PIPA/Knowledge Networks Polls.

La Nación. 2009. Jefe negociador de Costa Rica ve complicada posición de Unión Europea; 'Posición de UE es complicada'. *La Nación*, March 25. Available at:

———. 2010. Daniel Ortega fustiga Acuerdo con la Unión Europea. *La Nación*, May 1. Available at: http://www.nacion.com/economia/Daniel-Ortega-Acuerdo-Union-Europea_0_1119688065.html

Labor Advisory Committee. 2007. The U.S.-Korea Free Trade Agreement. Report of the Labor Advisory Committee for Trade Negotiations and Trade Policy (LAC). Washington, D.C.: LAC.

Lacey, Marc. 2001. Bush Seeking to Modify Pact on Trade With Jordan. *New York Times*, April 11. Available at: http://www.nytimes.com/2001/04/11/world/bush-seeking-to-modify-pact-on-trade-with-jordan.html

Lake, David A. 1988. The state and American trade strategy in the pre-hegemonic era. *International Organization* 42 (01):33-58.

———. 2009. Open economy politics: A critical review. *Review of International Organisation* 4 (3):219-244.

Lamy, Pascal. 1999. The EU's approach to trade and core labour standards in the New WTO Round. *Speech to the ICFTU, Seattle*, November 29. Available at:

Langille, Brian A. 1997. Eight Ways to think about International Labour Standards. *Journal of World Trade* 31 (4):27-53.

———. 2005. Core Labour Rights - The True Story (Reply to Alston). *European Journal of International Law* 16 (3):409-437.

Lee, Donna, and Rorden Wilkinson. 2007. *The WTO after Hong Kong: Progress in, and Prospects for, the Doha Development Agenda*. Abingdon: Routledge.

Lee, Eddy. 1997. Globalization and Labour Standards: a review of issues. *International Labour Review* 136 (2):173-189.

Lee, Frances E. 2016. *Insecure Majorities: Congress and the Perpetual Campaign*. Chicago: University of Chicago Press.

Lee, Thea M. 2006. Testimony on the Proposed U.S.-South Korea Free Trade Agreement. Submitted by the American Federation of Labor and Congress of Industrial Organizations. Washington, D.C.: American Federation of Labor and Congress of Industrial Organizations.

Leeg, Tobias. 2018. Negotiating sustainable trade: explaining the difference in social standards in US and EU preferential trade agreements. *Contemporary Politics* 24 (4):398-417.

Leeg, Tobias 2014. Normative Power Europe? The EU in the Negotiations on a Free Trade Agreement with India. *European foreign affairs review* 19 (3):335-355.

Lerer, Lisa, and Victoria McGrane. 2008. Venezuela scolds Bush over Colombia deal. *Politico*, September 4. Available at: http://www.politico.com/story/2008/04/venezuela-scolds-bush-over-colombia-deal-009473

Levendusky, Matthew. 2009. *The Partisan Sort: How Liberals Became Democrats and Conservatives Became Republicans*. Chicago: University of Chicago Press.

Levin, Sander M. 2002. The FTAA: A Chance to Shape the Rules of International Trade. *Economic Perspectives: An Electronic Journal of the US. Department of State* 7 (3):37-40.

Lichtenstein, Nelson. 2010. Ideology and Interest on the Social Policy Home Front. In *The Presidency of George W. Bush: A First Historical Assessment*, edited by J. E. Zelizer. Princeton: Princeton University Press.

Lohmann, Susanne, and Sharyn O'Halloran. 1994. Divided government and US trade policy: theory and evidence. *International Organization* 48 (4):595-632.

Los Angeles Times. 2005. U.S., Others Agree to Rework CAFTA Rules. *Los Angeles Times*, July 20. Available at: http://articles.latimes.com/2005/jul/20/business/fi-cafta20

Lundsgaarde, Erik. 2013. *The Domestic Politics of Foreign Aid*. Abingdon: Routledge.

Lütz, Susanne. 2011. Back to the future? The domestic sources of transatlantic regulation. *Review of International Political Economy* 18 (4):iii-xxii.

Madani, Dorsati. 1999. A Review of the Role and Impact of Export Processing Zones. In *Policy Research Working Papers*. Washington, D.C.: World Bank Group.

Magee, Stephen P. 1980. Three Simple Test of the Stolper Samuelson Theorem. In *Issues in International Economics*, edited by P. Oppenheimer. London: Oriel Press London.

Magee, Stephen P., William A. Brock, and Leslie Young. 1989. *Black Hole Tariffs and Endogenous Policy Theory*. New York: Cambridge University Press.

Mahoney, James, and Gary Goertz. 2006. A Tale of Two Cultures: Contrasting Quantitative and Qualitative Research. *Political Analysis* 14 (3):227-249.

Mandelson, Peter. 2005. Open markets, open trade: Europe's global challenge. *Speech at Market Access Symposium, Brussels*, September 19.

———. 2006. Trade policy and Decent Work. *Intervention by Peter Mandelson at the EU Decent Work Conference*, Brussels, December 5. Available at:

Manger, Mark S. 2009. *Investing in Protection. The Politics of Preferential Trade Agreements between North and South*. Cambridge: Cambridge University Press.

Manger, Mark S., and Kenneth C. Shadlen. 2012. Political Trade Dependence and North–South Trade Agreements. *International Studies Quarterly* 58 (1):79-91.

Mann, Michael. 1996. Brittan bids to dovetail trade rules with environment laws. *Politico*, February 21. Available at: http://www.politico.eu/article/brittan-bids-to-dovetail-trade-rules-with-environment-laws/

Manners, Ian. 2002. Normative Power Europe: A Contradiction in Terms? *Journal of Common Market Studies* 40 (2):235-258.

———. 2009. The Social Dimension of EU Trade Policies: Reflections from a Normative Power Europe Perspective. *European foreign affairs review* 14 (5):785-803.

———. 2011. The European Union's normative power. In *Normative Power Europe: Empirical and Theoretical Perspectives*, edited by R. G. Whitman. Basingstoke: Palgrave.

Mansfield, Edward D., and Marc L. Busch. 1995. The political economy of nontariff barriers: a cross-national analysis. *International Organization* 49 (4):723 - 749.

Mansfield, Edward D., Helen V. Milner, and Jon C. Pevehouse. 2007. Vetoing Cooperation: The Impact of Veto Players on Preferential Trading Arrangements. *British Journal of Political Science* 37 (3):403 - 432.

Mansfield, Edward D., Helen V. Milner, and Peter B. Rosendorff. 2002. Why Democracies Cooperate More: Electoral Control and International Trade Agreements. *International Organization* 56 (3):477-513.

Manyin, Mark E. 2007. South Korea-U.S. Economic Relations. In *CRS Report for Congress*. Washington, D.C.: Congressional Research Service.

Manyin, Mark E., and Dick K. Nanto. 2011. The Kaesong North-South Korean Industrial Complex. In *CRS Report for Congress*. Washington, D.C.: Congressional Research Service.

Marx, Axel, Brecht Lein, and Nicolas Brando. 2016. The Protection of Labour Rights in Trade Agreements: The Case of the EU-Colombia Agreement *Journal of World Trade* 50 (4):587-610.

Mayhew, David R. 1974. *Congress: The Electoral Connection*. Yale: Yale University Press.

McCormick, J. 1995. *The Global Environmental Movement*. Bloominton: John Wiley & Sons Incorporated.

Melo Araujo, Billy A. 2013. Intellectual Property and the EU's Deep Trade Agenda. *Journal of International Economic Law* 16 (2):439-474.

Menon, Anand, and Martin A. Schain. 2006. *Comparative Federalism: The European Union and the United States in Comparative Perspective*. Oxford: Oxford University Press.

Meunier, Sophie. 2000. What Single Voice? European Institutions and EU–U.S. Trade Negotiations. *International Organization* 54 (1):103–135.

———. 2005. *Trading Voices: The European Union in International Commercial Negotiations*. Princeton: Princeton University Press.

———. 2007. Managing Globalization? The EU in International Trade Negotiations. *Journal of Common Market Studies* 45 (4):905–926.

Milner, Helen V. 1988. *Resisting Protectionism: Global Industries and the Politics of International Trade*. Princeton: Princeton University Press.

———. 1991. Resisting the Protectionist Temptation: Industry and the Making of Trade Policy in France and the United States during the 1970s. In *International Political Economy: Perspectives on Global Power and Wealth*, edited by J. Frieden and D. A. Lake. New York: St. Martin's.

———. 1999. The Political Economy of International Trade. *Annual Review of Political Science* 2:91-114.

———. 2006. Why multilateralism? Foreign aid and domestic principal-agent problems. In *Delegation and Agency in International Organizations*, edited by D. G. Hawkins, D. A. Lake, D. L. Nielson and M. J. Tierney. New York: Cambridge University Press.

Milner, Helen V., and Benjamin Judkins. 2004. Partisanship, Trade Policy, and Globalization: Is There a Left–Right Divide on Trade Policy? *International Studies Quarterly* 48 (1):95-120.

Milner, Helen V., and Keiko Kubota. 2005. Why the Move to Free Trade? Democracy and Trade Policy in the Developing Countries. *International Organization* 59 (1):107-143.

Milner, Helen V., and Edward D. Mansfield. 2012. *Votes, Vetoes, and the Political Economy of International Trade Agreements*. Princeton: Princeton University Press.

Milner, Helen V., and Peter B. Rosendorff. 1997. Democratic Politics and International Trade Negotiations: Elections and Divided Government as Constraints on Trade Liberalization. *Journal of Conflict Resolution* 41 (1):117-146.

Milner, Helen V., and Dustin H. Tingley. 2010. The Political Economy of U.S. Foreign Aid: American Legislators and the Domestic Politics of Aid. *Economics & Politics* 22 (2):200-232.

Mincetur. 2009. Acuerdo Comercial entre la Unión Europea - Peru y Colombia. Tercera Ronda de Negociaciones, Bruselas, Bélgica del 4 al 8 de Mayo 2009: Ministerio de Comercio Exterior y Turismo de Peru.

Moravcsik, Andrew. 1993. Introduction: Integrating International and Domestic Theories of International Bargaining. In *Double-Edged Diplomacy: International Bargaining and Domestic Politics* edited by P. B. Evans, H. K. Jacobson and R. D. Putnam. Berkley and Los Angeles: University of California Press.

———. 1997. Taking preferences seriously: A liberal theory of international politics. *International Organization* 51 (4):513-553.

Motaal, Abdel. 2001. Multilateral Environmental Agreements (MEAs) and WTO Rules. *Journal of World Trade* 35 (6):1215-1233.

Müller-Rommel, Ferdinand, and Thomas Poguntke, eds. 2002. *Green Parties in National Governments*. London: Frank Cass.

Murillo, Álvaro. 2007. Centroamérica y la UE discrepan hasta en el saludo. *El País*, October 31. Available at: http://internacional.elpais.com/internacional/2007/10/31/actualidad/1193785206_850215.html

———. 2008. La corte de La Haya, nuevo escollo entre la UE y Centroamérica. *El País*, March 14. Available at: http://internacional.elpais.com/internacional/2008/03/14/actualidad/1205449203_850215.html

———. 2008. Stagno critica 'hipocresía' de UE contra armamento. *La Nación*, April 11. Available at: http://www.nacion.com/nacional/Stagno-critica-hipocresia-UE-armamento_0_969703066.html

Mutch, Robert E. 2016. *Campaign Finance: What Everyone Needs to Know*. Oxford: Oxford University Press.

Narlikar, Amrita. 2004. The ministerial process and power dynamics in the World Trade Organization: understanding failure from Seattle to Cancún. *New Political Economy* 9 (3):413-428.

———. 2010. New powers in the club: the challenges of global trade governance. *International Affairs* 86 (3):717-728.

Nassmacher, Karl-Heinz. 2014. The Established Anglophone Democracies. In *Funding of Political Parties and Election Campaigns. A Handbook on Political Finance*, edited by E. Falguera, S. Jones and M. Ohman. Stockholm: International Institute for Democracy and Electoral Assistance.

Needham, Vicki. 2013. US, Guatemala resolve labor enforcement concerns. *The Hill*, April 11. Available at: http://thehill.com/policy/finance/293511-us-guatemala-resolve-labor-enforcement-concerns

———. 2014. US ramps up pressure on Guatemala over labor rights. *The Hill*, September 18. Available at: http://thehill.com/policy/finance/218225-us-moves-forward-on-labor-case-with-guatemala

———. 2014. US trade officials give Guatemala more time to install labor overhaul. *The Hill*, August 25. Available at: http://thehill.com/policy/finance/215913-us-trade-officials-give-guatemala-more-time-to-install-labor-overhaul

New York Times. 2005. Applauding the Cafta 15. *New York Times*, July 29. Available at: http://www.nytimes.com/2005/07/29/opinion/applauding-the-cafta-15.html

Newell, Peter. 2005. The Political Economy of Trade and the Environment. In *The Political Economy of International Trade in the Twenty-First Century. Actors, Issues and Regional Dynamics*, edited by D. Kelly and W. Grant. New York: Palgrave Macmillian.

Nicolaïdis, Kalypso. 1998. Minimizing agency costs in two-level games: Lessons from the trade authority controversies in the United States and the European Union. In *Negotiating on Behalf of Others*, edited by R. H. Mnookin and L. E. Susskind. Thousand Oaks: Sage.

Nielson, Daniel L. 2003. Supplying Trade Reform: Political Institutions and Liberalization in Middle-Income Presidential Democracies. *American Journal of Political Science* 47 (3):470-491.

Novitz, Tonia. 2009. In search of a coherent social policy. EU import and export of ILO labour standards? In *The European Union and the Social Dimension of Globalization. How the EU influences the World*, edited by J. Orbie and L. Tortell. Abingdon: Routledge.

O'Brien, Robert. 2000. Workers and world order: the tentative transformation of the international union movement. *Review of International Studies* 26 (04):533-555.

O'Halloran, Sharyn. 1994. *Politics, Process and American Trade Policy*. Ann Arbor: University of Michigan Press.

O'Reilly, Robert F. 2005. Veto Points, Veto Players, and International Trade Policy. *Comparative Political Studies* 38 (6):652-675.

Oatley, Thomas. 2010. *International Political Economy: Interests and Institutions in the Global Economy*. New York: Longman.

Obach, B. K. 2004. *Labor and the Environmental Movement: The Quest for Common Ground*. Cambridge: MIT Press.

Oberthür, Sebastian, and Claire Roche Kelly. 2008. EU Leadership in International Climate Policy: Achievements and Challenges. *The International Spectator* 43 (3):35-50.

OECD. 1996. *Trade, Employment, and Labour Standards: A Study of Core Workers' Rights and International Trade*. Paris: Organization for Economic Cooperation and Development.

———. 2007. *Environment and Regional Trade Agreements*. Paris: OECD Publishing.

Olivet, Cecilia, and Paulina Novo. 2011. Time for Europe to put values and human rights above commercial advantage. Policy Brief: Why EU–Colombia/Peru Free Trade Agreements should not be ratified. In *Policy Brief*. Amsterdam: Transnational Institute.

Olsen, Kelly. 2007. South Korea, EU Launch Free Trade Talks. *Washington Post*, May 6. Available at: http://www.washingtonpost.com/wp-dyn/content/article/2007/05/05/AR2007050501260.html

———. 2007. U.S., South Korea Reach Free Trade Deal. *Washington Post*, April 2. Available at: http://www.washingtonpost.com/wp-dyn/content/article/2007/04/02/AR2007040200273_pf.html

Olson, Mancur. 1965. *The logic of Collective Action. Public Goods and the Theory of Groups*. Harvard: Harvard University Press.

Orbie, Jan, and Olufemi Babarinde. 2008. The Social Dimension of Globalization and EU Development Policy: Promoting Core Labour Standards and Corporate Social Responsibility. *Journal of European Integration* 30 (3):459-477.

Orbie, Jan, Martins Gistelinck, and Bart Kerremans. 2009. The social dimension of EU trade policies. In *The European Union and the Social Dimension of Globalization. How the EU influences the world*, edited by J. Orbie and L. Tortell. Abingdon: Routledge.

Orbie, Jan, Deborah Martens, Myriam Oehri, and Lore Van den Putte. 2016. Promoting sustainable development or legitimising free trade? Civil society mechanisms in EU trade agreements. *Third World Thematics: A TWQ Journal* 1 (4):526–546.

Orbie, Jan, and Lisa Tortell. 2009. From the social clause to social dimension of globalization. In *The EU and the Social Dimension of Globalization. How the EU influences the world*, edited by J. Orbie and L. Tortell. Abingdon: Routledge.

———. 2009. The New GSP Beneficiaries: Ticking the Box or Truly Consistent with ILO Findings. *European foreign affairs review* 14 (5):663-681.

Orbie, Jan, Lisa Tortell, Robert Kissack, Sieglinde Gstöhl, Jan Wouters, and Nicolas Hachez. 2009. JESP Symposium: The European Union's global social role. *Journal of European Social Policy* 19 (2):99–116.

Orbie, Jan, Hendrik Vos, and Liesbeth Taverniers. 2005. EU Trade Policy and a Social Clause: A Question of Competences? *Politique européenne* 17 (3):159-187.

Page, Benjamin I., and Martin Gilens. 2017. *Democracy in America?: What Has Gone Wrong and What We Can Do About It*. Chicago: University of Chicago Press.

Palmer, Doug. 2004. Colombia top priority in Andean trade talks - U.S. *Reuters*, September 29. Available at: http://www.citizenstrade.org/ctc/wp-content/upload s/2011/05/reuters_colombiapriority_09292004.pdf.

———. 2007. Bush trade agenda at risk as Democrats take over. *Washington Post*, January 4. Available at: http://www.washingtonpost.com/wp-dyn/content/article /2007/01/04/AR2007010400863_pf.html

Pearson, K. 2015. *Party Discipline in the U.S. House of Representatives*. Michigan: University of Michigan Press.

Peruvian Times. 2007. Peru president proposes creation of Environment Ministry. *Peruvian Times*, December 21. Available at: http://www.peruviantimes.com/21/pe ru-president-proposes-creation-of-environment-ministry/76/

Phillips, Leigh. 2009. Brussels' commitment to Latin American integration questioned. *EU observer*, September 30. Available at: https://euobserver.com/economi c/28749

———. 2009. Human rights no block to EU-Colombia talks. *EU observer*, May 4. Available at: https://euobserver.com/foreign/28062

Phillips, Nicola. 2007. The Limits of 'Securitization': Power, Politics and Process in US Foreign Economic Policy. *Government and Opposition* 42 (2):158–189.

Piccio, Daniela R. 2014. Northern, Western and Southern Europe. In *Funding of Political Parties and Election Campaigns. A Handbook on Political Finance*, edited by E. Falguera, S. Jones and M. Ohman. Stockholm: International Institute for Democracy and Electoral Assistance.

Pickel, Gert, and Susanne Pickel. 2009. Qualitative Interviews als Verfahren des Ländervergleichs. In *Methoden der vergleichenden Politikwissenschaft: Eine Einführung*, edited by S. Pickel, G. Pickel, H.-J. Lauth and D. Jahn. Wiesbaden: VS Verlag für Sozialwissenschaften.

Pierson, Paul, and Theda Skocpol. 2007. *The Transformation of American Politics: Activist Government and the Rise of Conservatism*. Princeton: Princeton University Press.

Pinto, Pablo M., and Santiago M. Pinto. 2008. The Politics of Investment: Partisanship and the sectoral Allocation of Foreign Direct Investment. *Economics and Politics* 20 (2):216-254.

Poletti, Arlo, and Dirk De Biévre. 2013. The political science of European trade policy: A literature review with a research outlook. *Comparative European Politics* 12 (1):101-119.

Poletti, Arlo, and Daniela Sicurelli. 2012. The EU as Promoter of Environmental Norms in the Doha Round. *West European Politics* 35 (4):911-932.

———. 2016. The European Union, Preferential Trade Agreements, and the International Regulation of Sustainable Biofuels. *JCMS: Journal of Common Market Studies* 54 (2):249-266.

Politi, James, Demetri Sevastopulo, and Jude Webber. 2018. Trump hails Canada-US deal to revamp Nafta 'historic'. *Financial Times*, October 1st. Available at: https://www.ft.com/content/8a43c9f4-c51e-11e8-8670-c5353379f7c2

Politi, James, Andrew Ward, and Edward Luce. 2008. Bush sets scene for Colombia trade fight. *Financial Times*, April 7. Available at: http://www.ft.com/intl/cms/s/0/8d439084-04dc-11dd-a2f0-000077b07658.html#axzz3wvKorAXx

Pollack, Mark , and Gregory Shaffer, eds. 2001. *Transatlantic Governance in the Global Economy*. Lanham, MD: Rowman & Littlefield.

Porges, Amelia. 2011. Dispute Settlement. In *Preferential Trade Agreement Policies for Development. A Handbook*, edited by J.-P. Chauffour and J.-C. Maur. Washington, D.C.: The World Bank.

Portela, C. 2009. *European Union Sanctions and Foreign Policy: When and Why Do They Work?* Abingdon: Routledge.

Portela, Clara, and Jan Orbie. 2014. Sanctions under the EU Generalised System of Preferences and foreign policy: coherence by accident? *Contemporary Politics* 20 (1):63-76.

Portman, Rob. 2005. Remarks of Ambassador Rob Portman, United States Trade Representative. *Speech at IDB Donor Conference*, Washington, D.C., July 19. Available at:

Postnikov, Evgeny. 2014. The design of social standards in EU and US preferential trade agreements. In *Handbook of the international political economy of trade*, edited by D. A. Deese. Cheltenham: Edward Elgar Publishing.

Postnikov, Evgeny, and Ida Bastiaens. 2014. Does dialogue work? The effectivness of labor standards in EU preferential trade agreements. *Journal of European Public Policy* 21 (6):923-940.

Pruzin, Daniel. 2002. Costa Rican Minister Says Government Open To Labor, Environmental Provisions in CAFTA. *Bloomberg International Trade Reporter*, October 17. Available at:

R. V., Anuradha 2011. Environment. In *Preferential Trade Agreement Policies for Development. A Handbook*, edited by J.-P. Chauffour and J.-C. Maur. Washington, D.C.: The World Bank.

Ramstad, Evan 2010. After Attack, South's Talks with U.S. Accelerated. *Wall Street Journal*, December 4. Available at: http://www.wsj.com/articles/SB100014240527 4870398900457565367205169803 4

Ramstad, Evan, and John W. Miller. 2010. South Korea and EU Near Free-Trade Pact. *Wall Street Journal*, March 25. Available at: http://www.wsj.com/articles/SB1 23789624042424463

Rangel. 2009. Moving Forward: A New, Bipartisan Trade Policy That Reflects American Values. *Harvard Journal on Legislation* 45 (2):377–419.

Ravenhill, John. 2010. The 'new East Asian regionalism': A political domino effect. *Review of International Organisation* 17 (2):178-208.

Reuters. 2004. No plans to change CAFTA labor provisions -US aide. *Reuters*, May 5. Available at: http://www.citizenstrade.org/ctc/wp-content/uploads/2011/05/re uters_caftalabor_may2004.pdf

―――. 2008. Colombia, Peru Presidents Urge Quick EU Trade Deal. *Reuters*, September 22. Available at: http://arhiva.dalje.com/en-economy/colombia-peru-presidents-urge-quick-eu-trade-deal/184861

Richards, John E. 1999. Toward a Positive Theory of International Institutions: Regulating International Aviation Markets. *International Organization* 53 (1):1-37.

Rickard, Stephanie J. 2015. Electoral Systems and Trade. In *The Oxford Handbook of the International Political Economy of Trade*, edited by L. L. Martin. Oxford: Oxford University Press.

Rittberger, Berthold. 2012. Institutionalizing Representative Democracy in the European Union: The Case of the European Parliament. *Journal of Common Market Studies* 50 (s1):18-37.

Rodrik, Dani. 1997. *Has Globalization Gone Too Far?* Washington, D.C.: Institute for International Economics.

Rogowski, Ronald. 1987. Trade and the variety of democratic institutions. *International Organization* 41 (2):203-223.

―――. 1989. *Commerce and Coalitions. How Trade Affects Domestic Alignments.* Princeton: Princeton University Press.

―――. 1999. Institutions as Constraints on Strategic Choice. In *Strategic Choice and International Relations*, edited by D. A. Lake and R. Powell. Princeton: Princeton University Press.

Rosen, Howard. 2004. Free Trade Agreements as Foreign Policy Tools: The US-Israel and US-Jordan FTAs In *Free Trade Agreements: US Strategies and Priorities*, edited by J. J. Schott. Washington, D.C.: Institute for International Economics.

Ross, George. 2011. European Center-Lefts and the Mazes of European Integration. In *What's Left of the Left. Democrats and Social Democrats in Challenging Times*, edited by J. Cronin, G. Ross and J. Shoch. Durham and London: Duke University Press.

Rowland, Kara. 2011. Three free-trade agreements linked to aid for workers. *Washington Times*, June 28. Available at: http://www.washingtontimes.com/news/2011/jun/28/iowa-obama-touts-economic-progress/?page=all

Sachs, Noah. 2006. Planning the Funeral at the Birth: Extended Producer Responsibility in the European Union and the United States. *Harvard Environmental Law Review* 30 (51):51-98.

Salazar-Xirinachs, Jose M. , and Jaime Granados. 2004. The US-Central America Free Trade Agreement: Opportunities and Challenges In *Free Trade Agreements: US Strategies and Priorities*, edited by J. J. Schott. Washington, D.C.: Institute for International Economics.

Sang-Hun, Choe. 2008. South Korea and U.S. reach deal on beef imports. *New York Times*, June 22. Available at: http://www.nytimes.com/2008/06/22/world/asia/22korea.html?mtrref=undefined&gwh=32B027F445364CE33467A4668786F12A&gwt=pay

———. 2009. Seoul Says European Trade Deal Is Near. *New York Times*, July 13. Available at: http://www.nytimes.com/2009/07/14/business/global/14trade.html?_r=0

Sanger, David E. 2001. Bush links Trade with Democracy at Quebec Talks. *New York Times*, April 22. Available at: http://www.nytimes.com/2001/04/22/world/bush-links-trade-with-democracy-at-quebec-talks.html

Sapir, André. 2007. Europe and the Global Economy. In *Fragmented Power: Europe and the Global Economy*, edited by A. Sapir. Brussels: Bruegel.

Sbragia, Alberta. 2010. The EU, the US, and trade policy: competitive interdependence in the management of globalization. *Journal of European Public Policy* 17 (3):368–382.

Schattschneider, Elmer E. 1935. *Politics, Pressures, and the Tariff*. New York: Prentice-Hall.

Scherrer, Christof. 1998. Protecting labor in the global economy: A social clause in trade agreements? *New Political Science* 20 (1):53-68.

Scherrer, Christof, Thomas Greven, Aaron Leopold, and Elisabeth Molinari. 2009. An Analysis of the relative Effectivness of Social and Environmental Norms in Free Trade Agreements. Brussels: European Parliament.

Schirm, Stefan A. 2010. Leaders in need of followers: Emerging powers in global governance. *European Journal of International Relations* 16 (2):197–221.

Schnietz, Karen E. 2000. The Institutional Foundation of U.S. Trade Policy: Revisiting Explanations for the 1934 Reciprocal Trade Agreements Act. *Journal of Policy History* 12 (4):417-444.

Schott, Jeffrey J. 2004. Assessing US FTA Policy. In *Free Trade Agreements: US Strategies and Priorities*, edited by J. J. Schott. Washington, D.C.: Institute for International Economics.

———. 2017. US Trade Policy Options in the Pacific Basin: Bigger Is Better. In *Policy Brief*. Washington, D.C.: Peterson Institute of International Economics.

Schott, Jeffrey J., Scott C. Bradford, and Thomas Moll. 2006. Negotiating the Korea–United States Free Trade Agreement. In *Policy Briefs in International Economics*. Washington, D.C.: Institute for International Economics.

Schott, Jeffrey J., and Cathleen Cimino. 2013. Crafting a Transatlantic Trade and Investment Partnership: What Can Be Done. In *Policy Briefs in International Economics*. Washington, D.C.: Peterson Institute for International Economics

Sek, Leonore. 2003. Trade Promotion Authority (Fast-Track Authority for Trade Agreements): Background and Developments in the 107th Congress. In *Issue Brief for Congress*. Washington, D.C.: Congressional Research Service.

Seligman, Dan. 2001. Transcript from a Panel Session at the Society of Environmental Journalists' 10th National Conference. *Speech at KING-TV Seattle*. Available at: http://www.sierraclub.org/trade/articles/debate.asp

Semuels, Alana, and Tom Hamburger. 2011. On South Korea trade deal, Obama and chamber are on same side. *Los Angeles Times*, January 24. Available at: http://articles.latimes.com/2011/jan/24/business/la-fi-korea-fta-20110125

Shaffer, Greg. 2003. *Defending Interests. Public-Private Partnerships in W.T.O. Litigation*. Washington, D.C.: Brookings Institution Press.

Shapiro, Hal. 2006. *Fast Track: A Legal, Historical, and Political Analysis International Law and Development*. Ardsley, NY: Transnational Publishers.

Shear, Michael D. 2017. Trump Will Withdraw U.S. From Paris Climate Agreement. *New York Times*, June 1st. Available at: https://www.nytimes.com/2017/06/01/climate/trump-paris-climate-agreement.html

Shoch, James. 2000. Contesting Globalization: Organized Labor, NAFTA, and the 1997 and 1998 Fast-Track Fights. *Politics & Society* 28 (1):119-150.

———. 2001. Organized Labor versus Globalization. NAFTA, Fast Track, and PNTR with China. In *Rekindling the Movement. Labor's Quest for Relevance in the Twenty-First Century*, edited by L. Turner, H. C. Katz and R. W. Hurd. Ithaca: Cornell University Press.

———. 2001. *Trading Blows: Party Competition and U.S. Trade Policy in a Globalizing Era*. Chapel Hill and London: University of North Carolina Press.

Sierra Club. 2011. Sierra Club Letter Opposing Korea Colombia Panama FTAs. *Letter to Congress*, October 6. Washington, D.C.: Sierra Club. Available at: http://www.citizen.org/documents/sierra-club-letter-opposing-korea-colombia-panama-ftas-october-2011.pdf.

———. 2015. TPP Text Analysis: Environment Chapter Fails to Protect the Environment. Washinton, D.C.: Sierra Club.

Sierra Club, and Friends of the Earth. 2008. Statement on the US-Colombia Free Trade Agreement. *Press Release*, March 12. Available at: www.citizenstrade.org/ctc/wp-content/uploads/2011/05/envirocolombiaFTAsign-onhouse.pdf

Siles-Brügge, Gabriel. 2013. The Power of Economic Ideas: A Constructivist Political Economy of EU Trade Policy. *Journal of Contemporary European Research* 9 (4):597-617.

———. 2014. *Constructing European Union Trade Policy. A Global Idea of Europe*. New York: Palgrave Macmillian.

———. 2014. Explaining the resilience of free trade: The Smooth-Hawley myth and the crisis. *Review of International Political Economy* 21 (3):535-574.

Singh, J.P. 2008. *Negotiation and the Global Information Economy*. Cambridge: Cambridge University Press.

Sokou, Katerina, and Howard Schneider. 2013. U.S. suspends Bangladesh's trade privileges due to labor concerns. *Washinton Post*, June 27. Available at: https://www.washingtonpost.com/business/economy/us-to-suspend-trade-privileges-with-bangladesh/2013/06/27/16171f08-df3d-11e2-963a-72d740e88c12_story.html

Song, Yeongkwan. 2011. KORUS FTA vs. Korea-EU FTA: Why the Differences? In *Academic Paper Series Vol. 6 No. 5*. Washington, D.C.: Korea Economic Institute.

Standing, Guy. 2008. The ILO: An Agency for Globalization? *Development and Change* 39 (3):355-384.

Stark, Pete. 2001. Don't Make Same Errors On This Trade Agreement. *Roll Call*, May 7. Available at:

Steffenson, Rebecca. 2005. *Managing EU-US Relations: Actors, Institutions and the New Transatlantic Agenda*. Manchester: Manchester University Press.

Stiles, Andrew. 2010. Business dials up trade efforts. *The Hill*, July 13. Available at: http://thehill.com/business-a-lobbying/108605-business-dials-up-free-trade-efforts

Stolper, Wolfgang, and Paul A. Samuelson. 1941. Protection and Real Wages. *Review of Economic Studies* 9 (1): 58–73.

Stout, David. 2008. Bush to Force Vote on Colombia Trade. *New York Times*, April 7. Available at: http://www.nytimes.com/2008/04/07/washington/07cnd-trade.html

Strauch, Nicolas, and Robertas Pogorelis. 2011. Electoral systems. The link between governance, elected members and voters. Brussels: European Parliament.

Suranovic, Steven. 2002. International Labour and Environmental Standards Agreements: Is This Fair Trade? *The World Economy* 25 (2):231-245.

———. 2010. *International Trade: Theory and Policy*. Nyack: Flat World Knowledge, L.L.C.

Swann, Christopher. 2005. Sugar lobby deal mooted to save trade pact. *Financial Times*, April 12. Available at: http://www.ft.com/intl/cms/s/0/caecfb9e-aaf0-11d9-98d7-00000e2511c8.html#axzz3yuKqURup

Swanson, Ian. 2007. Labor Groups Differ on Peru Free Trade Deal. *The Hill*, September 18. Available at: http://thehill.com/business-a-lobbying/3274-labor-groups-differ-on-peru-free-trade-deal

Teffer, Peter. 2015. EU wants promises on labour, environment in US trade pact. *EU observer*, November 6. Available at: https://euobserver.com/economic/131002

The Economic Times. 2009. Labour pangs likely to hold up India-EU free-trade agreement. *The Economic Times*, November 7. Available at: http://articles.economictimes.indiatimes.com/2009-11-07/news/28434950_1_india-eu-trade-india-and-eu-india-eu-free-trade-agreement

The Economist. 2007. Trade, timber and tribes. *The Economist*, October 4. Available at: http://www.economist.com/node/9910163

————. 2009. Low expectations exceeded. *The Economist*, April 30. Available at: http://www.economist.com/node/13578834

The Hankyoreh. 2007. Gov't says bracing itself for renegotiation on FTA. *The Hankyoreh*, May 23. Available at: http://english.hani.co.kr/arti/english_edition/e_business/211306.html

————. 2007. U.S. may seek FTA renegotiations on labor, environment. *The Hankyoreh*, May 12. Available at: http://english.hani.co.kr/arti/english_edition/e_business/208805.html

The White House. 2001. Bush Says Labor, Environmental Concerns Should Not Hamper Trade Deals. Washington, D.C.: Office of the Press Secretary.

————. 2001. The President's 2001 International Trade Agenda Washington, D.C.: Office of the Press Secretary.

Tico Times. 2010. EU and Central America begin new rounds of talk for association agreement, this time including Panama. *Tico Times*, October 7. Available at: http://www.ticotimes.net/2010/03/19/eu-and-central-america-begin-new-round-of-talks-for-association-agreement-this-time-including-panama

Toner, Robin. 2007. For Democrats, New Challenge in Age-Old Rift. *New York Times*, May 8. Available at: http://www.nytimes.com/2007/05/08/washington/08trade.html?_r=0&f

Trampusch, Christine, and Bruno Palier. 2016. Between X and Y: how process tracing contributes to opening the black box of causality. *New Political Economy* 21 (5):437-454.

Trottman, Melanie. 2010. Unions Make Vote Push. *Wall Street Journal*, October 4. Available at: http://www.wsj.com/articles/SB10001424052748703431604575521940172598182

Tsebelis, George. 1995. Decision Making in Political Systems: Veto Players in Presidentialism, Parliamentarism, Multicameralism and Multipartyism. *British Journal of Political Science* 25 (3):289-325.

Tsogas, George. 1999. Labour standards in international trade agreements: an assessment of the arguments. *The International Journal of Human Resource Management* 10 (2):351-375.

U.S. Chamber of Commerce. 2000. U.S. Chamber Hails Free Trade Talks with Chile. *Press Release*, November 29. Washington, D.C.: U.S. Chamber of Commerce. Available at: https://www.uschamber.com/press-release/us-chamber-hails-free-trade-talks-chile

————. 2001. U.S. Chamber Pulls Out All Stops For Trade Ad Campaign Starts Final Week Before Congress Votes. *Press Release*, November 28. Washington, D.C.: U.S. Chamber of Commerce. Available at: https://www.uschamber.com/press-release/us-chamber-pulls-out-all-stops-trade-ad-campaign-starts-final-week-congress-votes

————. 2003. Statement by U.S. Chamber Vice President for Asia Myron Brilliant before the International Trade Commission on the Impact of the United States-Singapore Free Trade Agreement. Washington, D.C.: U.S. Chamber of Commerce.

————. 2007. Chamber Welcomes Bipartisan Deal to Move Trade Agenda Forward. *Press Statement*, May 9. Washington, D.C.: U.S. Chamber of Commerce. Available at: https://www.uschamber.com/press-release/chamber-welcomes-bipartisan-deal-move-trade-agenda-forward

U.S. Department of Labor. 2012. Union members 2011. *News Release*, January 27. Available at: http://www.bls.gov/news.release/archives/union2_01272012.pdf.

UNCED. 1992. Agenda 21. The United Nations Programme of Action from Rio. Rio de Janeiro: United Nations Conference on Environment and Development.

UNICE. 1998. UNICE Comments on International Trade and Labour Standards. *Position paper*, June 11. Brussels: Union of Industrial and Employers' Confederation of Europe. Available at: https://www.businesseurope.eu/sites/buseur/files/media/imported/2002-03080-E.pdf.

————. 1999. UNICE and the WTO Millennium Round. *Executive Summary*, September 1999. Brussels: Union of Industrial and Employers' Confederations of Europe. Available at: https://www.businesseurope.eu/sites/buseur/files/media/imported/2002-03310-E.pdf.

————. 2001. The new WTO round. *UNICE Fact Sheets*, October 2001. Brussels: Union of Industrial and Employers' Confederations of Europe. Available at: https://www.businesseurope.eu/sites/buseur/files/media/imported/2002-03850-E.pdf.

————. 2006. UNICE Strategy on a EU Approach to Free Trade Agreements. *Position Paper*, December 7. Available at: http://www.bilaterals.org/?unice-strategy-on-an-eu-approach&lang=en

USCIB. 2001. Statement of the United States Council for International Business on Recommendations for a Broad-Based WTO Negotiation. May 10. Washington, D.C.: US Council for International Business. Available at: http://www.jmcti.org/2000round/US/USTR_comment/USCIB.pdf.

————. 2007. Labor and Employment. *Position Paper*, Washington, D.C.: US Council for International Business. Available at: http://www.uscib.org/index.asp?documentID=825

————. 2007. USCIB Welcomes Bipartisan Trade Policy Accord. *Press Release*, May 14. Washington, D.C.: US Council for International Business. Available at: http://www.uscib.org/uscib-welcomes-bipartisan-trade-policy-accord-ud-3699/

Usi, Eva. 2012. Humala: "queremos industrializar el Perú". *Deutsche Welle*, June 12. Available at: http://www.dw.com/es/humala-queremos-industrializar-el-per%C3%BA/a-16017789

Van den Hoven, Adrian. 2004. Assuming Leadership in Multilateral Economic Institutions: The EU's 'Development Round' Discourse and Strategy. *West European Politics* 27 (2):256-283.

Van den Putte, Lore. 2015. Divided we stand: the European Parliament's position on social trade in the post-Lisbon era. In *Global Governance of Labour Rights. Assessing the Effectiveness of Transnational Public and Private Policy Initiatives*, edited by A. Marx, J. Wouters, G. Rayp and L. Beke. Cheltenham: Edward Elgar Publishing.

———. 2015. Involving Civil Society in Social Clauses and the Decent Work Agenda. *Global Labour Journal* 6 (2):221 - 235.

Van den Putte, Lore, Ferdi De Ville, and Jan Orbie. 2015. The European Parliament as an actor in international trade: from power to impact. In *The European Parliament and its International Relations*, edited by S. Stavridis and D. Irrera. Abingdon: Routledge.

Van den Putte, Lore, and Jan Orbie. 2015. EU Bilateral Trade Agreements and the Surprising Rise of Labour Provisions. *The International Journal of Comparative Labour Law and Industrial Relations* 31 (3):263–284.

Van den Putte, Lore, Jan Orbie, Fabienne Bossuyt, and Ferdi De Ville. 2014. Social norms in EU bilateral trade agreements: A comparative overview. In *Linking trade and non-commercial interests: the EU as a global role model?*, edited by T. Takács, A. Ott and A. Dimopoulos. The Hague: Centre for the Law of EU External Relations.

van Haute, Emilie, ed. 2016. *Green Parties in Europe*. Abingdon: Routledge.

van Schendelen, Rinus. 2005. *Machiavelli in Brussels. The Art of Lobbying the EU*. Amsterdam: Amsterdam University Press.

Vieth, Warren. 2005. Friends, Foes Made Over Trade Deal. *Los Angeles Times*, August 7. Available at: http://articles.latimes.com/print/2005/aug/07/nation/na-cafta7

Villareal, Angeles M. 2005. Andean-U.S. Free-Trade Agreement Negotiations. In *CRS Report for Congress*. Washington, D.C.: Congressional Research Service.

———. 2006. Andean-U.S. Free-Trade Agreement Negotiations. In *CRS Report for Congress*. Washington, D.C.: Congressional Research Service.

———. 2008. U.S.-Peru Economic Relations and the U.S.-Peru Trade Promotion Agreement. In *CRS Report for Congress*. Washington, D.C.: Congressional Research Service.

Vinagre, Emili. 2009. Merkel avala a Uribe y ofrece apoyo para pacificación en Colombia. *Deutsche Welle*, January 31. Available at: http://www.dw.com/es/merkel-avala-a-uribe-y-ofrece-apoyo-para-pacificaci%C3%B3n-en-colombia/a-3992973-0

Visser, Jelle. 2006. Union membership statistics in 24 countries. *Monthly Labor Review* January:38-49.

Vogel, David. 1997. *Trading Up: Consumer and Environmental Regulation in a Global Economy*. Cambridge and London: Harvard University Press.

———. 2012. *The Politics of Precaution: Regulating Health, Safety, and Environmental Risks in Europe and the United States*. Princeton: Princeton University Press.

Vogel, Toby. 2012. Member states and MEPs to clash over free-trade deal. *Politico*, March 7. Available at: http://www.politico.eu/article/member-states-and-meps-to-clash-over-free-trade-deal/

Vogler, John, and Hannes R. Stephan. 2007. The European Union in global environmental governance: Leadership in the making? *International Environmental Agreements: Politics, Law and Economics* 7 (4):389-413.

Vogt, Jeffrey S. 2014. Trade and Investment Arrangements and Labor Rights. In *Corporate Responsibility for Human Rights Impacts: New Expectations and Paradigms*, edited by L. Blecher, N. Kaymar Stafford and G. C. Bellamy. New York: ABA Book Publishing.

———. 2015. The Evolution of Labor Rights and Trade—A Transatlantic Comparison and Lessons for the Transatlantic Trade and Investment Partnership. *Journal of International Economic Law* 18 (4):827–860.

———. 2015. A Little Less Conversation: The EU and the (Non) Application of Labour Conditionality in the Generalized System of Preferences (GSP). *International Journal of Comparative Labour Law and Industrial Relations* 31 (3):285–304.

Wade, Robert Hunter. 2003. What strategies are viable for developing countries today? The World Trade Organization and the shrinking of 'development space'. *Review of International Political Economy* 10 (4):621-644.

Waer, Paul. 1996. Social Clauses in International Trade The Debate in the European Union. *Journal of World Trade* 30 (4):25-42.

Wall Street Journal. 2010. Obama's Outsourced Trade Policy. *Wall Street Journal*, September 15. Available at: http://www.wsj.com/articles/SB10001424052748703 376504575490944170692312

———. 2011. Democrats vs. Obama on Trade. *Wall Street Journal*, March 14. Available at: http://www.wsj.com/articles/SB1000142405274870429660457619648028 0412662

Wallach, Lori, and Michelle Sforza. 1999. *The WTO: Five Years of Reasons to Resist Corporate Globalization*. New York: Seven Stories Press.

Weisman, Steven R. 2007. Bush and Democrats in Accord on Trade Deals. *New York Times*, May 10. Available at: http://www.nytimes.com/2007/05/11/business/11trade.html?_r=0&pa

———. 2007. Partisan Disagreements Jeopardize New Trade Deals. *New York Times*, July 8. Available at: http://www.nytimes.com/2007/07/08/washington/08trade.html

———. 2007. Using Chávez as Counterpoint, Bush Pursues Latin Trade Pacts. *New York Times*, October 24. Available at: http://www.nytimes.com/2007/10/25/business/worldbusiness/25trade.html

Weissbrodt, David, and Matthew Mason. 2014. Compliance of the United States with International Labor Law. *Minnesota Law Review* 98 (5):1842-1878.

Weitzman, Hal. 2005. US and Peru end trade impasse with agreement. *Financial Times*, December 7. Available at: http://www.ft.com/intl/cms/s/0/02108266-6776-11da-a650-0000779e2340.html#axzz3xgQwp4IV

Wheeler, David. 2001. Racing to the Bottom? Foreign Investment and Air Pollution in Developing Countries. *Journal of Environment & Development* 10 (3):225-245.

Wilkinson, Rorden. 1999. Labour and trade-related regulation: beyond the trade-labour standards debate? *The British Journal of Politics and International Relations* 1 (2):165-191.

Williams, Brock R., Mark E. Manyin, Remy Jurenas, and Michaela D. Platzer. 2014. The U.S.-South Korea Free Trade Agreement (KORUS FTA): Provisions and Implementation. In *CRS Report for Congress*. Washington, D.C.: Congressional Research Service.

Williamson, Elizabeth. 2010. U.S. Sets Sweeping New Deal on Trade. *Wall Street Journal*, December 3. Available at: http://www.wsj.com/articles/SB100014240527 48703350104575652882154932888

———. 2010. U.S. Vows New Push in Korean Trade Pact. *Wall Street Journal*, June 25. Available at: http://www.wsj.com/articles/SB1000142405274870484600457 53 33303589295326

———. 2011. Trade Pacts Tied to Worker Aid. *Wall Street Journal*, May 17. Available at: http://www.wsj.com/articles/SB10001424052748703421204576327164110599 384

Williamson, Elizabeth, and Melanie Trottman. 2010. Obama Courts Labor Support for Trade Deal. *Wall Street Journal*, August 4. Available at: http://www.wsj.com/ar ticles/SB10001424052748704499604575407790047897522

Willis, Andrew. 2009. EU trade talks with Peru continue despite government violence. *EU observer*, June 17. Available at: https://euobserver.com/economic/28324

———. 2009. Honduran coup threatens to delay EU trade deal. *EU observer*, June 29. Available at: https://euobserver.com/foreign/28386

———. 2010. EU completes trade talks with Peru and Colombia. *EU observer*, March 2. Available at: https://euobserver.com/economic/29582

———. 2010. Landmark EU-Korea trade deal moves a step closer. *EU Observer*, June 23. Available at: https://euobserver.com/economic/30351

———. 2010. Parliament sets out concerns over Colombia trade deal. *EU observer*, February 2. Available at: https://euobserver.com/economic/29392

———. 2011. EU signs trade deals with Peru and Colombia. *EU observer*, April 14. Available at: https://euobserver.com/news/32177

Wolf, Martin. 2005. *Why Globalization Works*. Yale: Yale University Press.

Woll, Cornelia. 2009. Trade Policy Lobbying in the European Union: Who Captures Whom? In *Lobbying in the European Union: Institutions, Actors, and Issues*, edited by D. Coen and J. Richardson. Oxford: Oxford University Press.

———. 2012. The brash and the soft-spoken: Lobbying styles in a transatlantic comparison. *Interest Groups & Advocacy* 1 (2):193-214.

Woll, Cornelia, and Alvaro Artigas. 2007. When trade liberalization turns into regulatory reform: The impact on business–government relations in international trade politics. *Regulation & Governance* 1 (2):121-138.

Woolcock, Stephen. 2005. European Union Trade Policy: Domestic Institutions and Systemic Factors. In *The Politics of International Trade in the Twenty-First Century. Actors, Issues and Regional Dynamics*, edited by D. Kelly and W. Grant. New York: Palgrave Macmillian.

———. 2007. European Union policy towards Free Trade Agreements. In *ECIPE Working Paper*. Brussels: European Centre for International Political Economy.

———. 2010. The Treaty of Lisbon and the European Union as an actor in international Trade. In *ECIPE Working Paper*. Brussels: European Centre for International Political Economy.

———. 2011. *European Union Economic Diplomacy. The Role of the EU in External Economic Relations*. Farnham: Ashgate.

———. 2014. Differentiation within reciprocity: the European Union approach to preferential trade agreements. *Contemporary Politics* 20 (1):36-48.

———. 2014. EU Policy on Preferential Trade Agreements in the 2000s: A Reorientation towards Commercial Aims. *European Law Journal* 20 (6):718-732.

WTO. 1994. Agreement establishing the World Trade Organization. Marrakesh: World Trade Organization.

WWF. 2001. Environment & Trade in the European Union's Inter-regional Agreements. *Position Paper*, May 2001. Brussels: World Wildlife Fund European Policy Office. Available at: http://assets.panda.org/downloads/dgtrademikel3.pdf.

———. 2003. A League of Gentlemen. Who really runs EU Trade Decision-Making? *Report*, November 2003. Brussels. World Wildlife Fund European Policy Office. Available at: http://awsassets.panda.org/downloads/aleagueofgentlemenfinal.pdf.

Yandle, Bruce. 1983. Bootleggers and Baptists: The Education of a Regulatory Economist. *Regulation* (May/June):12-16.

Yerkey, Gary G. 2001. EU's Lamy Opposes Addressing Social Issues Such as Workers' Rights in Trade Agreements. *Bloomberg International Trade Reporter*, April 5. Available at:

Yoon, Esook 2003. South Korean Environmental Foreign Policy. *Asia-Pacific Review of Economic Studies* 13 (2):74-96.

Young, Alasdair R. 2004. The Incidental Fortress: The Single European Market and World Trade. *Journal of Common Market Studies* 42 (2):393–414.

Young, Alasdair R., and John Peterson. 2006. The EU and the new trade politics. *Journal of European Public Policy* 13 (6):795-814.

———. 2014. *Parochial Global Europe. 21st Century Trade Politics*. Oxford: Oxford University Press.

Zarocostas, John. 1994. US under pressure for attempt to link trade, labor rules. *Journal of Commerce*, March 28. Available at:

Zimmermann, Hubert. 2007. *Drachenzähmung. Die EU und die USA in den Verhandlungen um die Integration Chinas in den Welthandel*. Baden-Baden: Nomos.

———. 2007. Realist Power Europe? The EU in the Negotiations about China's and Russia's WTO Accession. *Journal of Common Market Studies* 45 (4):813-832.

———. 2008. How the EU Negotiates Trade and Democracy: The Cases of China's Accession to the WTO and the Doha Round. *European foreign affairs review* 13 (2):255-280.

Zoellick, Robert B. 2001. American Trade Leadership: What is at Stake. *Speech to the Institute for International Economics, Washington, D.C.*, September 24. Available at:

Interviews

Interview 1
U.S. academic, Washington, D.C., March 4th 2015

Interview 2
USTR official, Washington, D.C., March 9th 2015

Interview 3
AFL-CIO representative, Washington, D.C., March 10th 2015

Interview 4
International Brotherhood of Teamsters representative, Washington, D.C., March 12th 2015

Interview 5
Friends of the Earth representative, Washington, D.C., March 14th 2015

Interview 6
USTR official, Washington, D.C., March 17th 2015

Interview 7
U.S. Department of Labor official, Washington, D.C., March 27th 2015

Interview 8
Journalist Inside U.S. Trade, Washington, D.C., March 30th 2015

Interview 9
USTR official, Washington, D.C., April 2nd 2015

Interview 10
Think Tank representative, Washington, D.C., April 6th 2015

Interview 11
Republican congressional aide, Washington, D.C., April 7th 2015

Interview 12
Democratic congressional aide, Washington, D.C., April 8th 2015

Interview 13
Think Tank representative, Washington, D.C., April 9th 2015

Interview 14
Democratic congressional aide, Washington, D.C., April 13th 2015

Interview 15
National Association of Manufacturers representative, Washington, D.C., April 14th 2015

Interview 16
USTR official, Washington, D.C., April 16th 2015

Interview 17
   U.S. academic, Washington, D.C., April 20th 2015

Interview 18
   Alliance for American Manufacturing representative, Washington, D.C., April 22th 2015

Interview 19
   U.S. Chamber of Commerce representative, Washington, D.C., April 24th 2015

Interview 20
   BusinessEurope representative, Brussels, November 9th 2015

Interview 21
   S&D Member of the European Parliament, Brussels, November 10th 2015

Interview 22
   DG Trade official, Brussels, November 11th 2015

Interview 23
   EESC representative, Brussels, November 11th 2015

Interview 24
   ITUC representative, Brussels, November 12th 2015

Interview 25
   DG Trade and DG Employment officials, Brussels, November 12th 2015

Interview 26
   DG Trade official, Brussels, November 12th 2015

Interview 27
   DG Environment official, Brussels, November 13th 2015

Interview 28
   ETUC representative, Brussels, November 13th 2015

Interview 29
   DG Trade official, telephone interview, November 24th 2015

Interview 30
   DG Trade official, telephone interview, December 9th 2015

Interview 31
   Friends of the Earth Europe representative, telephone interview, December 11th 2015

Interview 32
   DG Trade official, telephone interview, February 2nd 2016